Jax Epoch and the Quicken Forbidden

Borrowed Magic

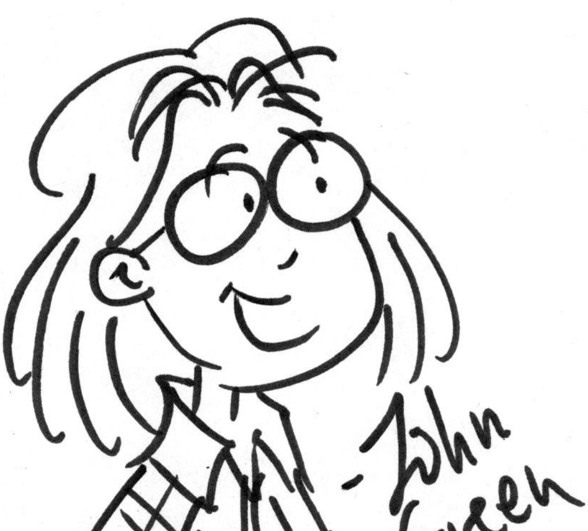
-John Green

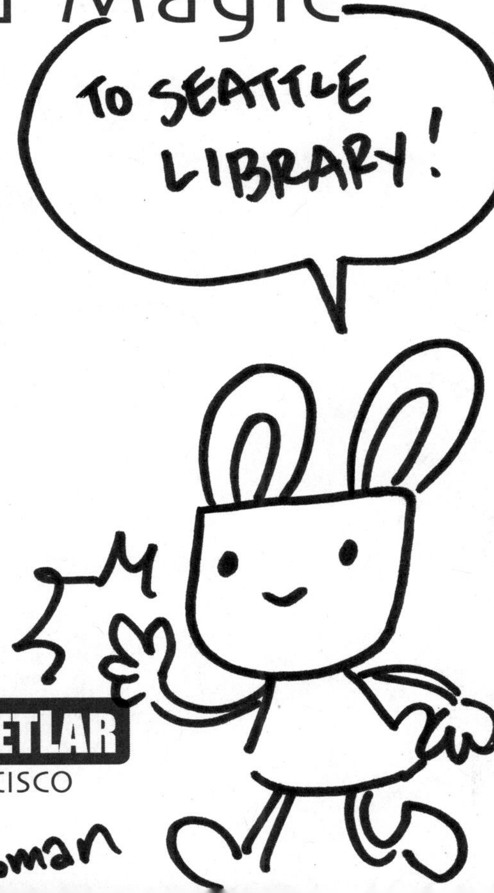
TO SEATTLE LIBRARY!
dave roman

AiT/PLANETLAR
SAN FRANCISCO

Jax Epoch and the Quicken Forbidden: Borrowed Magic

Published by AiT/Planet Lar.
Originally published by Cryptic Press as *Quicken Forbidden* #'s 1-5.

For more information about *Quicken Forbidden* write to:
Cryptic Press
365 Smith Street
Freeport, NY 11520
crypticpress@aol.com
www.quickenforbidden.com

For more information about AiT/Planet Lar write to:
AiT/Planet Lar
2034 47th Avenue
San Francisco, CA 94116
www.ait-planetlar.com

ISBN: 1-932051-11-2

Printed in Canada

Second Printing, July 2006

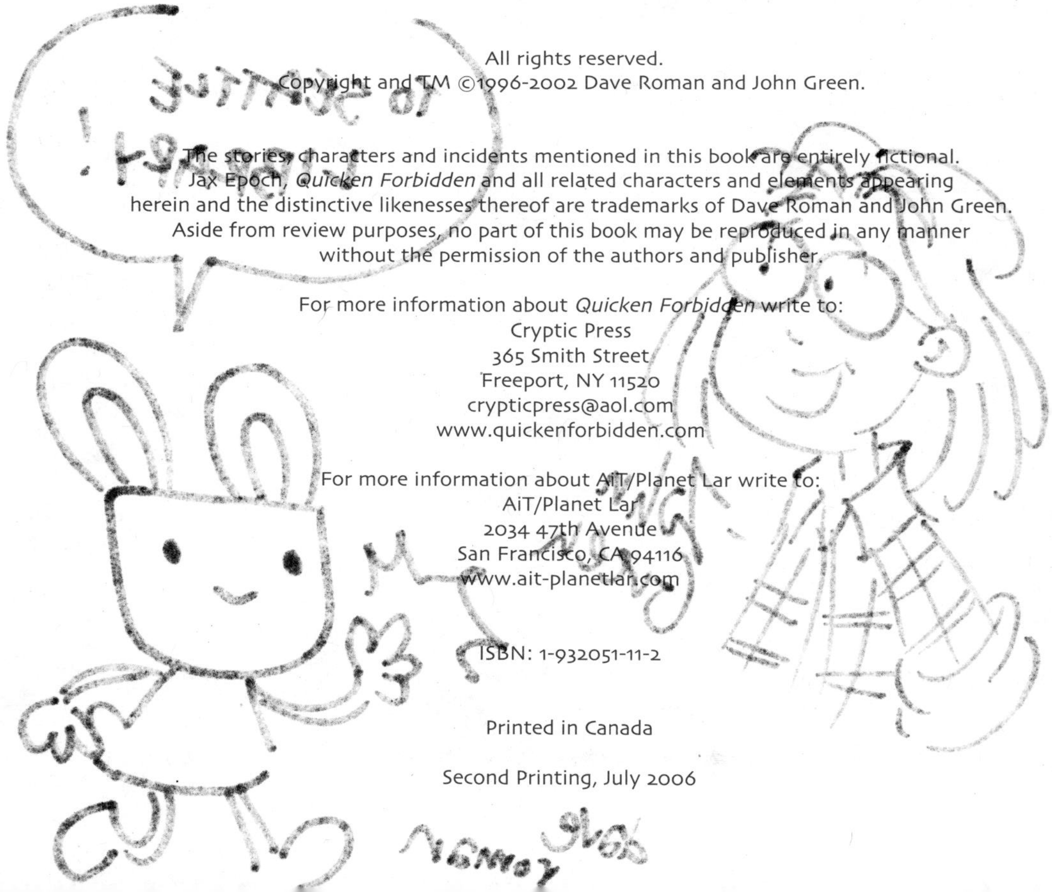

DAVE ROMAN
writer

JOHN GREEN
artist

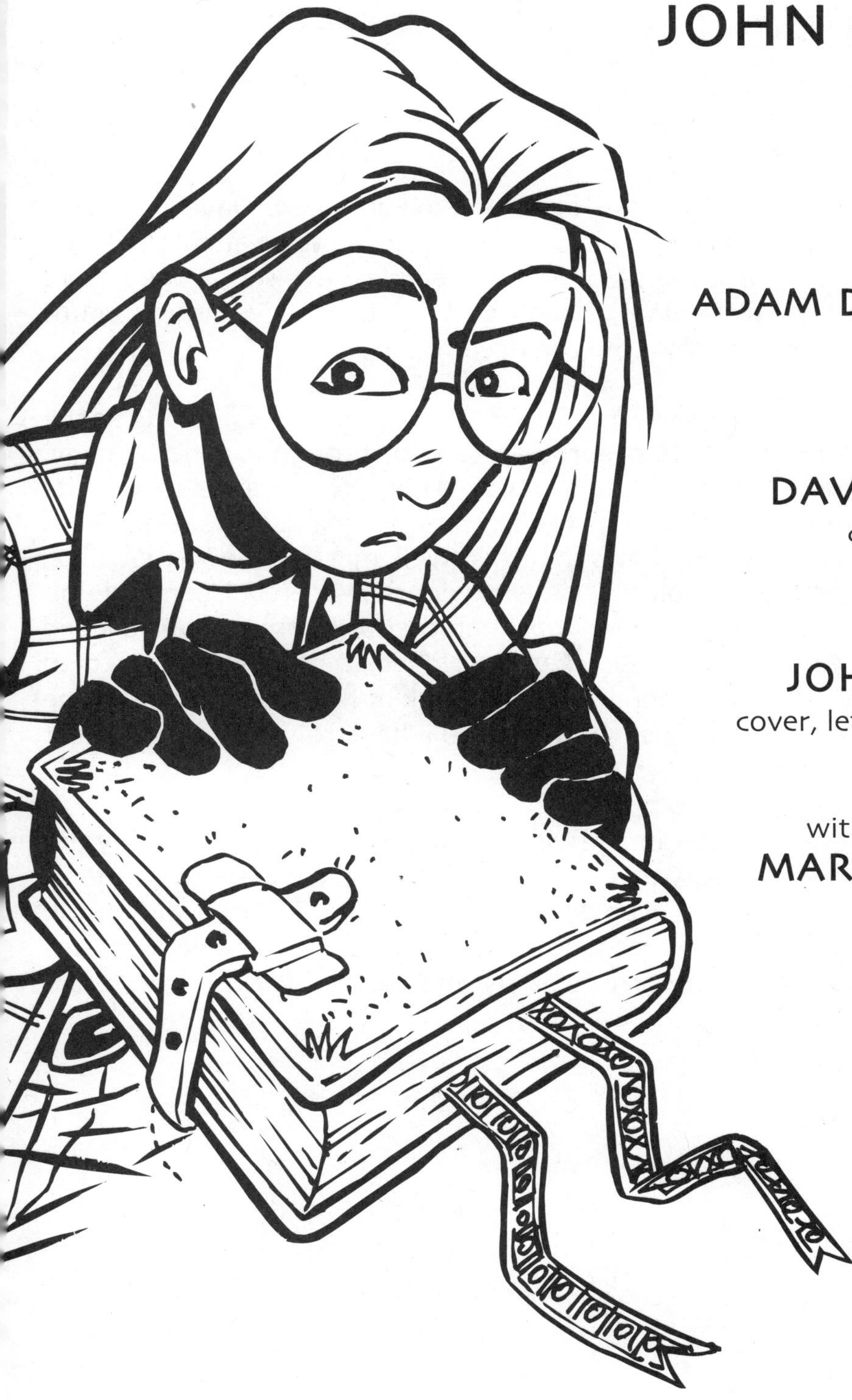

ADAM DEKRAKER
inker
pages 86-92

DAVE ROMAN
dream sequence
pages 49-53

JOHN GREEN
cover, letters and design

with a foreword by
MARK CRILLEY

FOREWORD

I'll never forget my first glimpse of *Quicken Forbidden.* Dave and John kindly sent me a copy of their debut issue, allowing me to be among the first lucky readers to get a glimpse of the incredible new series they were creating. John's bold black lines, Dave's crisp writing... everything about that comic was right, just the way it needed to be.

What a pleasure it is to be here, many marvelous issues later, looking at the first *Quicken Forbidden* trade paperback. As I go through it page by page, it's simply dazzling to see all the amazing creations this comic has shown its readers over the years: dragons in the skies of Manhattan, floating robot lawyers, spoons and marshmallows that talk (well, marshmallows that 'Eep', at any rate), trees that double as revolving doors... There is seemingly no end to what Dave and John can cook up when they join forces. Even a jaded comics fan will find things in *Quicken Forbidden* that are guaranteed to make his head pop like a balloon. (Come to think of it, there's a point in the series when Jax's head does just that, but you'll have to wait until the next trade to see that one.)

What makes these fantastic images soar so high is the fact that they are balanced by delightfully down-to-earth scenes in every issue: coffee shops, classrooms, office buildings; even the courthouse in a different dimension has a wonderfully commonplace water cooler. John Green's talent is such that he can render both the otherworldly and the *our*worldly with equal skill and enthusiasm.

And in a medium where the visual fireworks often steal the show, we've got to tip a hat to Dave Roman's dialogue and narration. Here's a good example: *"For the first time ever, I felt a little glad to be back in the 'real' world... especially one where I had the power to jump out of a thirty story building and live."* Here's another: *"Why would a being with the power to destroy all space and time disguise himself as a cheap gift shop souvenir?"* And we can't leave out this one, straight from the talking spoon himself: *"Gimme some sugar, baby, before I decide to run away with that dish... she's a hottie!"* Dave's light touch with lines such as these is a big part of what makes *Quicken Forbidden* sparkle.

So sit back and prepare yourself for a real treat. You're about to take a tour of a marvelous world you've never seen before– *several* worlds, actually– and with guides like Dave Roman and John Green, rest assured you're in for one heckuva trip.

-Mark Crilley, January 2003

Mark Crilley is the author of the *Akiko on the Planet Smoo* series of novels published by Random House as well writer an artist of the comic book series on which it is based (published by Sirius Entertainment).

"Reality is that which, when you stop believing in it, doesn't go away."

-Philip K. Dick

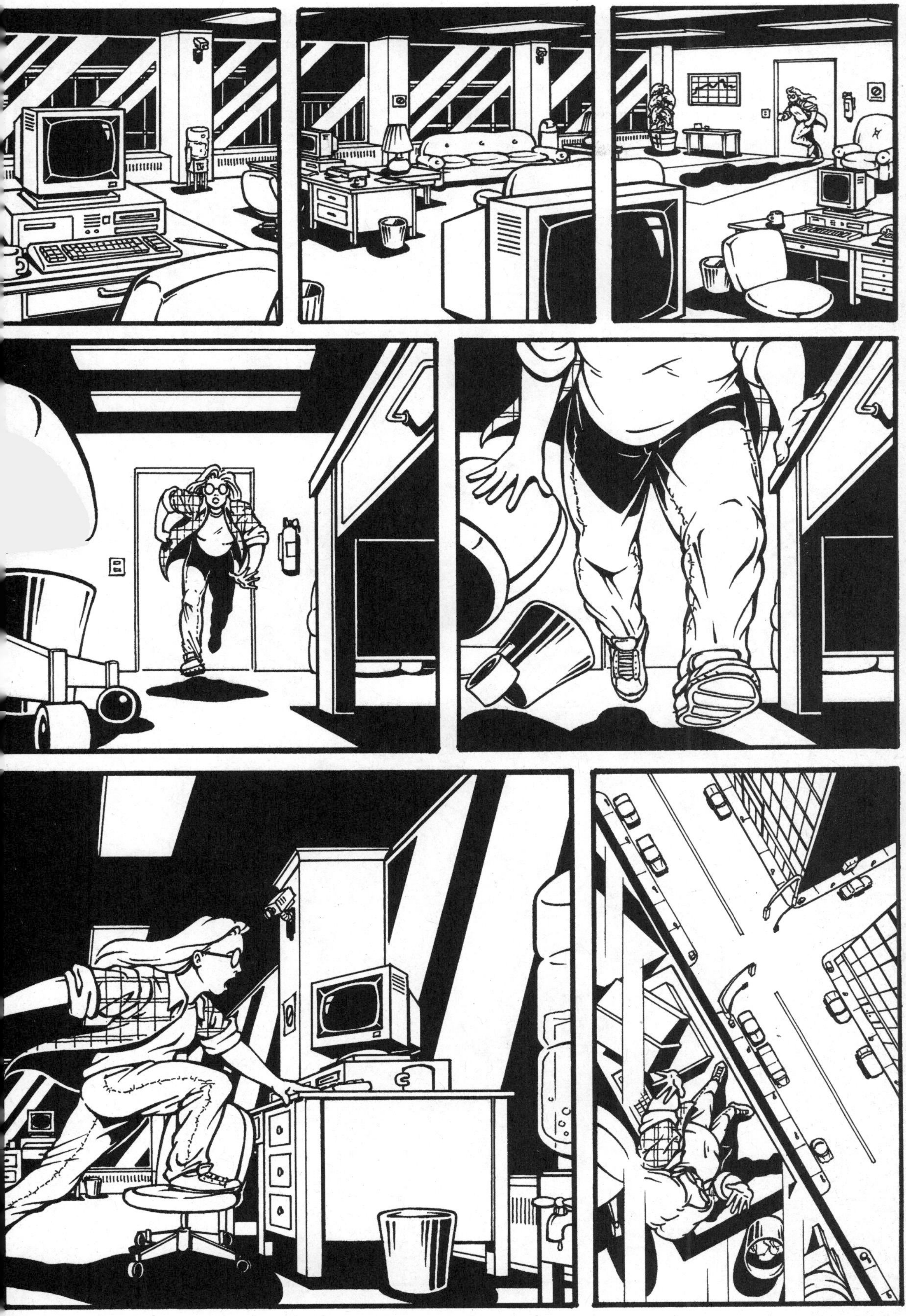

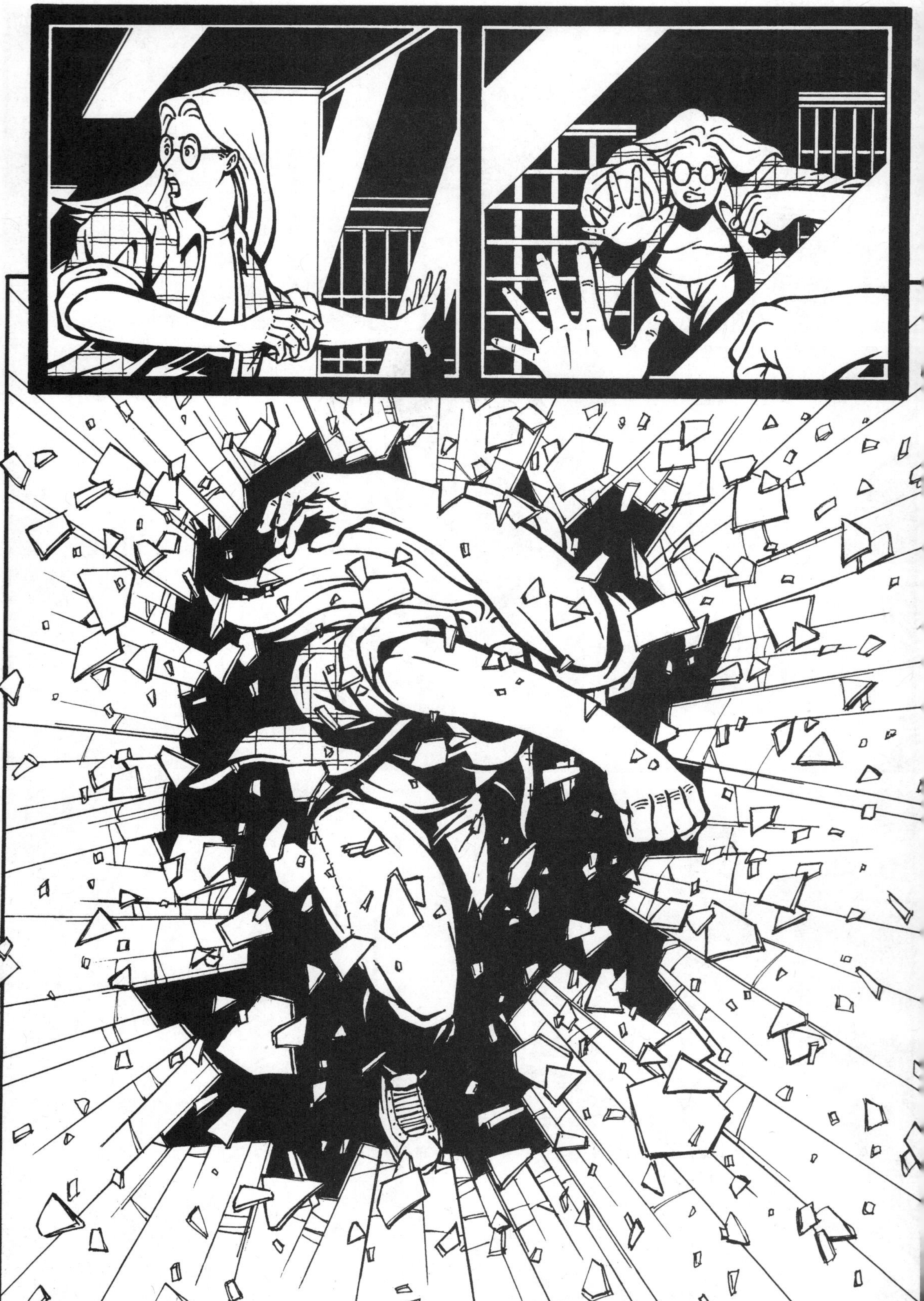

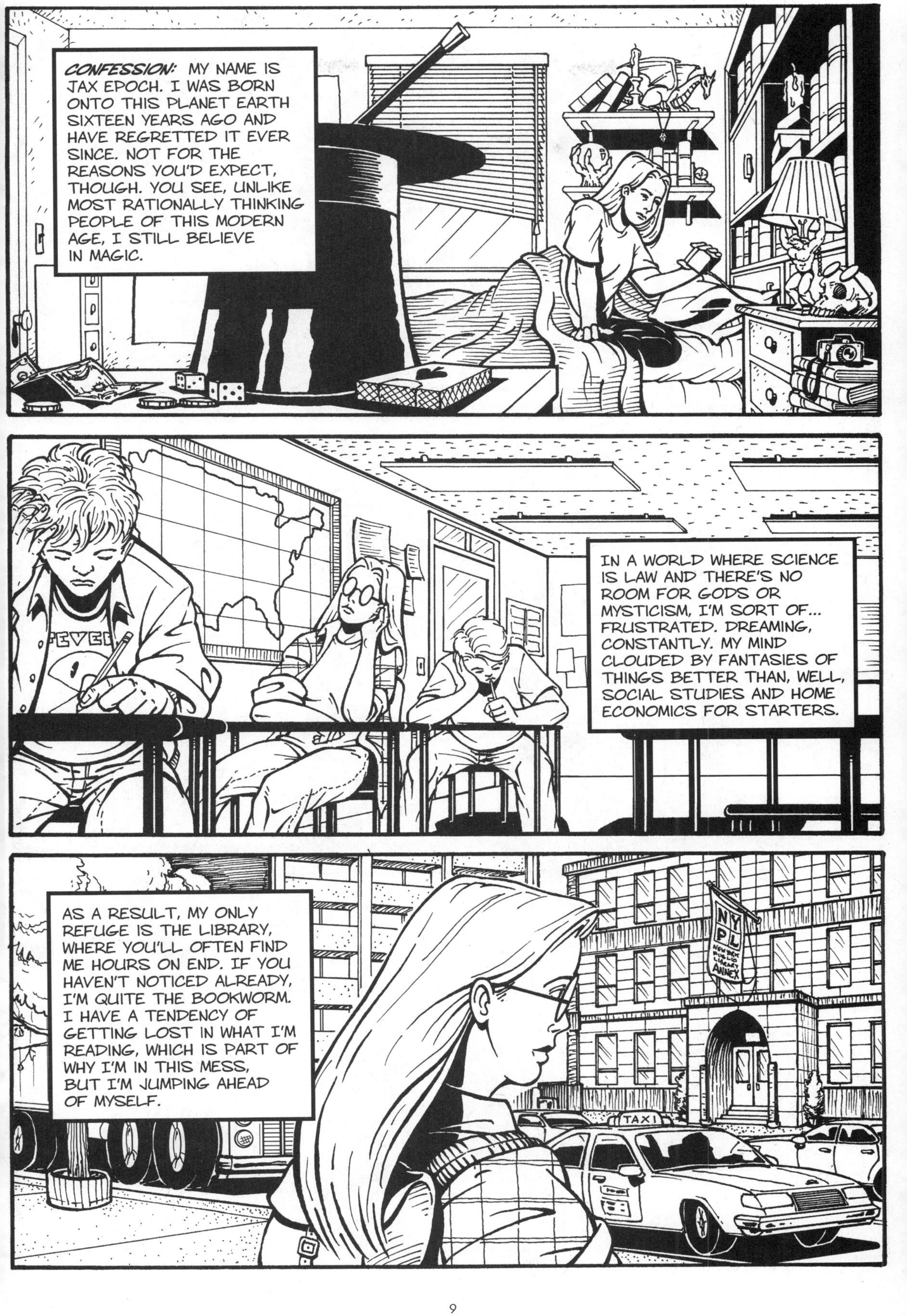
CONFESSION: MY NAME IS JAX EPOCH. I WAS BORN ONTO THIS PLANET EARTH SIXTEEN YEARS AGO AND HAVE REGRETTED IT EVER SINCE. NOT FOR THE REASONS YOU'D EXPECT, THOUGH. YOU SEE, UNLIKE MOST RATIONALLY THINKING PEOPLE OF THIS MODERN AGE, I STILL BELIEVE IN MAGIC.
IN A WORLD WHERE SCIENCE IS LAW AND THERE'S NO ROOM FOR GODS OR MYSTICISM, I'M SORT OF... FRUSTRATED. DREAMING, CONSTANTLY. MY MIND CLOUDED BY FANTASIES OF THINGS BETTER THAN, WELL, SOCIAL STUDIES AND HOME ECONOMICS FOR STARTERS.
AS A RESULT, MY ONLY REFUGE IS THE LIBRARY, WHERE YOU'LL OFTEN FIND ME HOURS ON END. IF YOU HAVEN'T NOTICED ALREADY, I'M QUITE THE BOOKWORM. I HAVE A TENDENCY OF GETTING LOST IN WHAT I'M READING, WHICH IS PART OF WHY I'M IN THIS MESS, BUT I'M JUMPING AHEAD OF MYSELF.
NY PL
ANNEX
TAXI

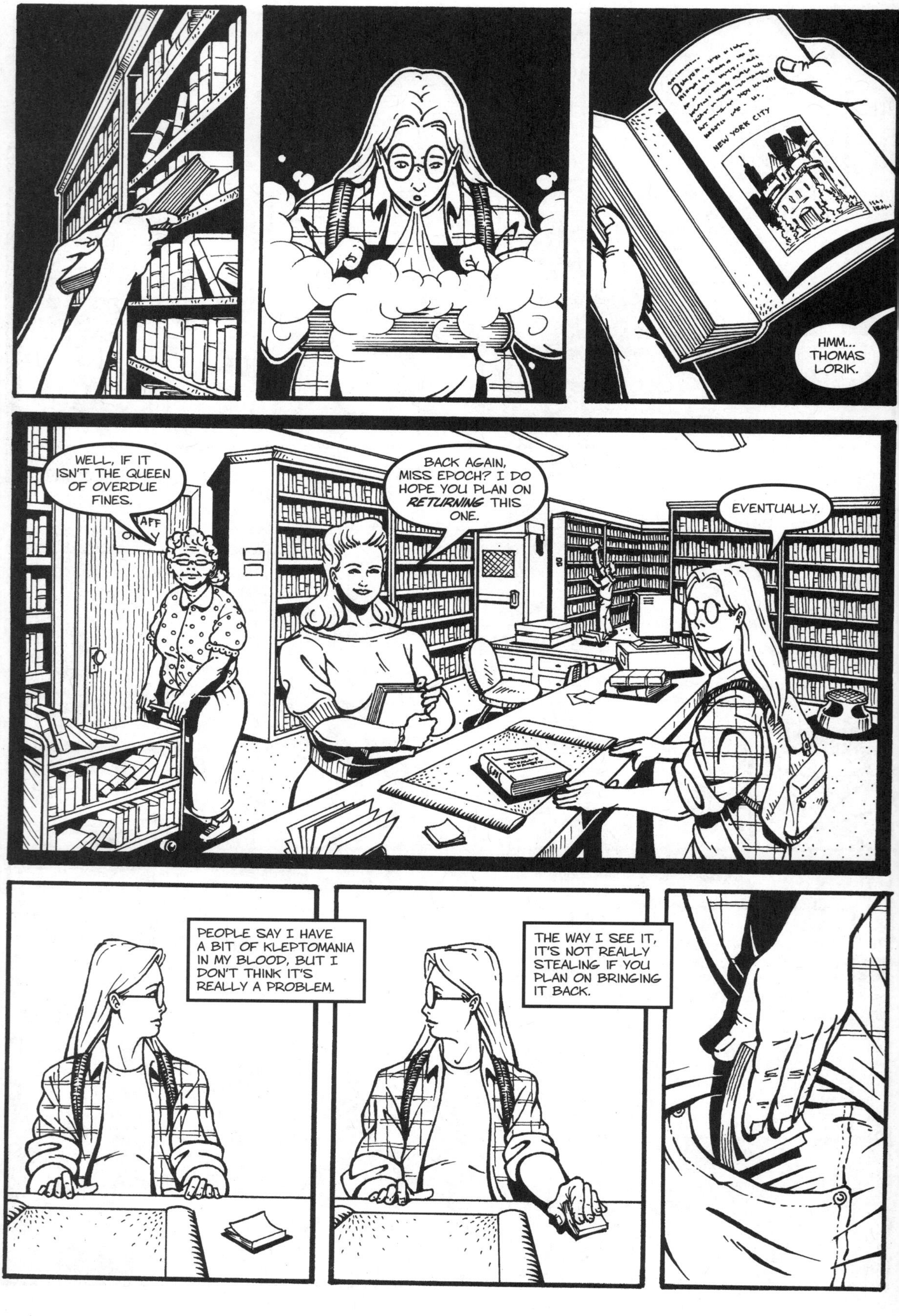
HMM... THOMAS LORIK.
WELL, IF IT ISN'T THE QUEEN OF OVERDUE FINES.
BACK AGAIN, MISS EPOCH? I DO HOPE YOU PLAN ON *RETURNING* THIS ONE.
EVENTUALLY.
PEOPLE SAY I HAVE A BIT OF KLEPTOMANIA IN MY BLOOD, BUT I DON'T THINK IT'S REALLY A PROBLEM.
THE WAY I SEE IT, IT'S NOT REALLY STEALING IF YOU PLAN ON BRINGING IT BACK.

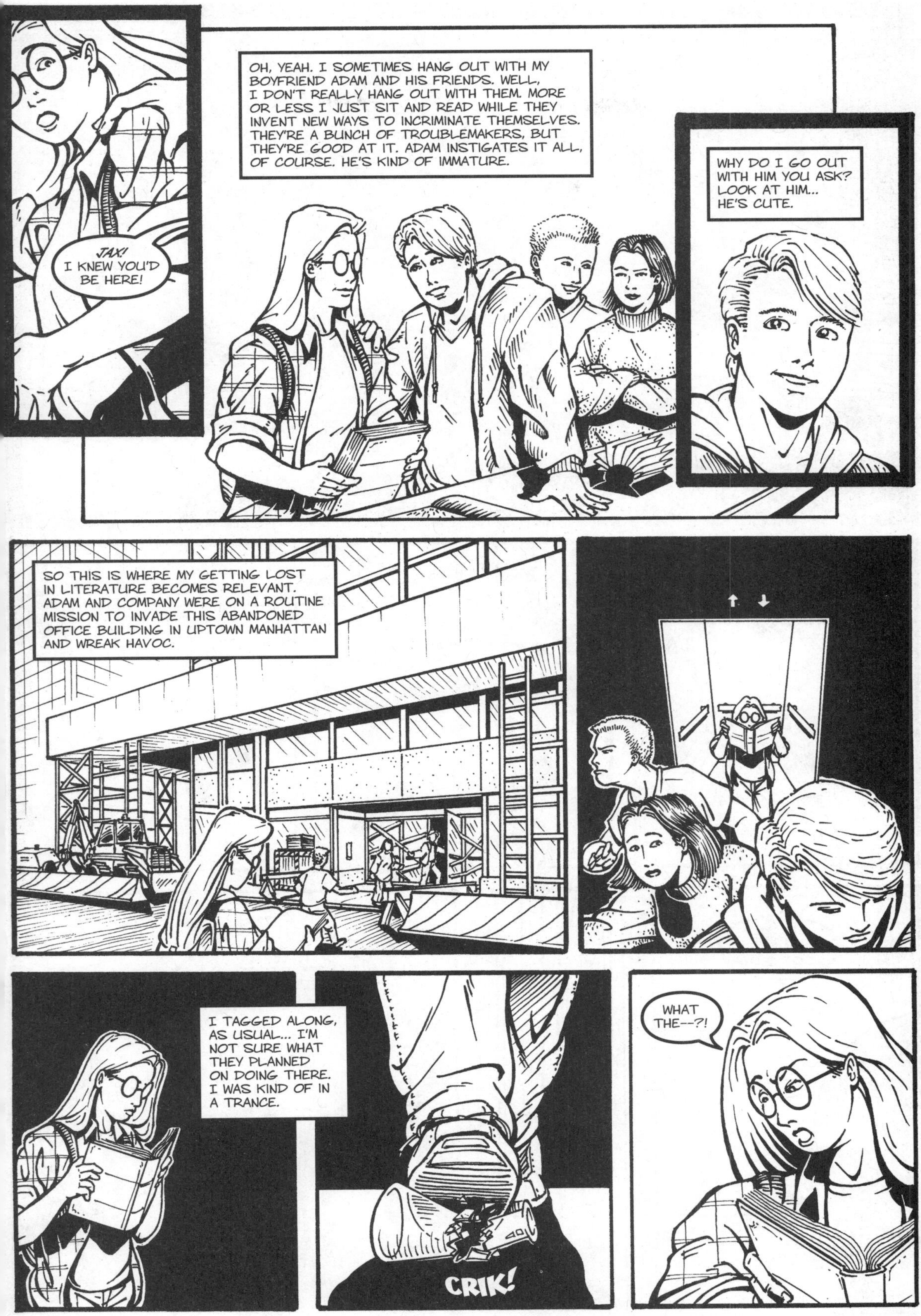
JAX!
I KNEW YOU'D
BE HERE!
OH, YEAH. I SOMETIMES HANG OUT WITH MY BOYFRIEND ADAM AND HIS FRIENDS. WELL, I DON'T REALLY HANG OUT WITH THEM. MORE OR LESS I JUST SIT AND READ WHILE THEY INVENT NEW WAYS TO INCRIMINATE THEMSELVES. THEY'RE A BUNCH OF TROUBLEMAKERS, BUT THEY'RE GOOD AT IT. ADAM INSTIGATES IT ALL, OF COURSE. HE'S KIND OF IMMATURE.
WHY DO I GO OUT WITH HIM YOU ASK? LOOK AT HIM... HE'S CUTE.
SO THIS IS WHERE MY GETTING LOST IN LITERATURE BECOMES RELEVANT. ADAM AND COMPANY WERE ON A ROUTINE MISSION TO INVADE THIS ABANDONED OFFICE BUILDING IN UPTOWN MANHATTAN AND WREAK HAVOC.
I TAGGED ALONG, AS USUAL... I'M NOT SURE WHAT THEY PLANNED ON DOING THERE. I WAS KIND OF IN A TRANCE.
CRIK!
WHAT THE--?!

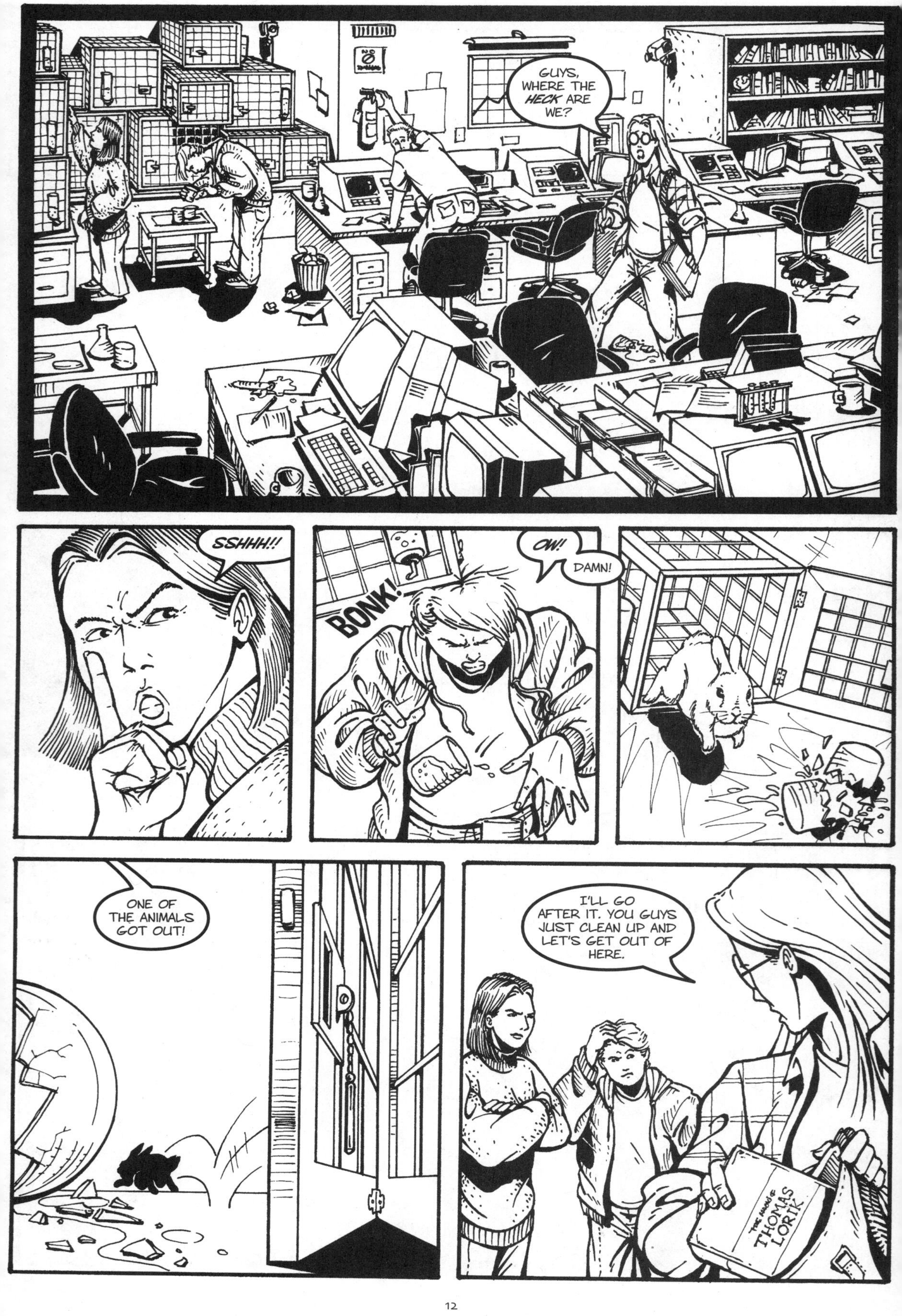
GUYS, WHERE THE *HECK* ARE WE?
SSHHH!!
BONK!
OW!
DAMN!
ONE OF THE ANIMALS GOT OUT!
I'LL GO AFTER IT. YOU GUYS JUST CLEAN UP AND LET'S GET OUT OF HERE.
THOMAS LORIK

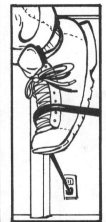

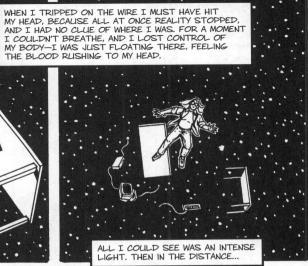

WHEN I TRIPPED ON THE WIRE I MUST HAVE HIT MY HEAD, BECAUSE ALL AT ONCE REALITY STOPPED, AND I HAD NO CLUE OF WHERE I WAS. FOR A MOMENT I COULDN'T BREATHE, AND I LOST CONTROL OF MY BODY—I WAS JUST FLOATING THERE, FEELING THE BLOOD RUSHING TO MY HEAD.

ALL I COULD SEE WAS AN INTENSE LIGHT. THEN IN THE DISTANCE...

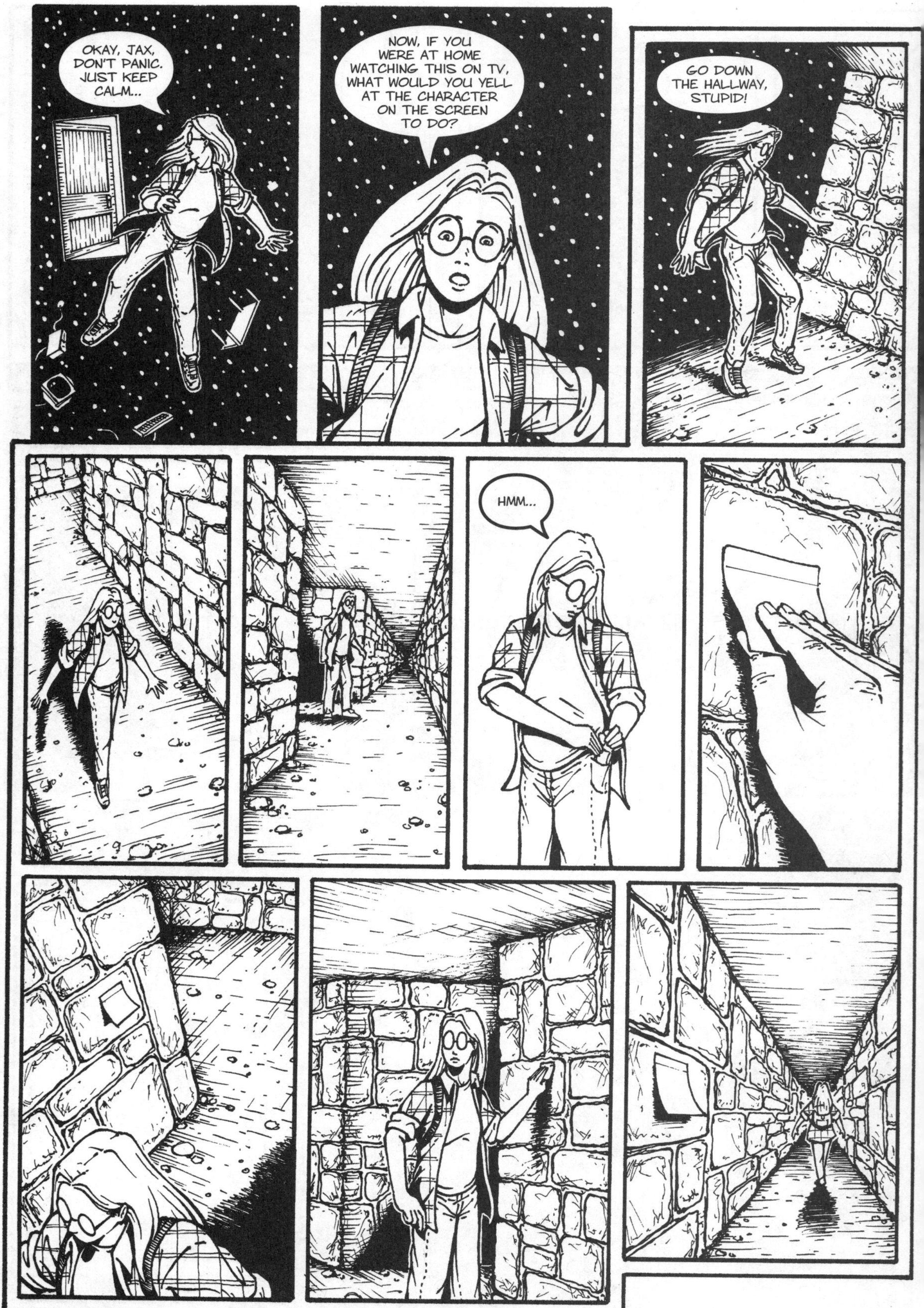
OKAY, JAX, DON'T PANIC. JUST KEEP CALM...
NOW, IF YOU WERE AT HOME WATCHING THIS ON TV, WHAT WOULD YOU YELL AT THE CHARACTER ON THE SCREEN TO DO?
GO DOWN THE HALLWAY, STUPID!
HMM...

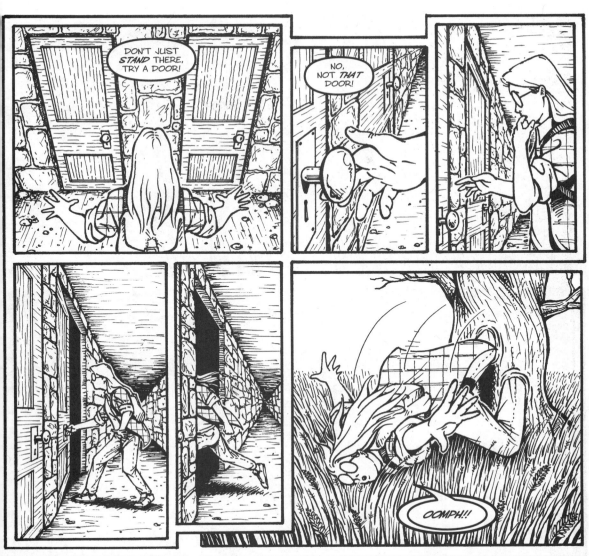

DON'T JUST *STAND* THERE, TRY A DOOR!

NO, NOT *THAT* DOOR!

OOMPH!!

ANY *SANE* PERSON WOULD'VE FREAKED OUT BY NOW...

...LUCKILY...

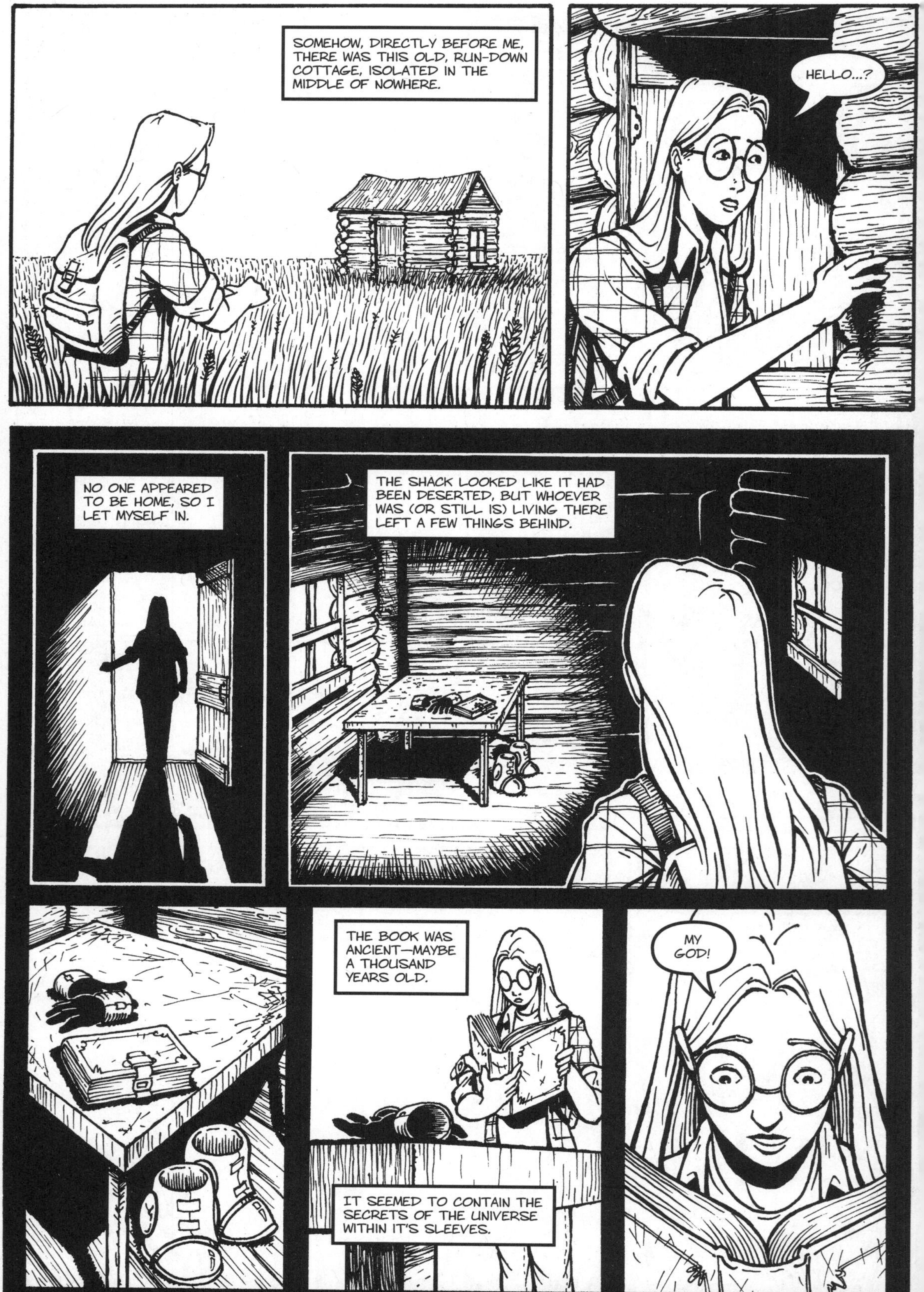
SOMEHOW, DIRECTLY BEFORE ME, THERE WAS THIS OLD, RUN-DOWN COTTAGE, ISOLATED IN THE MIDDLE OF NOWHERE.
HELLO...?
NO ONE APPEARED TO BE HOME, SO I LET MYSELF IN.
THE SHACK LOOKED LIKE IT HAD BEEN DESERTED, BUT WHOEVER WAS (OR STILL IS) LIVING THERE LEFT A FEW THINGS BEHIND.
THE BOOK WAS ANCIENT—MAYBE A THOUSAND YEARS OLD.
IT SEEMED TO CONTAIN THE SECRETS OF THE UNIVERSE WITHIN IT'S SLEEVES.
MY GOD!

I HAD TO HAVE IT, EVEN IF JUST FOR A LITTLE WHILE.

COOL!

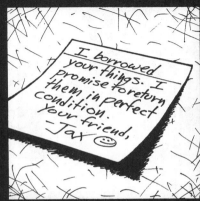

I borrowed your things. I promise to return them in perfect condition. Your friend, -Jax

WELL, I'D BETTER GET OUT OF HERE BEFORE THE THREE BEARS GET HOME.

HMM... I HOPE THIS TREE IS A REVOLVING DOOR...

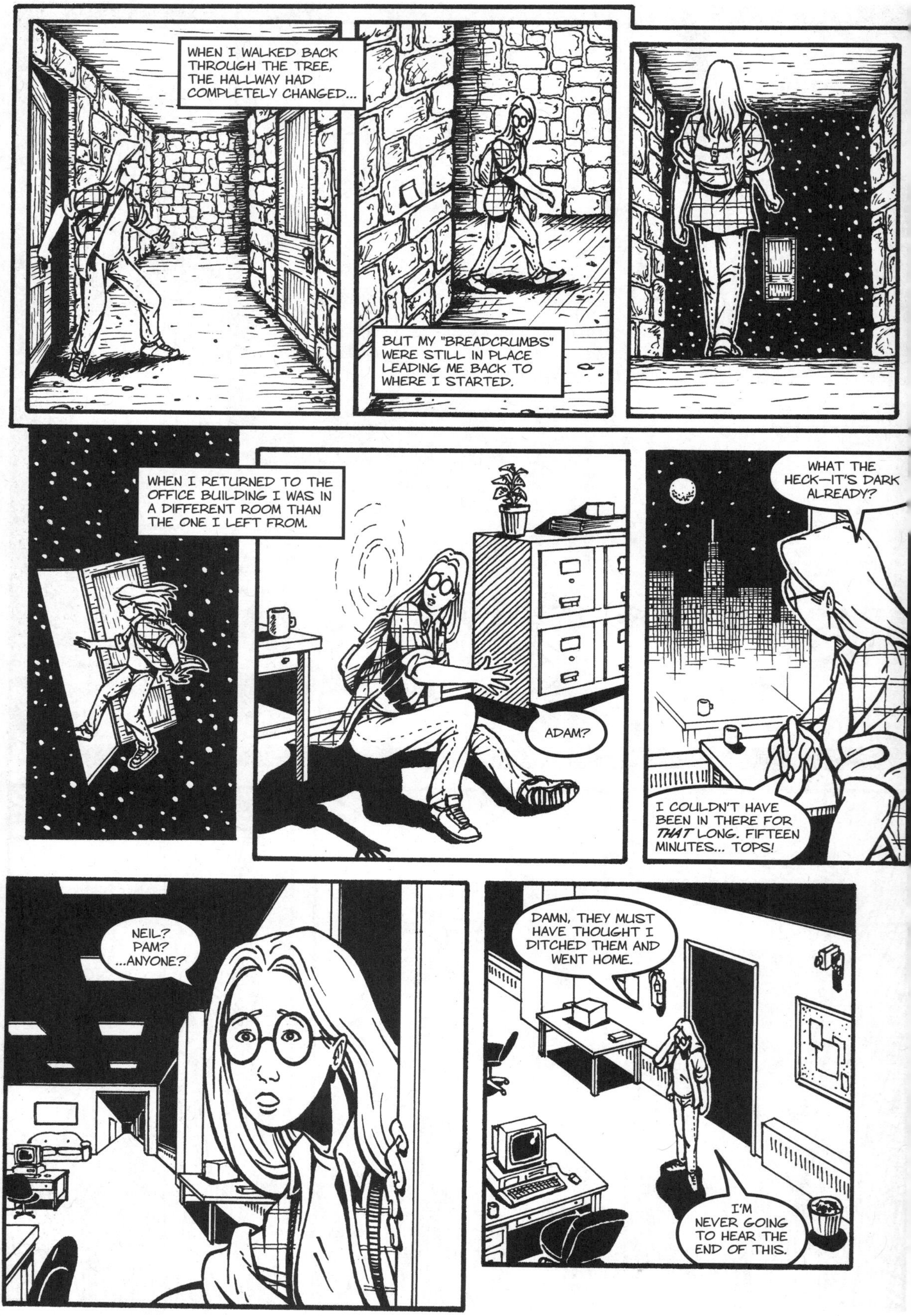
WHEN I WALKED BACK THROUGH THE TREE, THE HALLWAY HAD COMPLETELY CHANGED...
BUT MY "BREADCRUMBS" WERE STILL IN PLACE LEADING ME BACK TO WHERE I STARTED.
WHEN I RETURNED TO THE OFFICE BUILDING I WAS IN A DIFFERENT ROOM THAN THE ONE I LEFT FROM.
ADAM?
WHAT THE HECK—IT'S DARK ALREADY?
I COULDN'T HAVE BEEN IN THERE FOR *THAT* LONG. FIFTEEN MINUTES... TOPS!
NEIL? PAM? ...ANYONE?
DAMN, THEY MUST HAVE THOUGHT I DITCHED THEM AND WENT HOME.
I'M NEVER GOING TO HEAR THE END OF THIS.

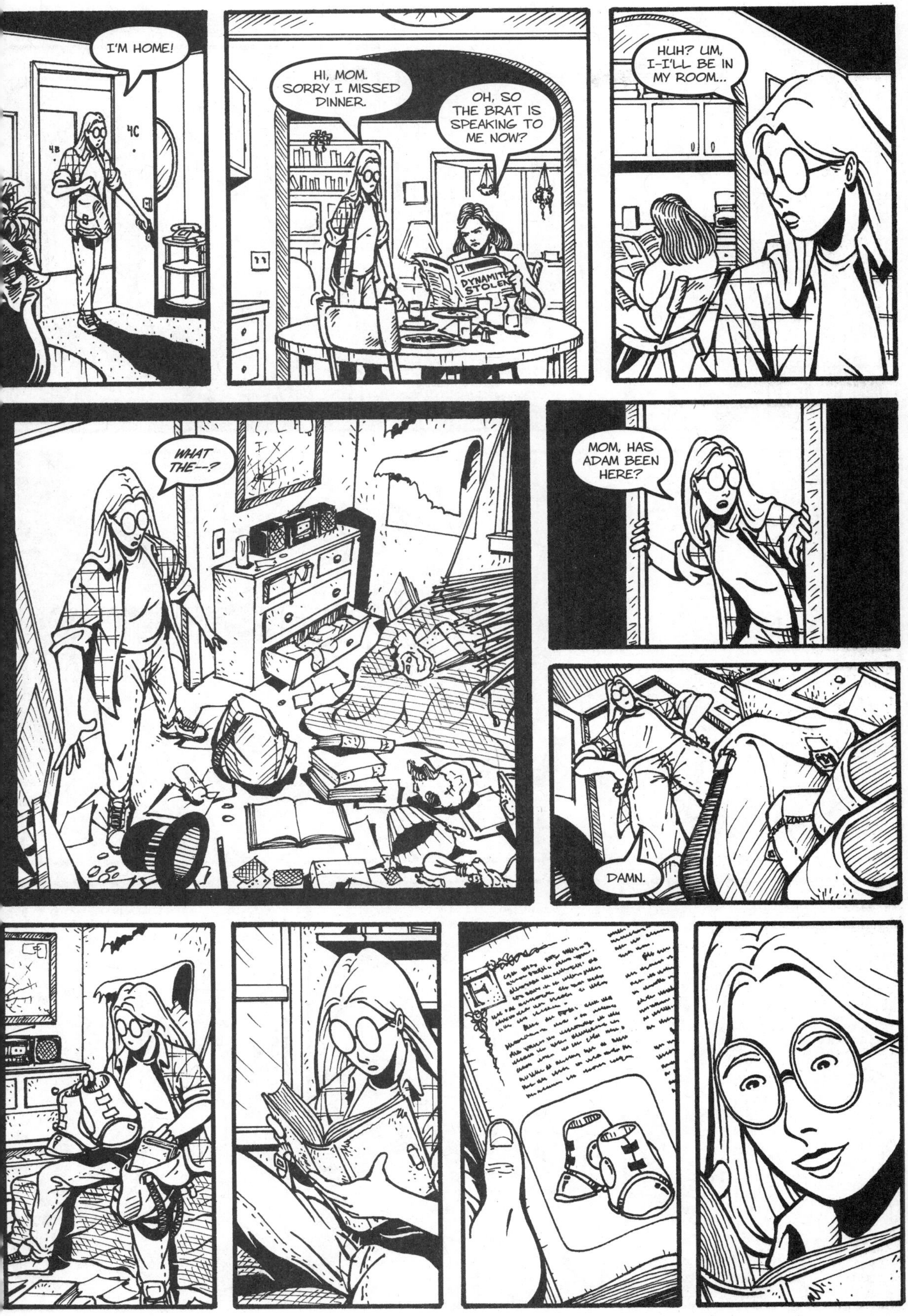
I'M HOME!
HI, MOM. SORRY I MISSED DINNER.
OH, SO THE BRAT IS SPEAKING TO ME NOW?
DYNAMITE STOLEN
HUH? UM, I-I'LL BE IN MY ROOM...
WHAT THE--?
MOM, HAS ADAM BEEN HERE?
DAMN.

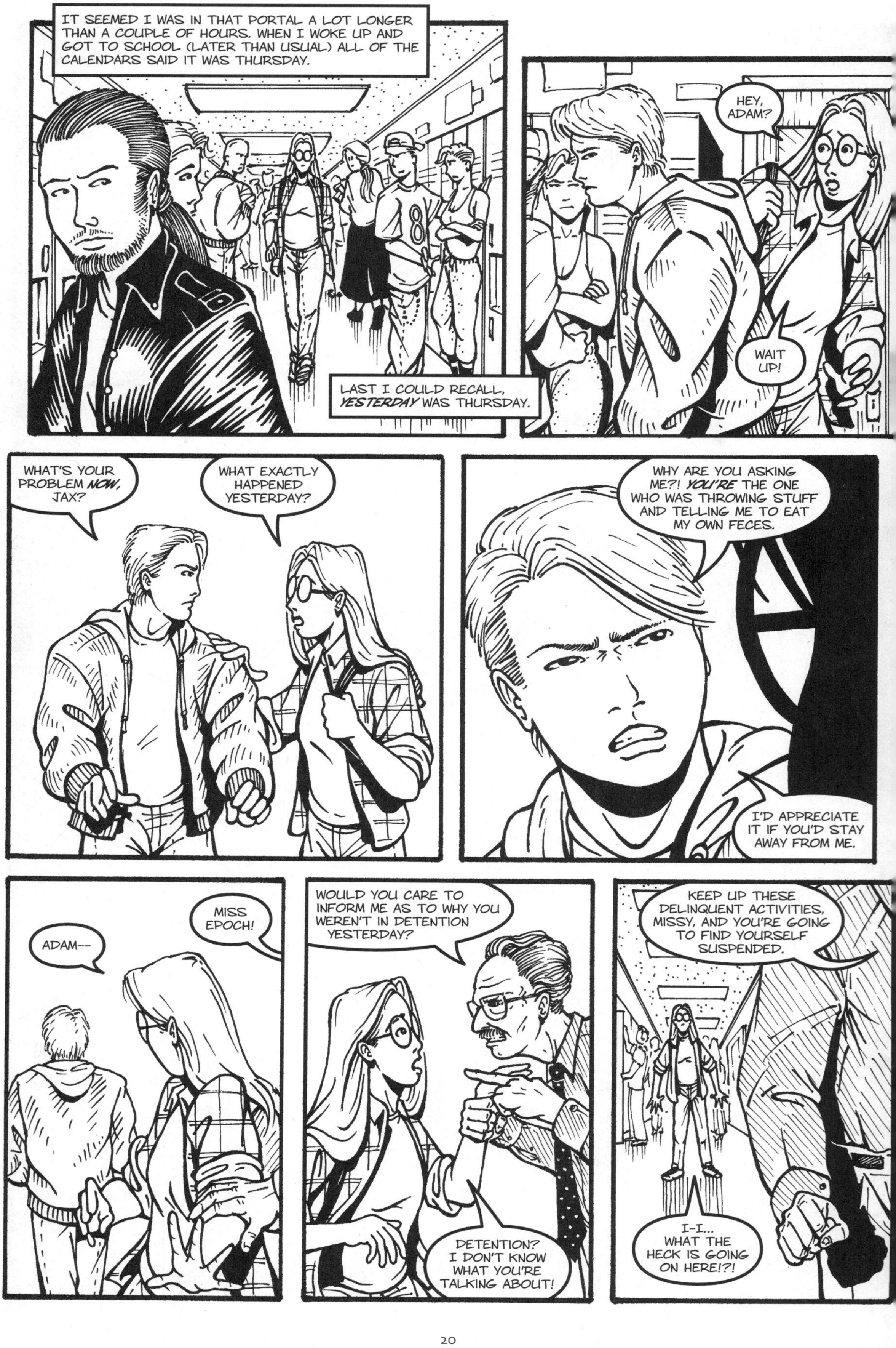

IT SEEMED I WAS IN THAT PORTAL A LOT LONGER THAN A COUPLE OF HOURS. WHEN I WOKE UP AND GOT TO SCHOOL (LATER THAN USUAL) ALL OF THE CALENDARS SAID IT WAS THURSDAY.
LAST I COULD RECALL, *YESTERDAY* WAS THURSDAY.
HEY, ADAM?
WAIT UP!
WHAT'S YOUR PROBLEM *NOW,* JAX?
WHAT EXACTLY HAPPENED YESTERDAY?
WHY ARE YOU ASKING ME?! *YOU'RE* THE ONE WHO WAS THROWING STUFF AND TELLING ME TO EAT MY OWN FECES.
I'D APPRECIATE IT IF YOU'D STAY AWAY FROM ME.
ADAM--
MISS EPOCH!
WOULD YOU CARE TO INFORM ME AS TO WHY YOU WEREN'T IN DETENTION YESTERDAY?
DETENTION? I DON'T KNOW WHAT YOU'RE TALKING ABOUT!
KEEP UP THESE DELINQUENT ACTIVITIES, MISSY, AND YOU'RE GOING TO FIND YOURSELF SUSPENDED.
I-I... WHAT THE HECK IS GOING ON HERE!?!

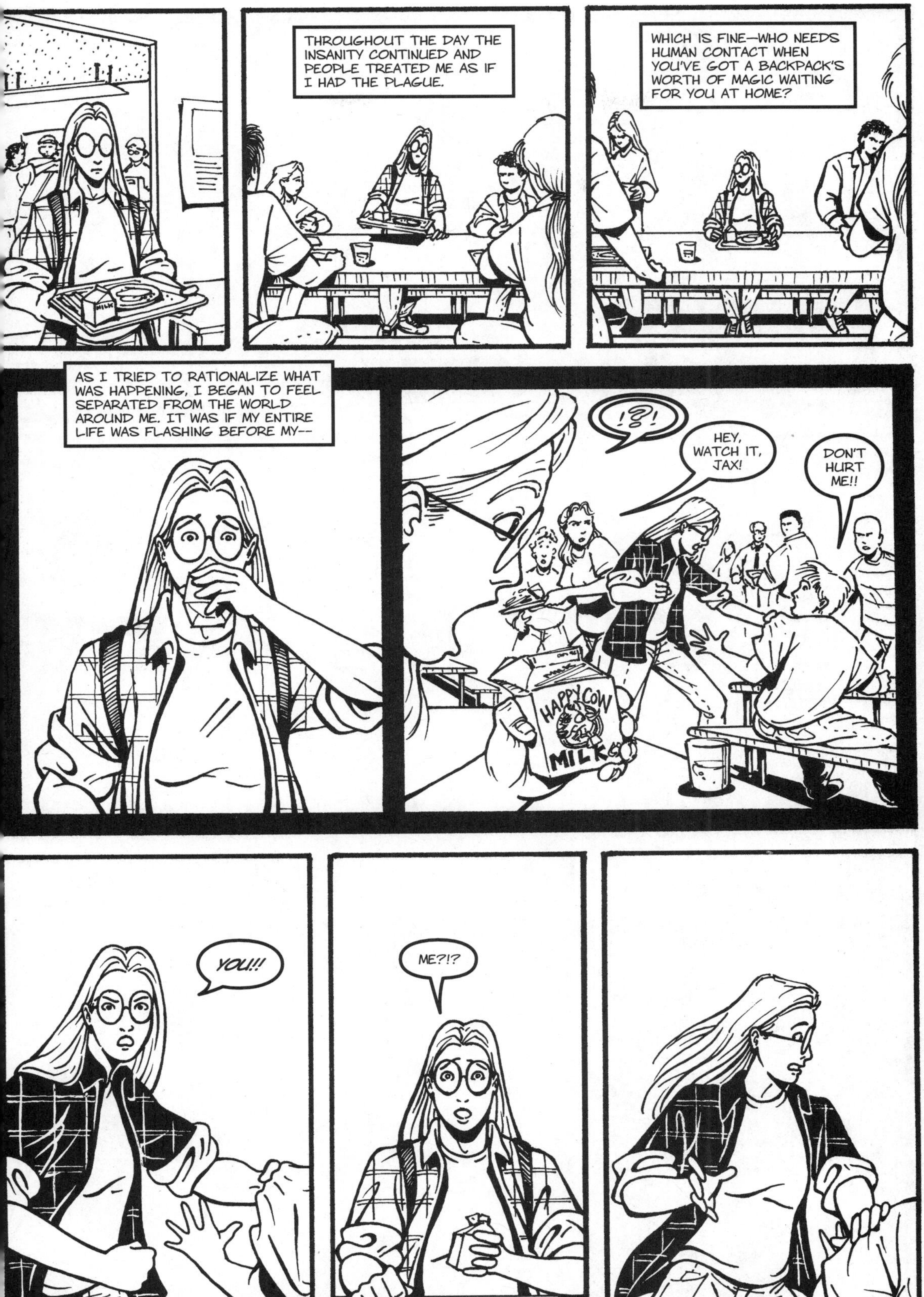
THROUGHOUT THE DAY THE INSANITY CONTINUED AND PEOPLE TREATED ME AS IF I HAD THE PLAGUE.
WHICH IS FINE—WHO NEEDS HUMAN CONTACT WHEN YOU'VE GOT A BACKPACK'S WORTH OF MAGIC WAITING FOR YOU AT HOME?
AS I TRIED TO RATIONALIZE WHAT WAS HAPPENING, I BEGAN TO FEEL SEPARATED FROM THE WORLD AROUND ME. IT WAS IF MY ENTIRE LIFE WAS FLASHING BEFORE MY--
!?!
HEY, WATCH IT, JAX!
DON'T HURT ME!!
HAPPY COW MILK
YOU!!
ME?!?

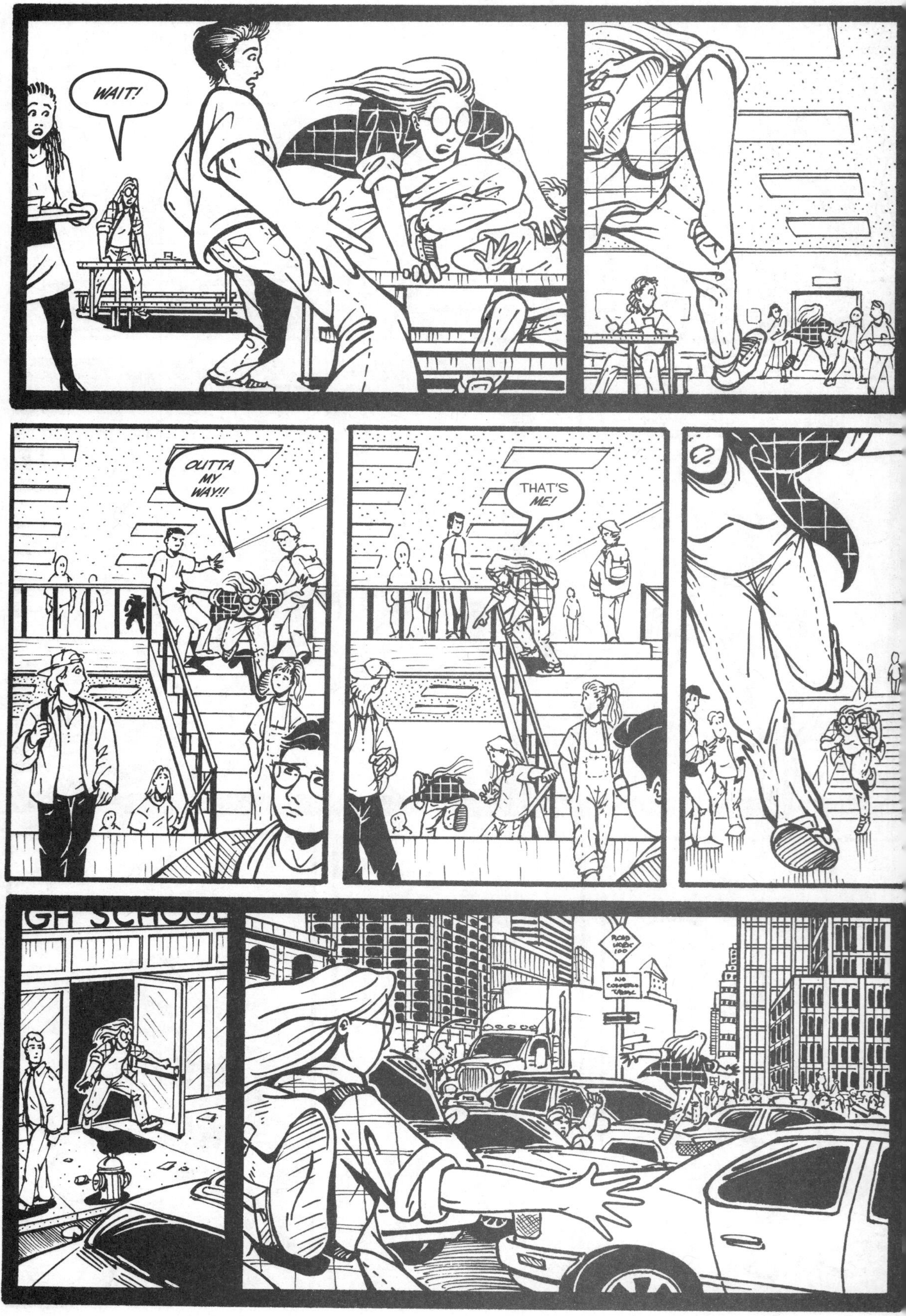
WAIT!
OUTTA MY WAY!!
THAT'S ME!
GH SCHOOL

SHE-SHE WANTS ME DEAD!

I COULD FEEL HER EMOTIONS... HEAR HER THOUGHTS AS SHE RAN FROM ME.

BUT WHY? SHE'S PART OF ME—NO! SHE *IS* ME! I CAN ALMOST SEE WHAT SHE'S SEEING... ALMOST. I HAVE TO FIND HER, EVEN IF SHE TRIES TO HURT ME. I NEED TO KNOW WHAT THIS IS ALL ABOUT. MAYBE SHE CAN MAKE SENSE OF IT ALL—THE HALLWAY, THE SHACK, THE... *ARMOR!*

ACCORDING TO THAT ANCIENT BOOK, THE GLOVES AND THE BOOTS FORM A PROTECTIVE ARMOR, A MAGICAL SHIELD THAT CAN BE USED TO DEFEND ME AGAINST... MYSELF.

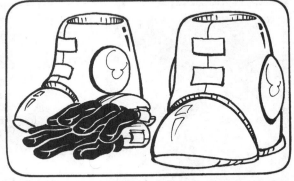

WHAT A MESS.

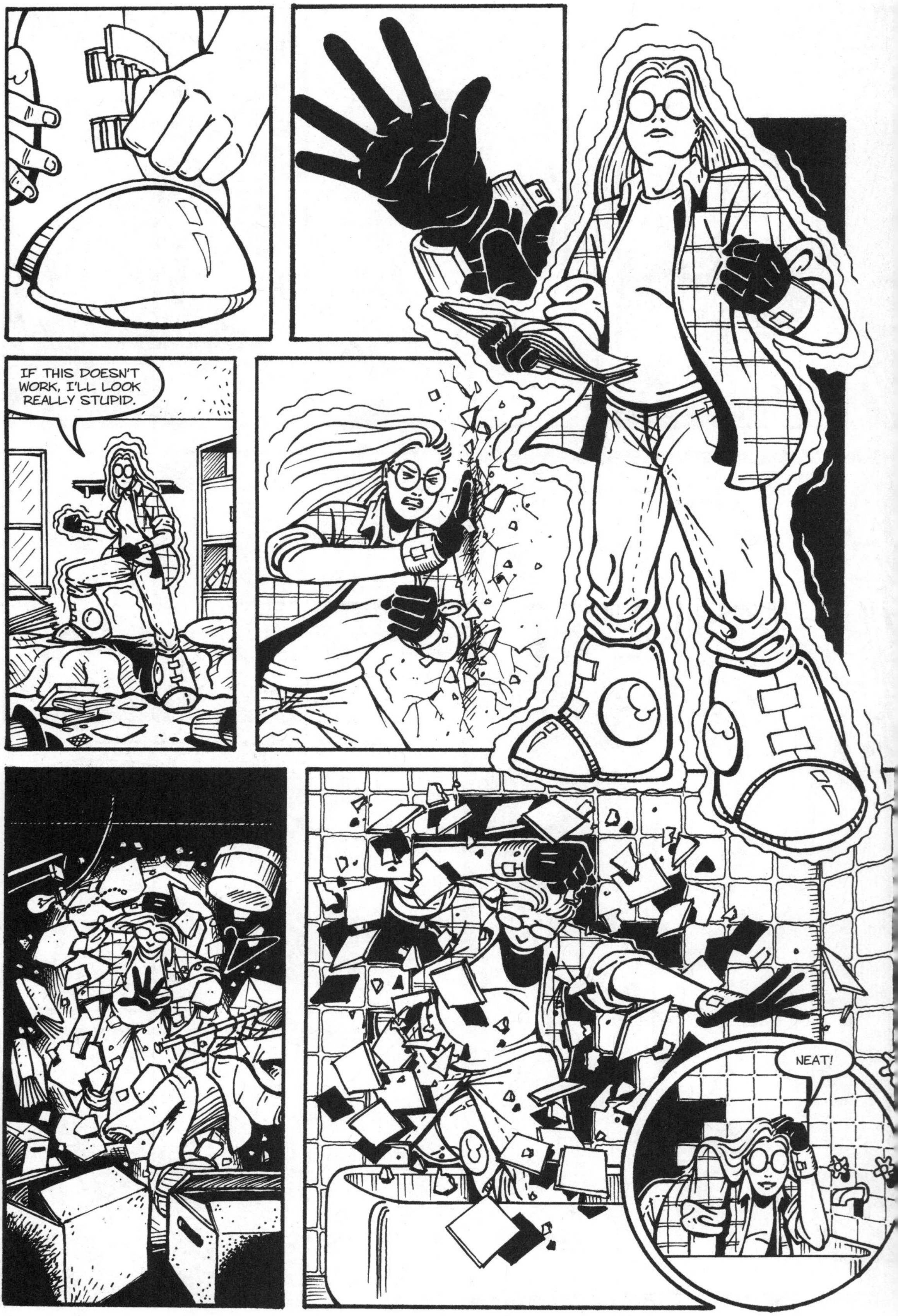
IF THIS DOESN'T WORK, I'LL LOOK REALLY STUPID.
NEAT!

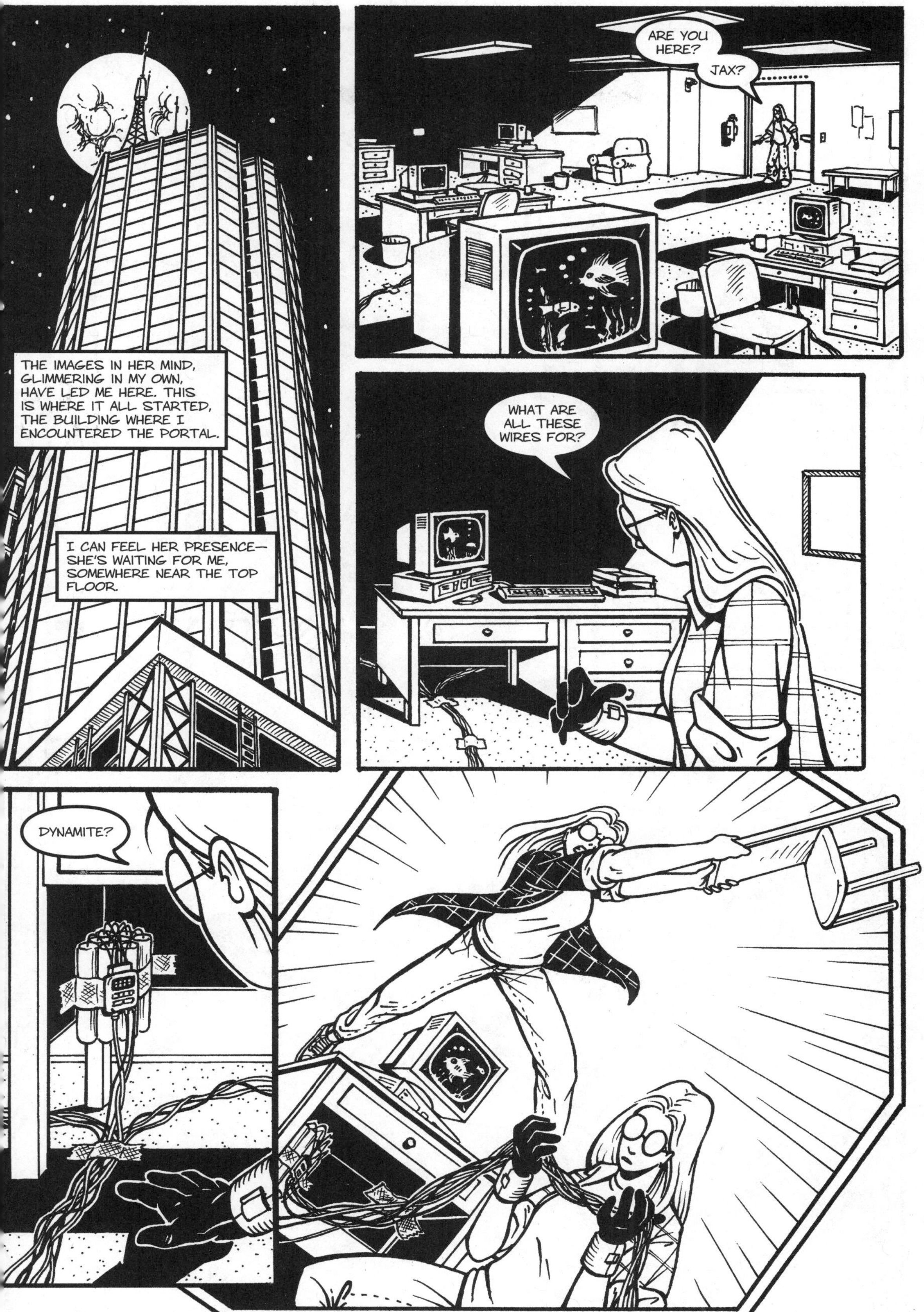
THE IMAGES IN HER MIND, GLIMMERING IN MY OWN, HAVE LED ME HERE. THIS IS WHERE IT ALL STARTED, THE BUILDING WHERE I ENCOUNTERED THE PORTAL.
I CAN FEEL HER PRESENCE—SHE'S WAITING FOR ME, SOMEWHERE NEAR THE TOP FLOOR.
ARE YOU HERE?
JAX?
WHAT ARE ALL THESE WIRES FOR?
DYNAMITE?

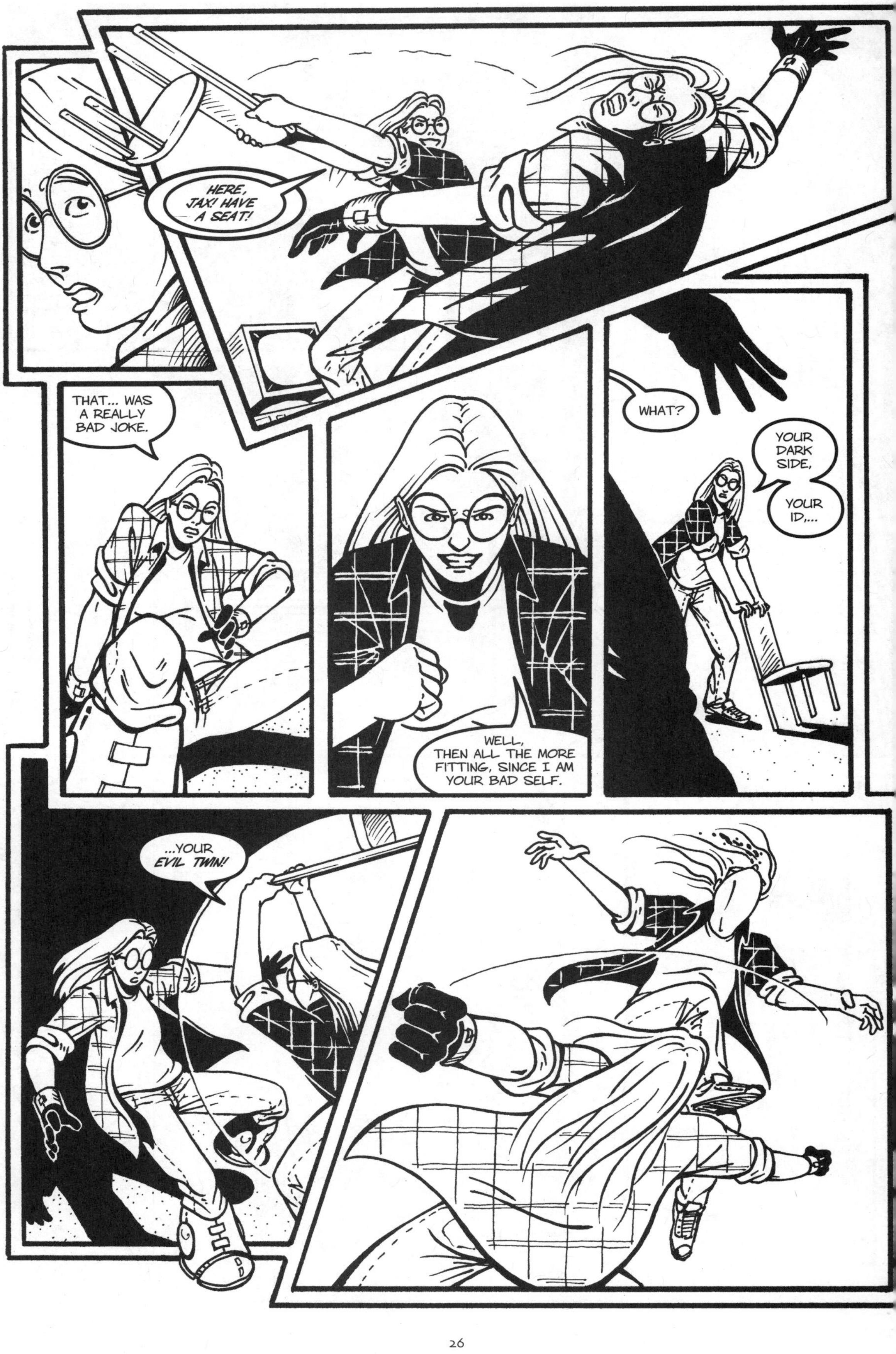
HERE, JAX! HAVE A SEAT!
THAT... WAS A REALLY BAD JOKE.
WELL, THEN ALL THE MORE FITTING, SINCE I AM YOUR BAD SELF.
WHAT?
YOUR DARK SIDE,
YOUR ID,...
...YOUR EVIL TWIN!

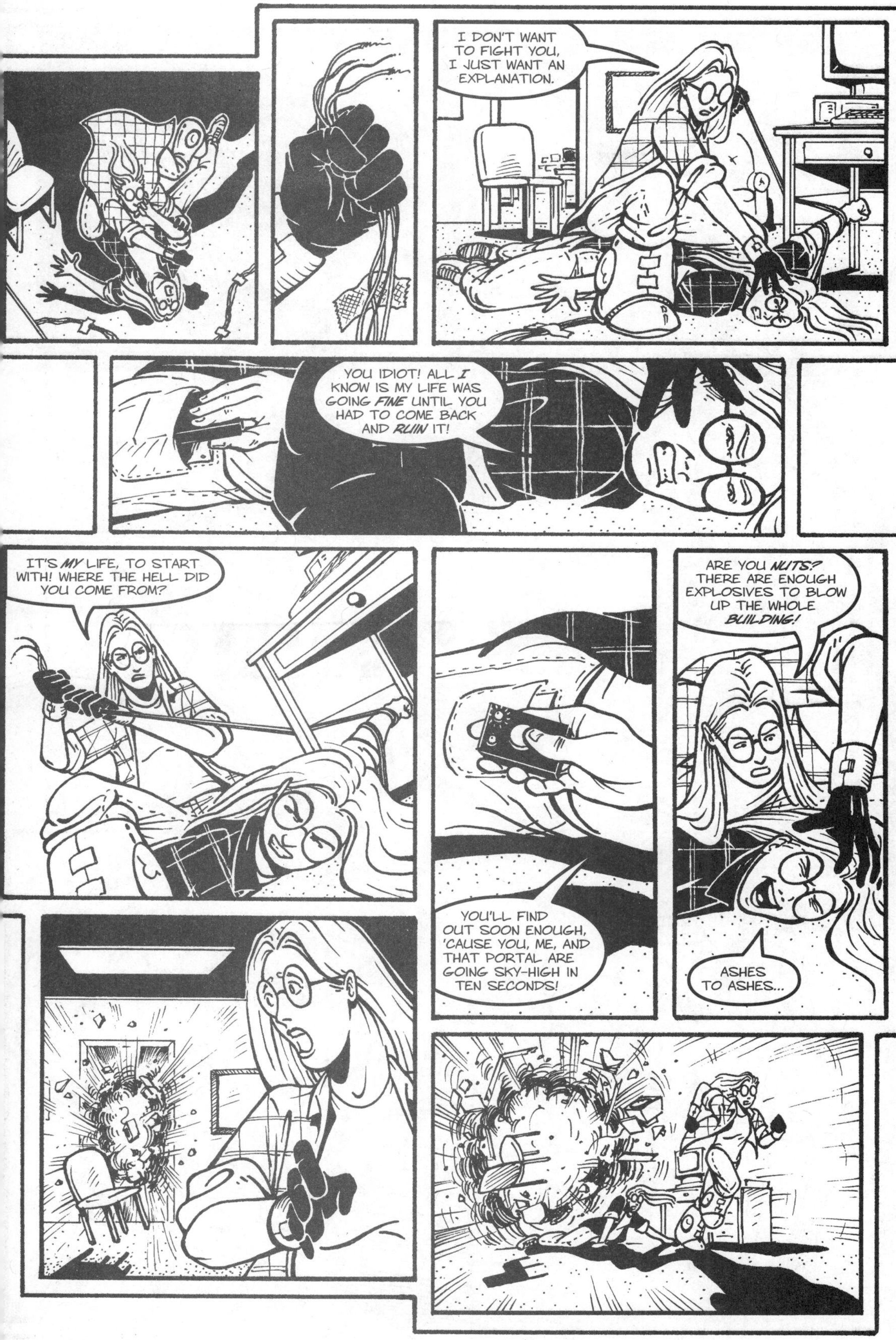
I DON'T WANT TO FIGHT YOU, I JUST WANT AN EXPLANATION.
YOU IDIOT! ALL *I* KNOW IS MY LIFE WAS GOING *FINE* UNTIL YOU HAD TO COME BACK AND *RUIN* IT!
IT'S *MY* LIFE, TO START WITH! WHERE THE HELL DID YOU COME FROM?
YOU'LL FIND OUT SOON ENOUGH, 'CAUSE YOU, ME, AND THAT PORTAL ARE GOING SKY-HIGH IN TEN SECONDS!
ARE YOU *NUTS?* THERE ARE ENOUGH EXPLOSIVES TO BLOW UP THE WHOLE *BUILDING!*
ASHES TO ASHES...

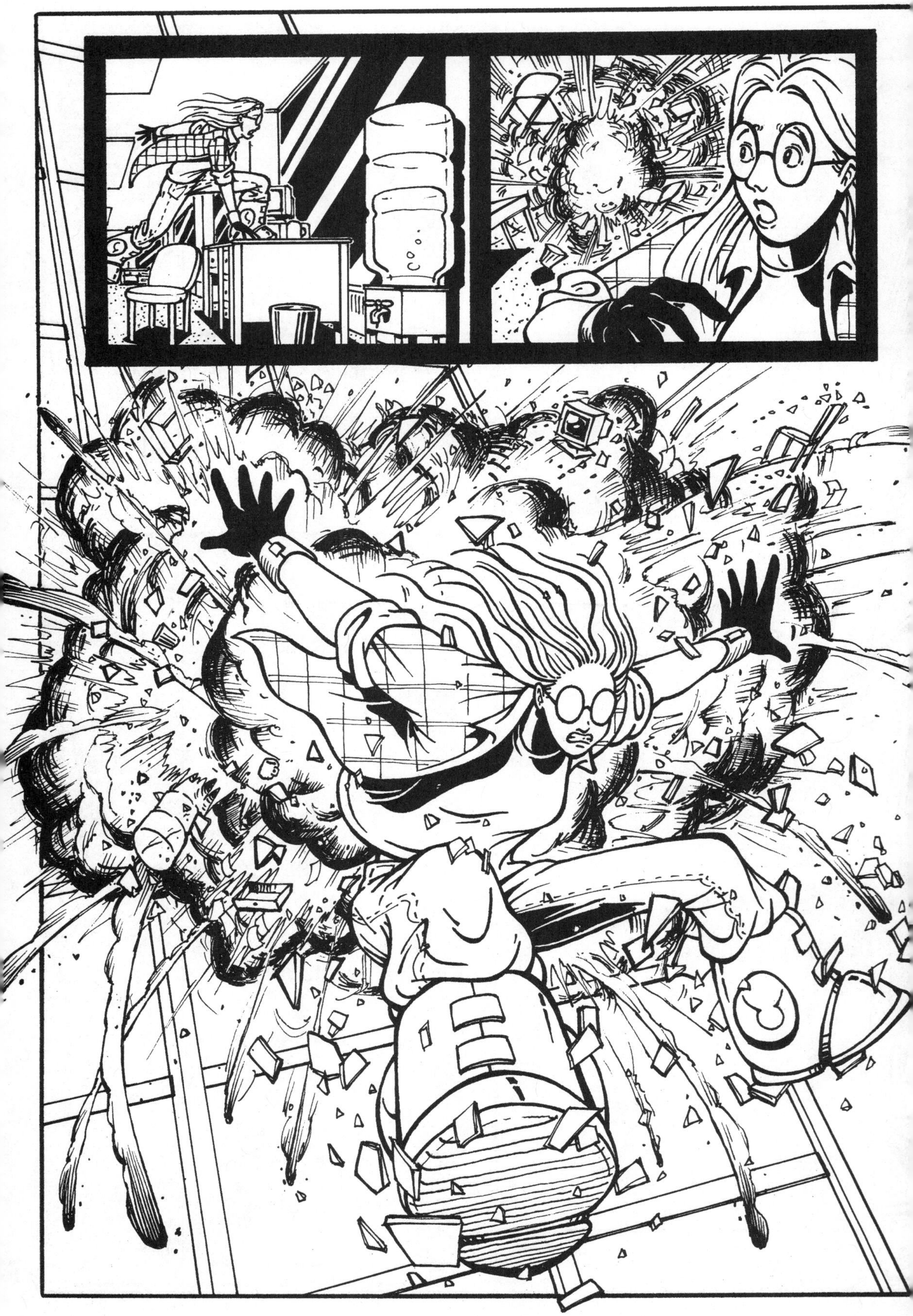

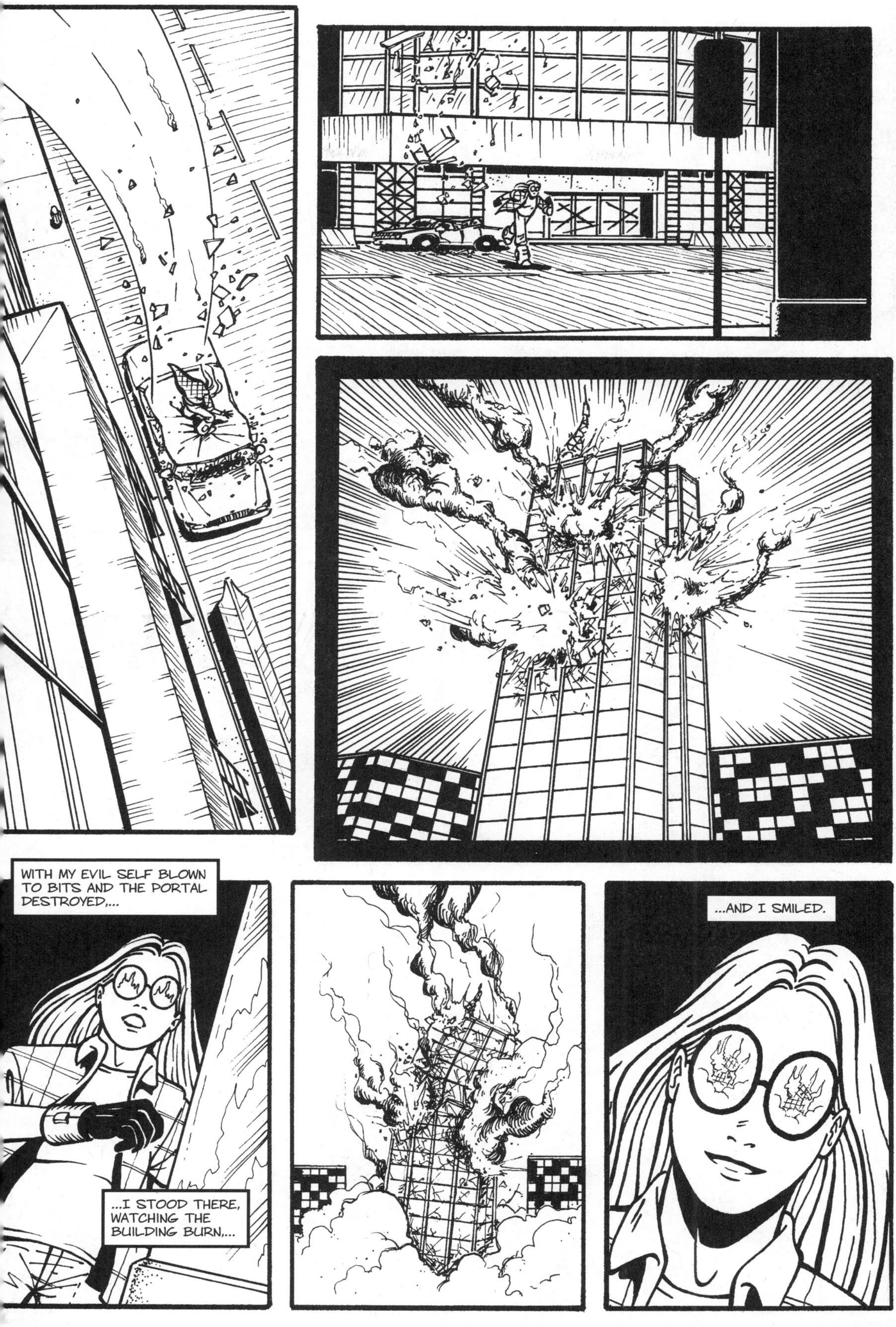
WITH MY EVIL SELF BLOWN TO BITS AND THE PORTAL DESTROYED,...
...I STOOD THERE, WATCHING THE BUILDING BURN,...
...AND I SMILED.

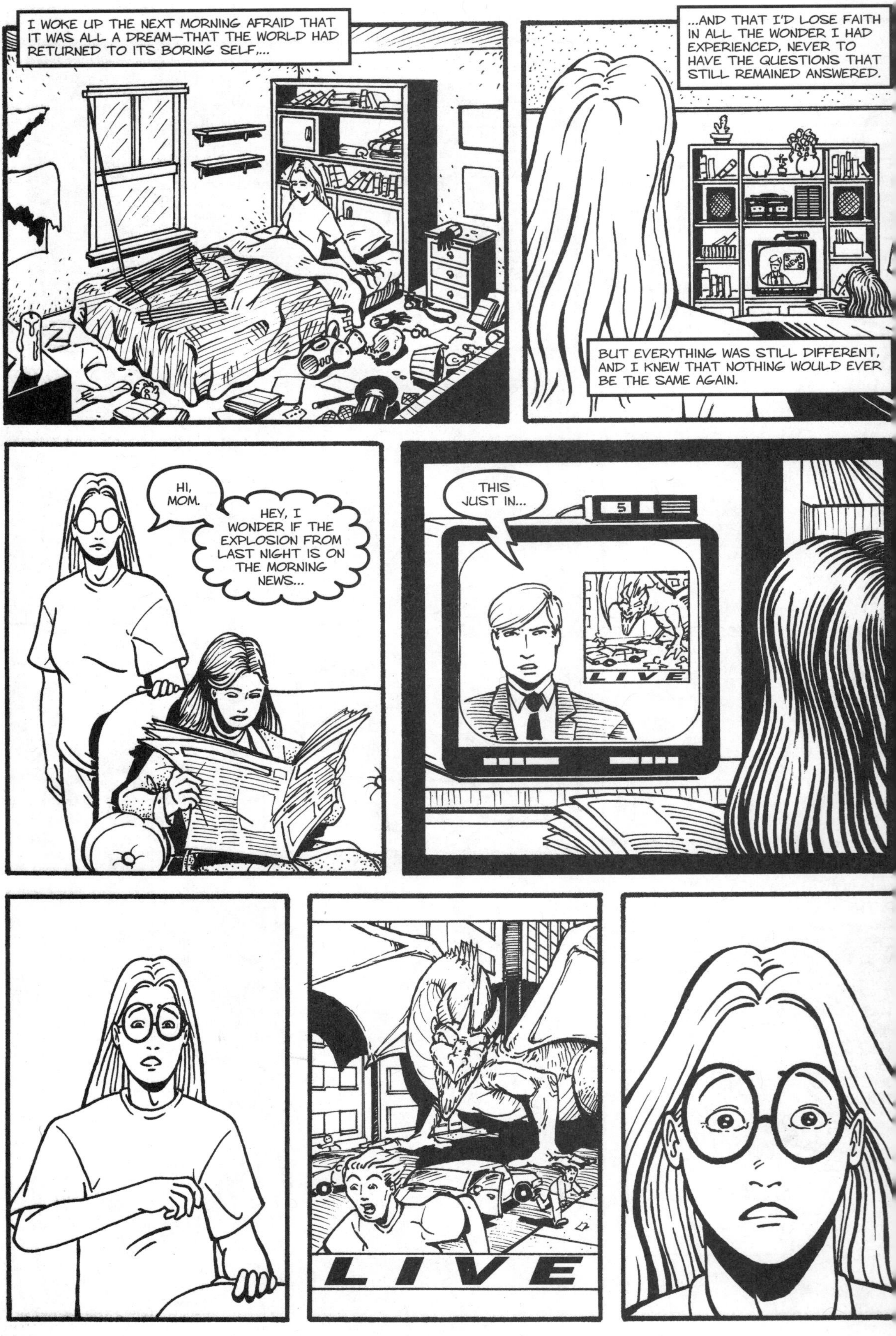
I WOKE UP THE NEXT MORNING AFRAID THAT IT WAS ALL A DREAM—THAT THE WORLD HAD RETURNED TO ITS BORING SELF,...
...AND THAT I'D LOSE FAITH IN ALL THE WONDER I HAD EXPERIENCED, NEVER TO HAVE THE QUESTIONS THAT STILL REMAINED ANSWERED.
BUT EVERYTHING WAS STILL DIFFERENT, AND I KNEW THAT NOTHING WOULD EVER BE THE SAME AGAIN.
HI, MOM.
HEY, I WONDER IF THE EXPLOSION FROM LAST NIGHT IS ON THE MORNING NEWS...
THIS JUST IN...
5
LIVE
LIVE

"I'M STILL JAX EPOCH—AT LEAST I HOPE I AM. AFTER LAST NIGHT, I MAY NEVER BE TOTALLY SURE. IF I *AM* ME, NOT BROKEN AND STILL SANE, THEN THE WORLD I ONCE KNEW IS COMPLETELY FALLING APART."

IN CASE YOU MISSED IT, I RECENTLY FELL THROUGH A HOLE IN SPACE (CORRECT ME IF I'M WRONG) WHICH LED ME TO A DARK HALLWAY WITH DOORS THAT CAN TRANSPORT YOU FROM OZ TO KANSAS.

THE ONLY PHYSICAL PROOF I HAVE OF MY EXPERIENCE IS AN ANCIENT BOOK AND A SPECIAL PAIR OF BOOTS AND GLOVES. SHAMEFULLY, I SORT OF TOOK THEM WITHOUT REALLY FINDING OUT WHO THEY BELONGED TO, BUT MY IMPULSES SCREAM LOUDER THAN MY CONSCIENCE CRICKETS.

WHEN I FOUND MY WAY BACK HOME THROUGH THE PORTAL, I DISCOVERED A WEEK MISSING FROM MY NORMALLY UNEVENTFUL LIFE. BUT DID ANYONE NOTICE I WAS GONE? NOPE. 'CAUSE, FOR REASONS STILL UNKNOWN TO ME, A PSYCHOTIC VERSION OF MYSELF HAD FILLED MY SNEAKERS IN MY ABSENCE. WHO WOULD'VE KNOWN CHASING A RABBIT WOULD HAVE SUCH CONSEQUENCES... SHUT UP, ALICE.

ALL I LEARNED WAS THAT SHE WAS OBSESSED WITH KILLING ME AND WAS THE EMBODIMENT OF MY DARK SIDE (THE PART WITH NO SENSE OF HUMOR). THANKS TO THE COOL BOOTS AND GLOVES I WAS ABLE TO SAVE MYSELF, BUT I WASN'T ABLE TO STOP HER FROM BLOWING UP THE BUILDING FROM WHICH THE PORTAL ORIGINATED, AND HERSELF WITH IT. GOT IT? DOES IT ALL MAKE SENSE? IF IT DOES, I'M IN SERIOUS TROUBLE.

I HAD WOKEN UP THAT NEXT MORNING TO CHECK AND SEE IF THE REMAINS OF THE CHAOS I HAD CAUSED THE NIGHT BEFORE HAD MADE THE EARLY NEWS. INSTEAD, IT SEEMED SOMETHING A LITTLE MORE EVENTFUL STOLE MY SPOTLIGHT...

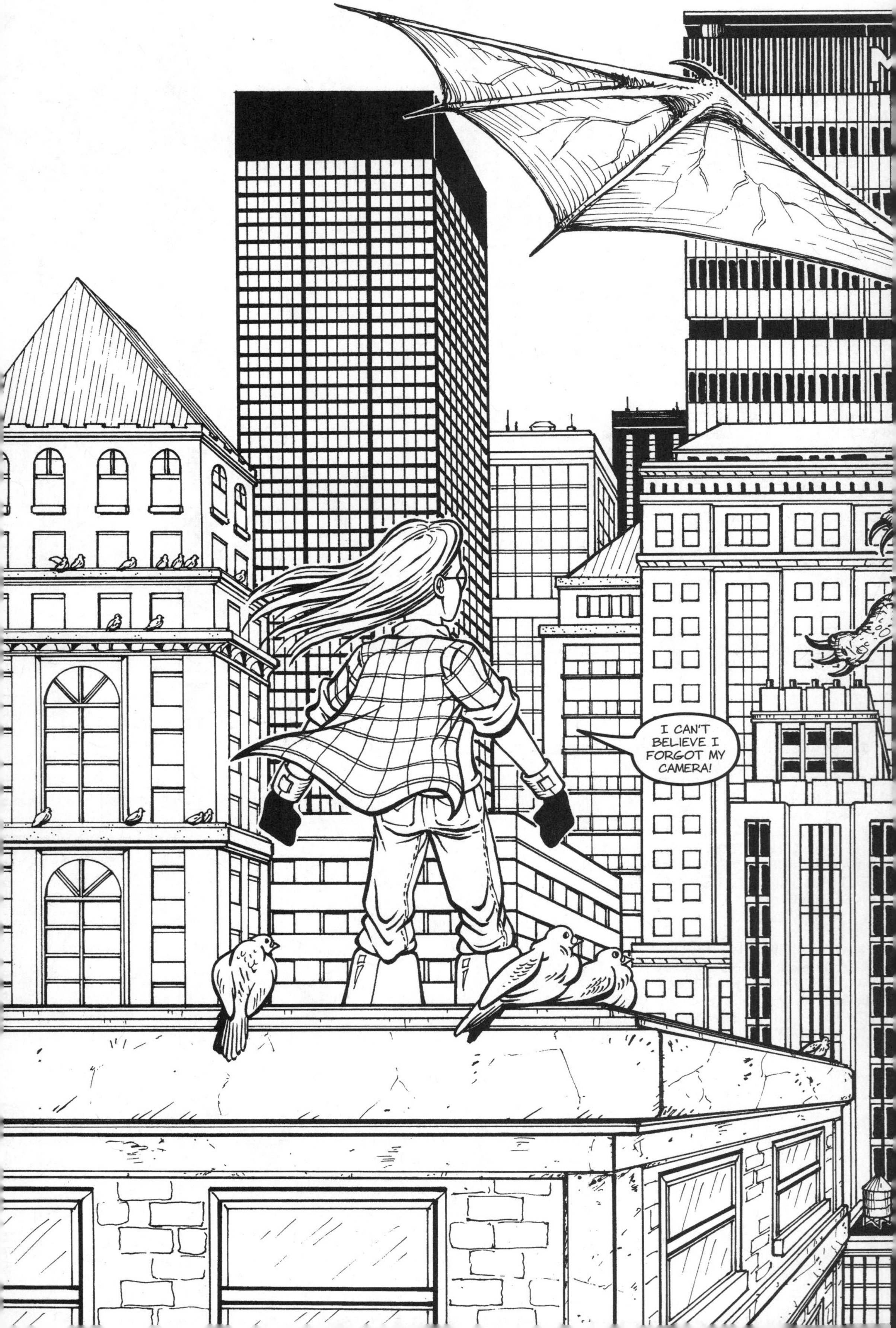
I CAN'T BELIEVE I FORGOT MY CAMERA!

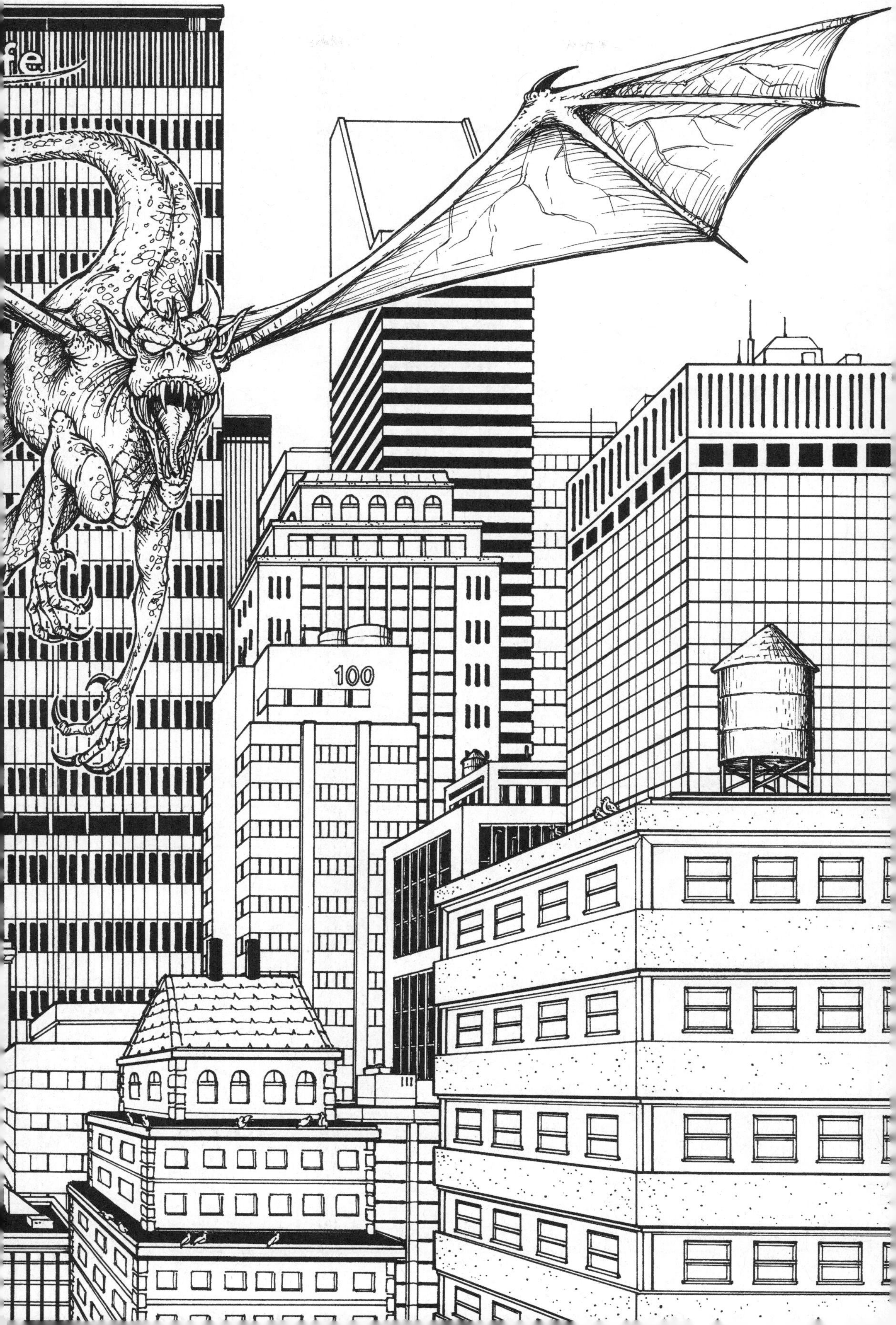
fe
100

WHY AM I SO SPELLBOUND? AFTER ALL I'VE BEEN THROUGH, YOU'D THINK *NOTHING* WOULD SURPRISE ME...

BUT A REAL, LIVE *DRAGON* FLYING OVER NEW YORK CITY IS JUST TOO MUCH!

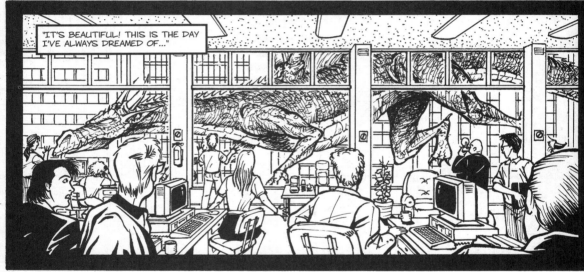

"IT'S BEAUTIFUL! THIS IS THE DAY I'VE ALWAYS DREAMED OF..."

UH, OH...

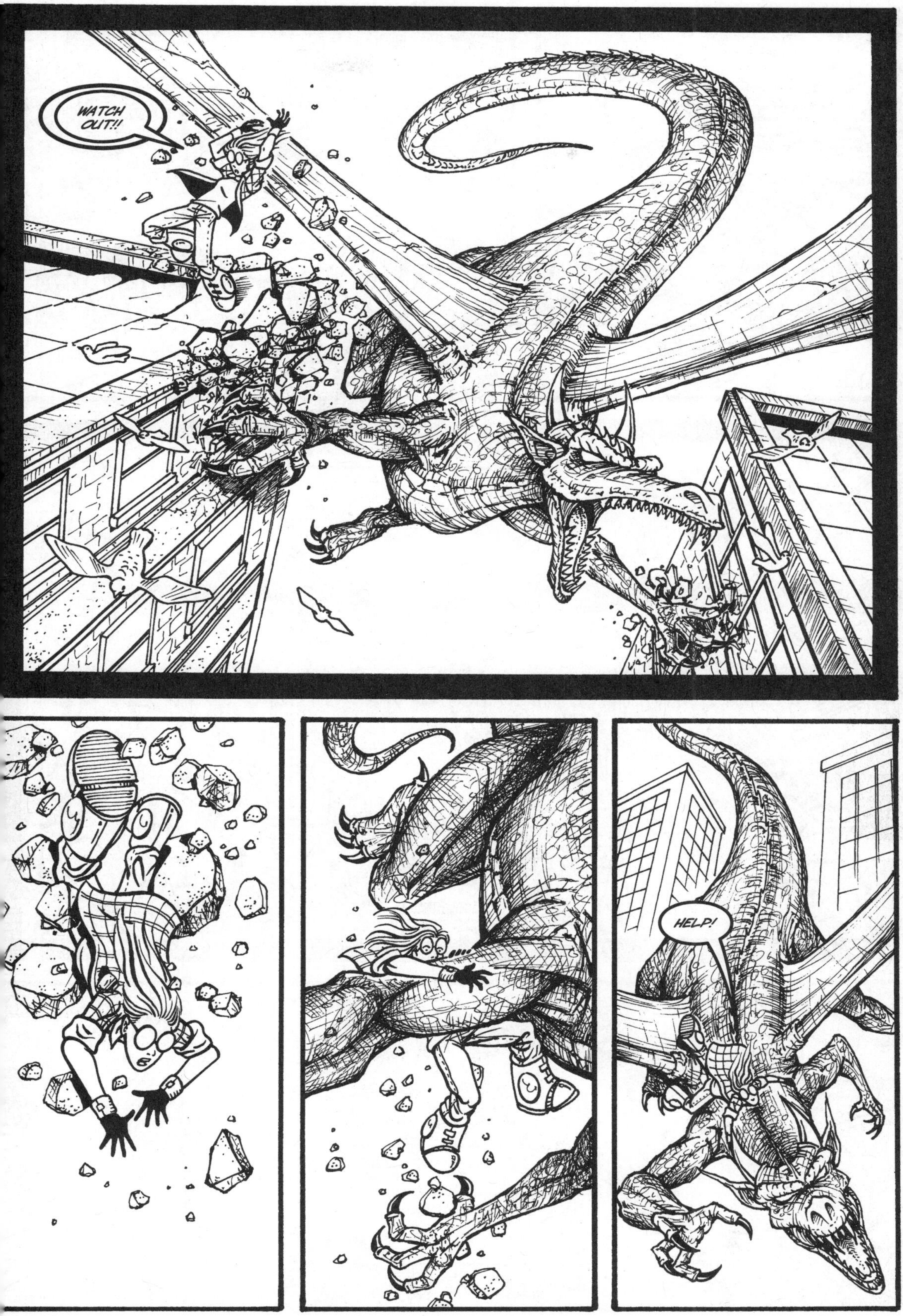
WATCH OUT!!
HELP!

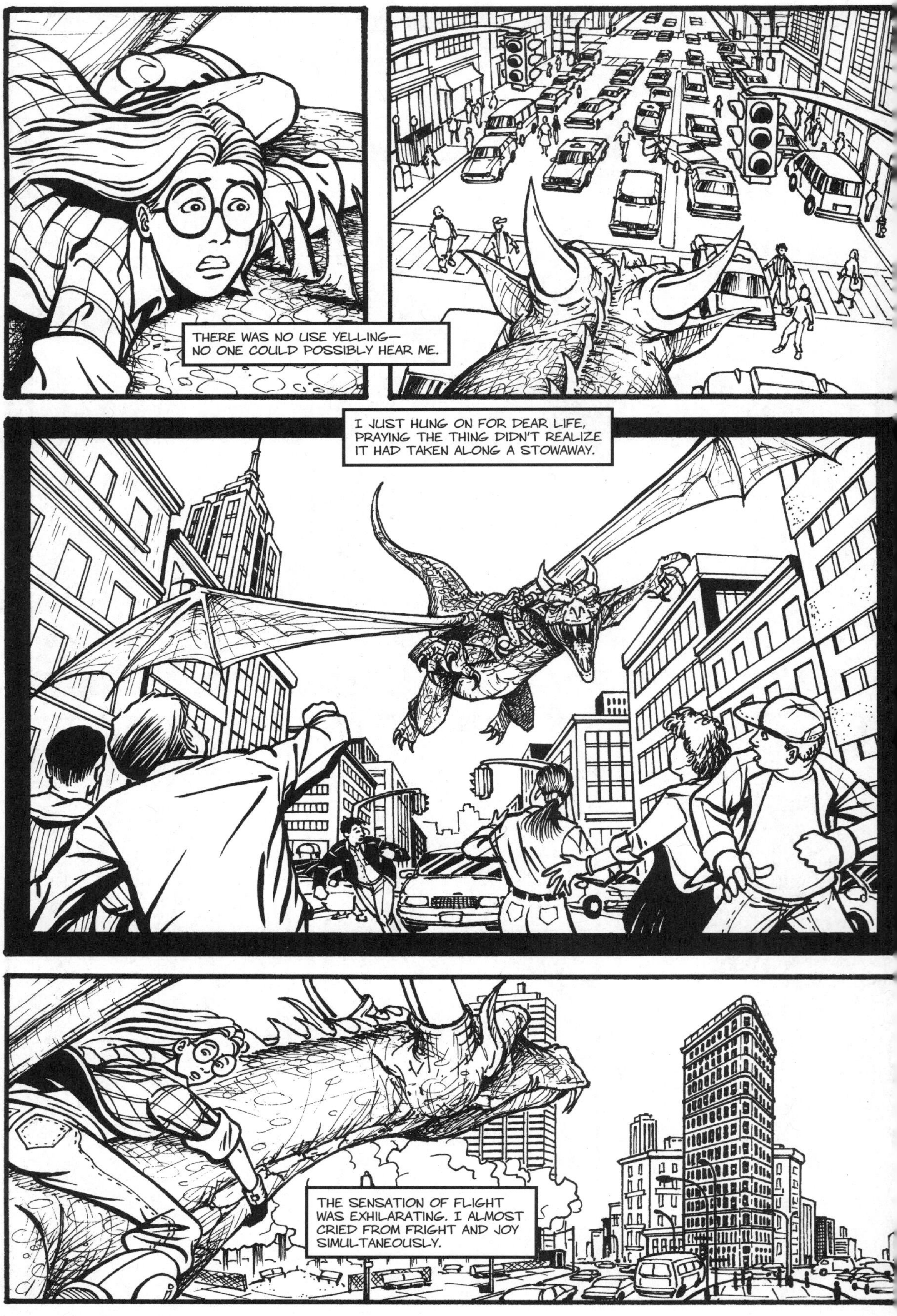
THERE WAS NO USE YELLING—
NO ONE COULD POSSIBLY HEAR ME.
I JUST HUNG ON FOR DEAR LIFE, PRAYING THE THING DIDN'T REALIZE IT HAD TAKEN ALONG A STOWAWAY.
THE SENSATION OF FLIGHT WAS EXHILARATING. I ALMOST CRIED FROM FRIGHT AND JOY SIMULTANEOUSLY.

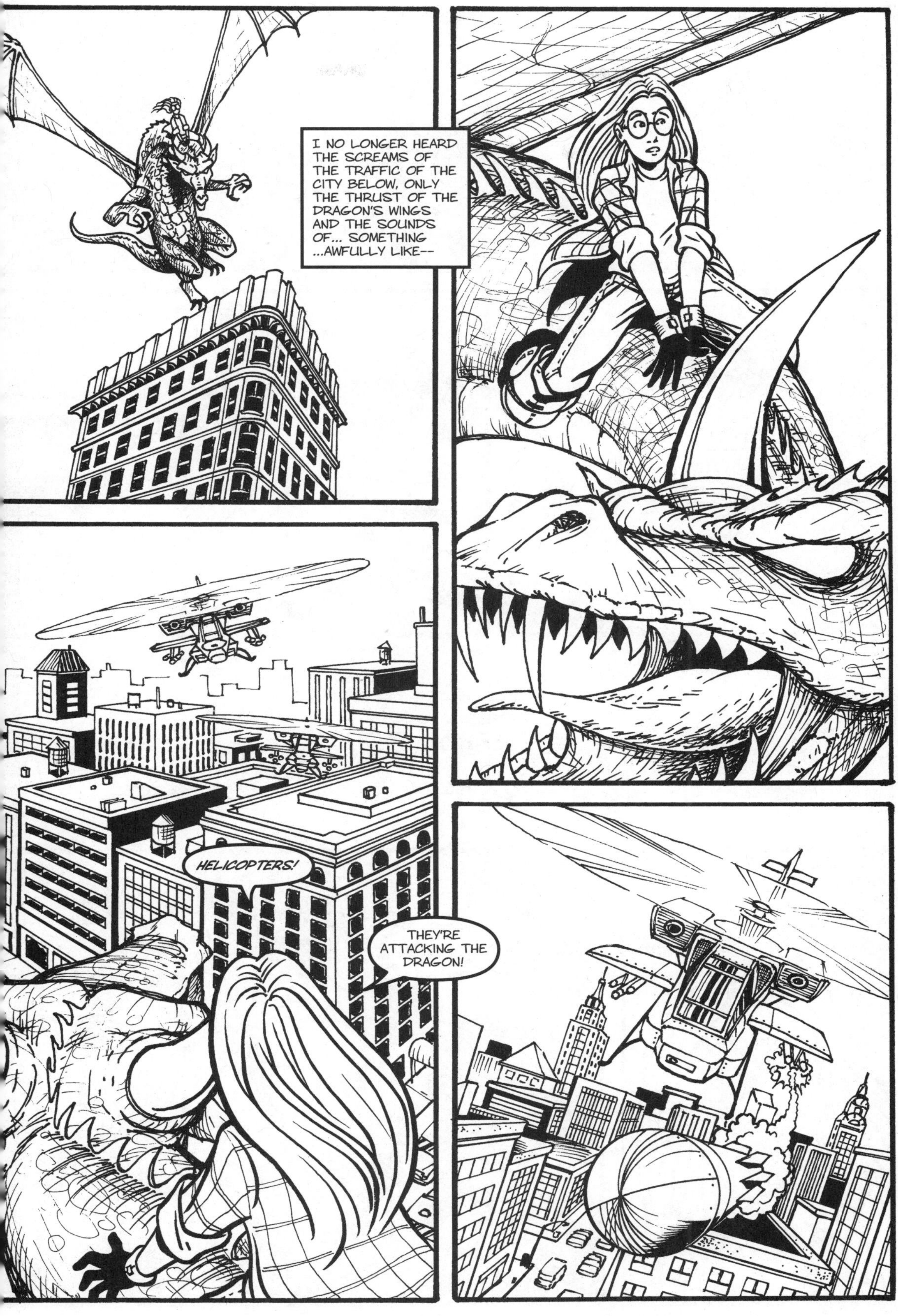
I NO LONGER HEARD THE SCREAMS OF THE TRAFFIC OF THE CITY BELOW, ONLY THE THRUST OF THE DRAGON'S WINGS AND THE SOUNDS OF... SOMETHING ...AWFULLY LIKE--
HELICOPTERS!
THEY'RE ATTACKING THE DRAGON!

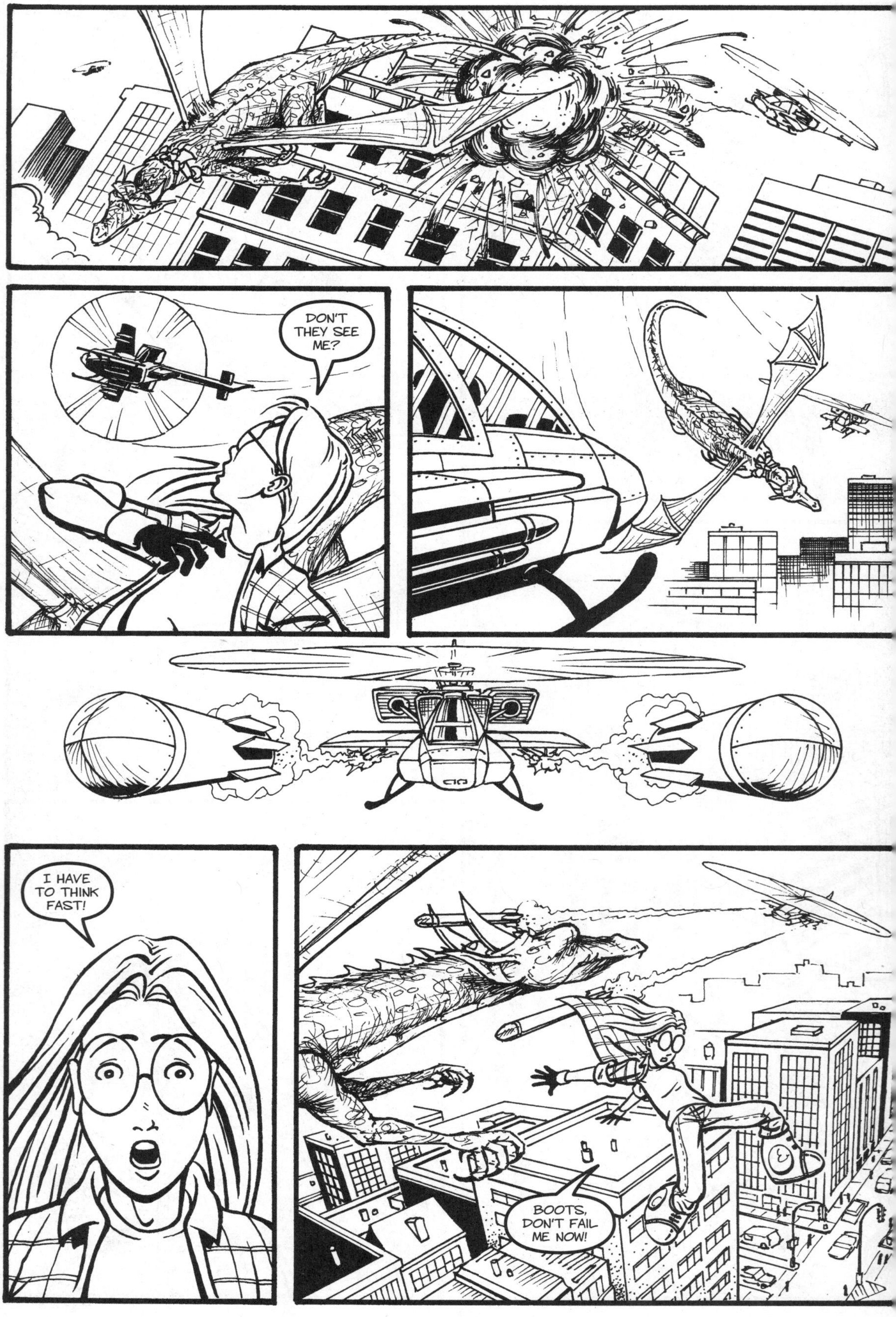
DON'T THEY SEE ME?
I HAVE TO THINK FAST!
BOOTS, DON'T FAIL ME NOW!

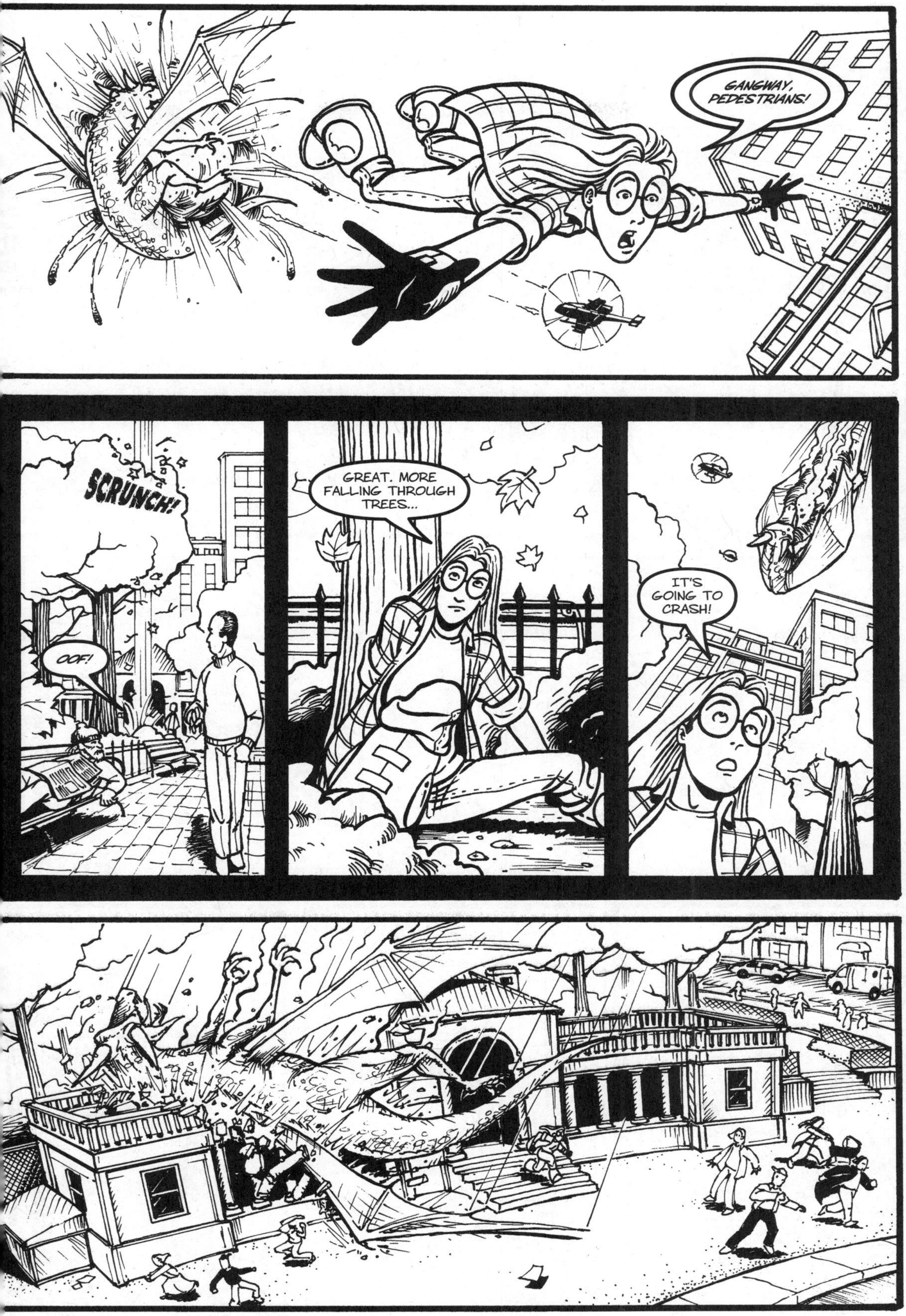
GANGWAY, PEDESTRIANS!
SCRUNCH!
OOF!
GREAT. MORE FALLING THROUGH TREES...
IT'S GOING TO CRASH!

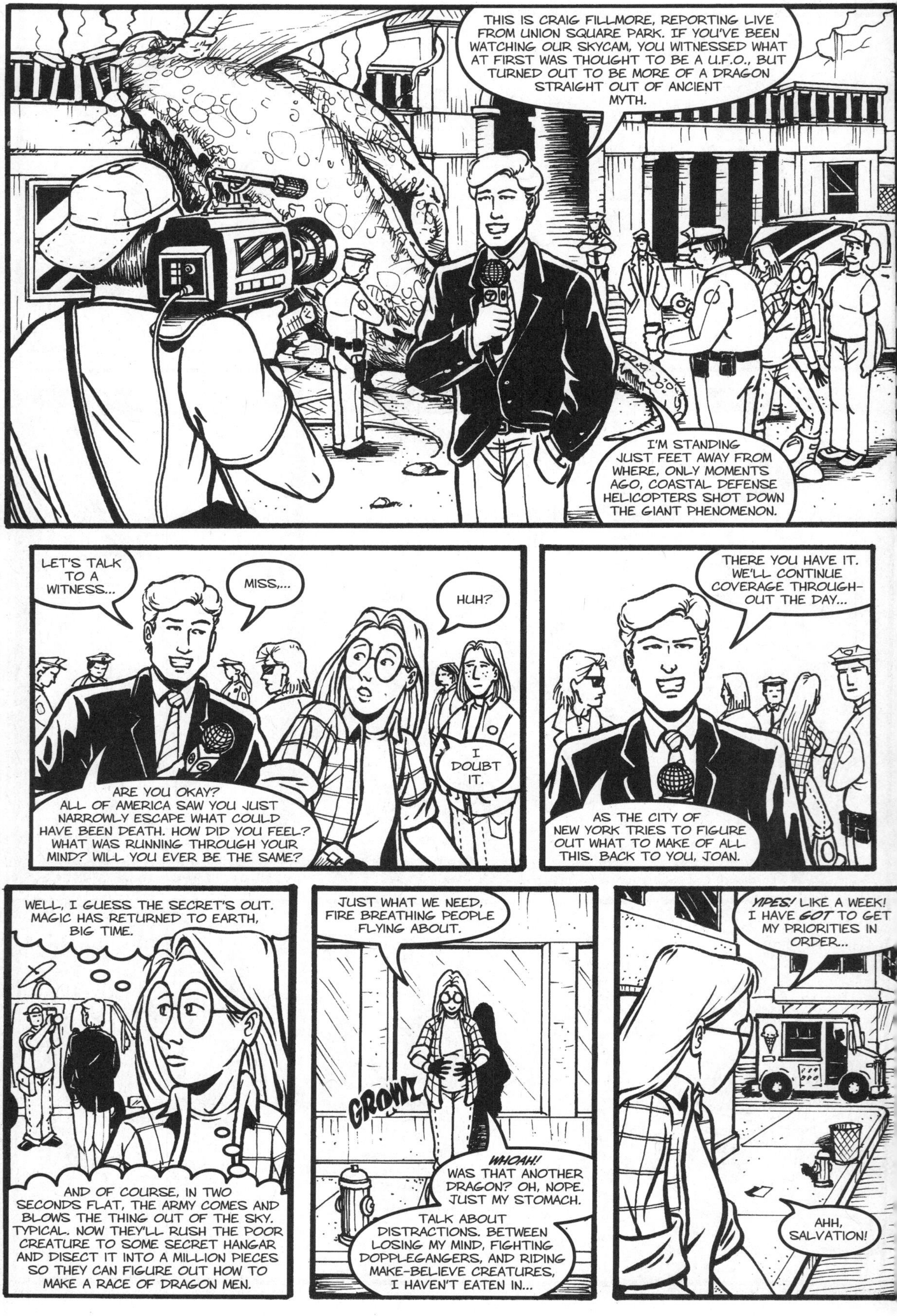
THIS IS CRAIG FILLMORE, REPORTING LIVE FROM UNION SQUARE PARK. IF YOU'VE BEEN WATCHING OUR SKYCAM, YOU WITNESSED WHAT AT FIRST WAS THOUGHT TO BE A U.F.O., BUT TURNED OUT TO BE MORE OF A DRAGON STRAIGHT OUT OF ANCIENT MYTH.
I'M STANDING JUST FEET AWAY FROM WHERE, ONLY MOMENTS AGO, COASTAL DEFENSE HELICOPTERS SHOT DOWN THE GIANT PHENOMENON.
LET'S TALK TO A WITNESS...
MISS,...
HUH?
ARE YOU OKAY? ALL OF AMERICA SAW YOU JUST NARROWLY ESCAPE WHAT COULD HAVE BEEN DEATH. HOW DID YOU FEEL? WHAT WAS RUNNING THROUGH YOUR MIND? WILL YOU EVER BE THE SAME?
I DOUBT IT.
THERE YOU HAVE IT. WE'LL CONTINUE COVERAGE THROUGH-OUT THE DAY...
AS THE CITY OF NEW YORK TRIES TO FIGURE OUT WHAT TO MAKE OF ALL THIS. BACK TO YOU, JOAN.
WELL, I GUESS THE SECRET'S OUT. MAGIC HAS RETURNED TO EARTH, BIG TIME.
AND OF COURSE, IN TWO SECONDS FLAT, THE ARMY COMES AND BLOWS THE THING OUT OF THE SKY. TYPICAL. NOW THEY'LL RUSH THE POOR CREATURE TO SOME SECRET HANGAR AND DISECT IT INTO A MILLION PIECES SO THEY CAN FIGURE OUT HOW TO MAKE A RACE OF DRAGON MEN.
JUST WHAT WE NEED, FIRE BREATHING PEOPLE FLYING ABOUT.
GROWL
WHOAH! WAS THAT ANOTHER DRAGON? OH, NOPE. JUST MY STOMACH.
TALK ABOUT DISTRACTIONS. BETWEEN LOSING MY MIND, FIGHTING DOPPLEGANGERS, AND RIDING MAKE-BELIEVE CREATURES, I HAVEN'T EATEN IN...
YIPES! LIKE A WEEK! I HAVE GOT TO GET MY PRIORITIES IN ORDER...
AHH, SALVATION!

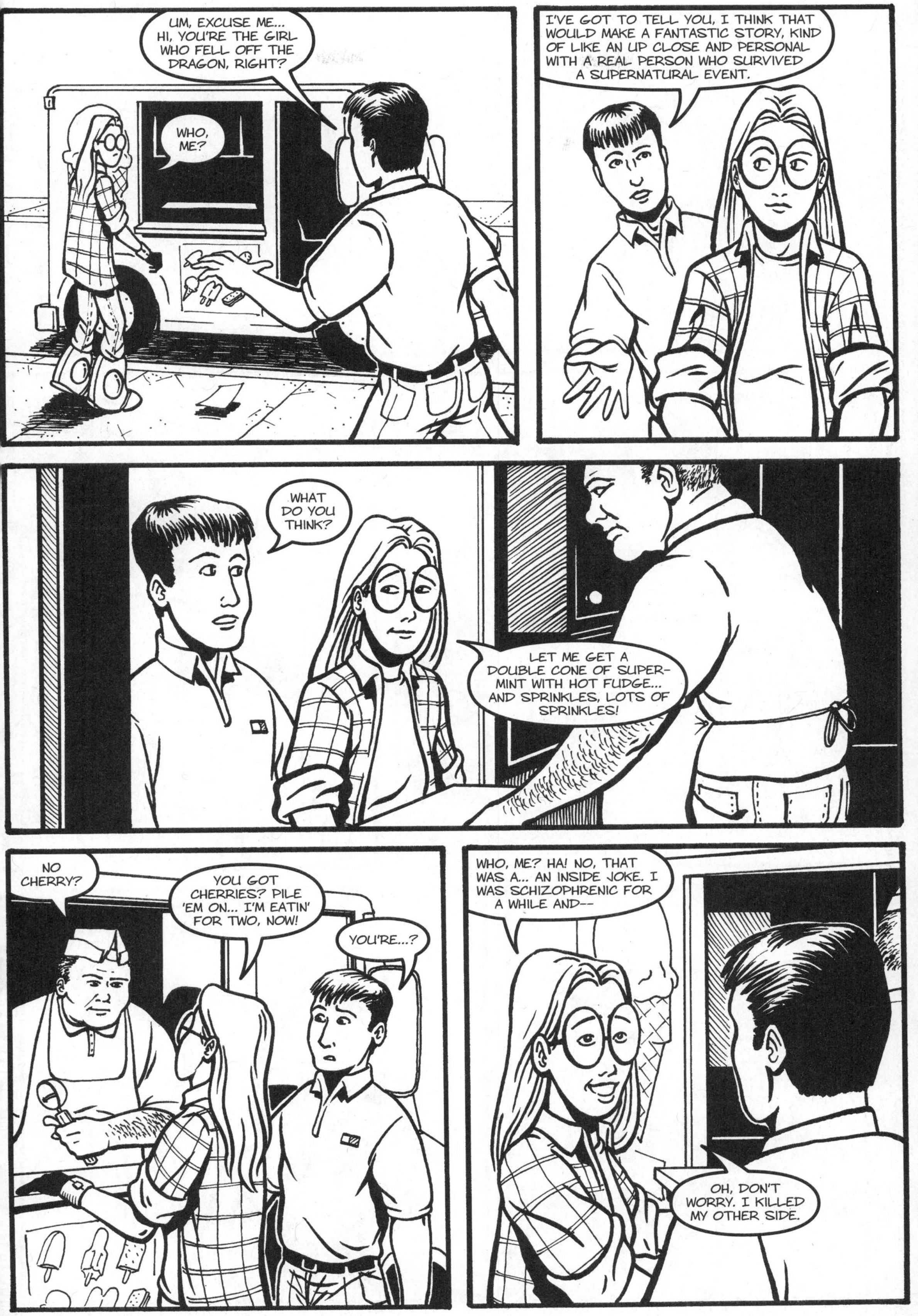
UM, EXCUSE ME... HI, YOU'RE THE GIRL WHO FELL OFF THE DRAGON, RIGHT?
WHO, ME?
I'VE GOT TO TELL YOU, I THINK THAT WOULD MAKE A FANTASTIC STORY, KIND OF LIKE AN UP CLOSE AND PERSONAL WITH A REAL PERSON WHO SURVIVED A SUPERNATURAL EVENT.
WHAT DO YOU THINK?
LET ME GET A DOUBLE CONE OF SUPER-MINT WITH HOT FUDGE... AND SPRINKLES, LOTS OF SPRINKLES!
NO CHERRY?
YOU GOT CHERRIES? PILE 'EM ON... I'M EATIN' FOR TWO, NOW!
YOU'RE...?
WHO, ME? HA! NO, THAT WAS A... AN INSIDE JOKE. I WAS SCHIZOPHRENIC FOR A WHILE AND--
OH, DON'T WORRY. I KILLED MY OTHER SIDE.

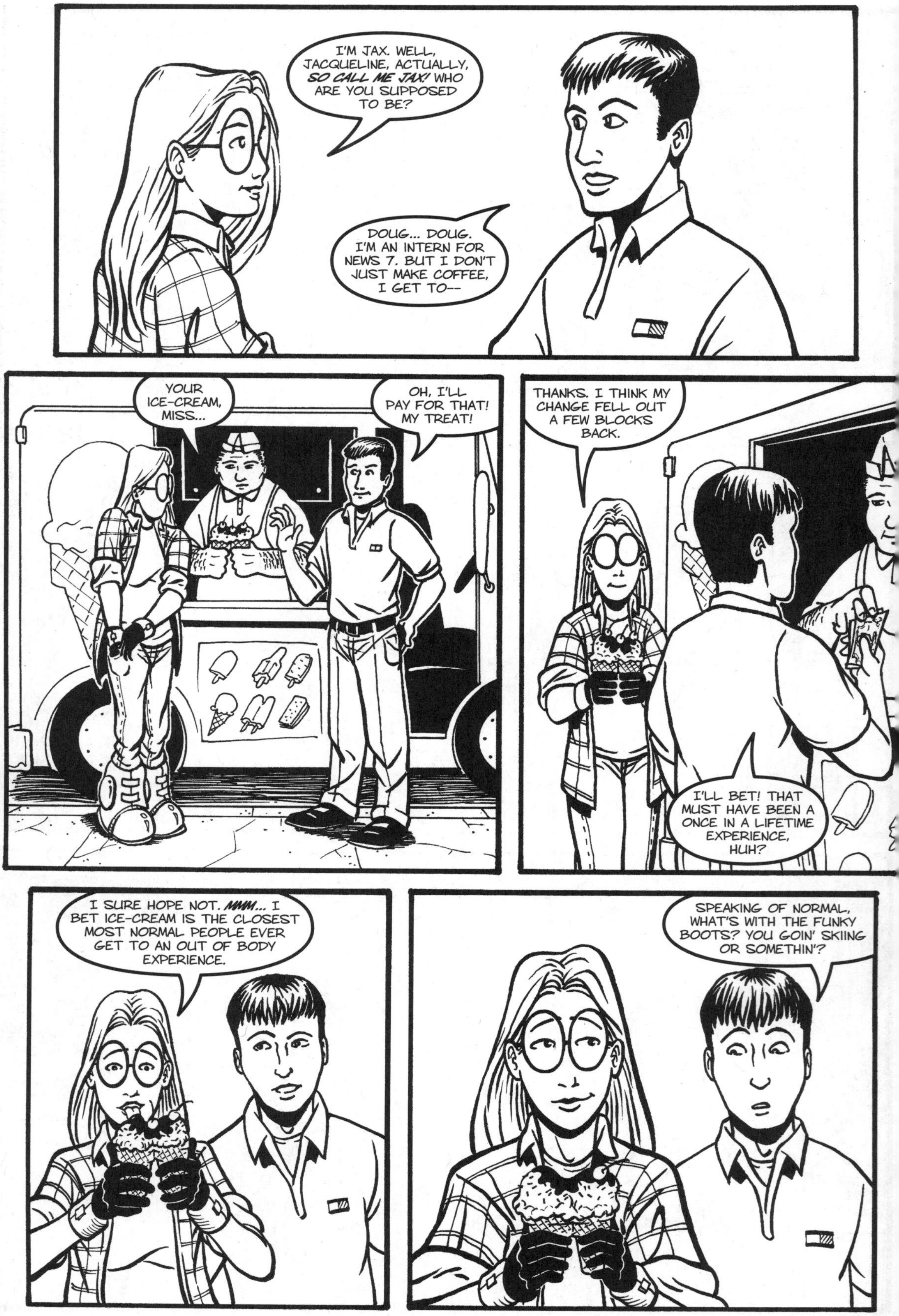
I'M JAX. WELL, JACQUELINE, ACTUALLY, ***SO CALL ME JAX!*** WHO ARE YOU SUPPOSED TO BE?
DOUG... DOUG. I'M AN INTERN FOR NEWS 7. BUT I DON'T JUST MAKE COFFEE, I GET TO--
YOUR ICE-CREAM, MISS...
OH, I'LL PAY FOR THAT! MY TREAT!
THANKS. I THINK MY CHANGE FELL OUT A FEW BLOCKS BACK.
I'LL BET! THAT MUST HAVE BEEN A ONCE IN A LIFETIME EXPERIENCE, HUH?
I SURE HOPE NOT. ***MMM...*** I BET ICE-CREAM IS THE CLOSEST MOST NORMAL PEOPLE EVER GET TO AN OUT OF BODY EXPERIENCE.
SPEAKING OF NORMAL, WHAT'S WITH THE FUNKY BOOTS? YOU GOIN' SKIING OR SOMETHIN'?

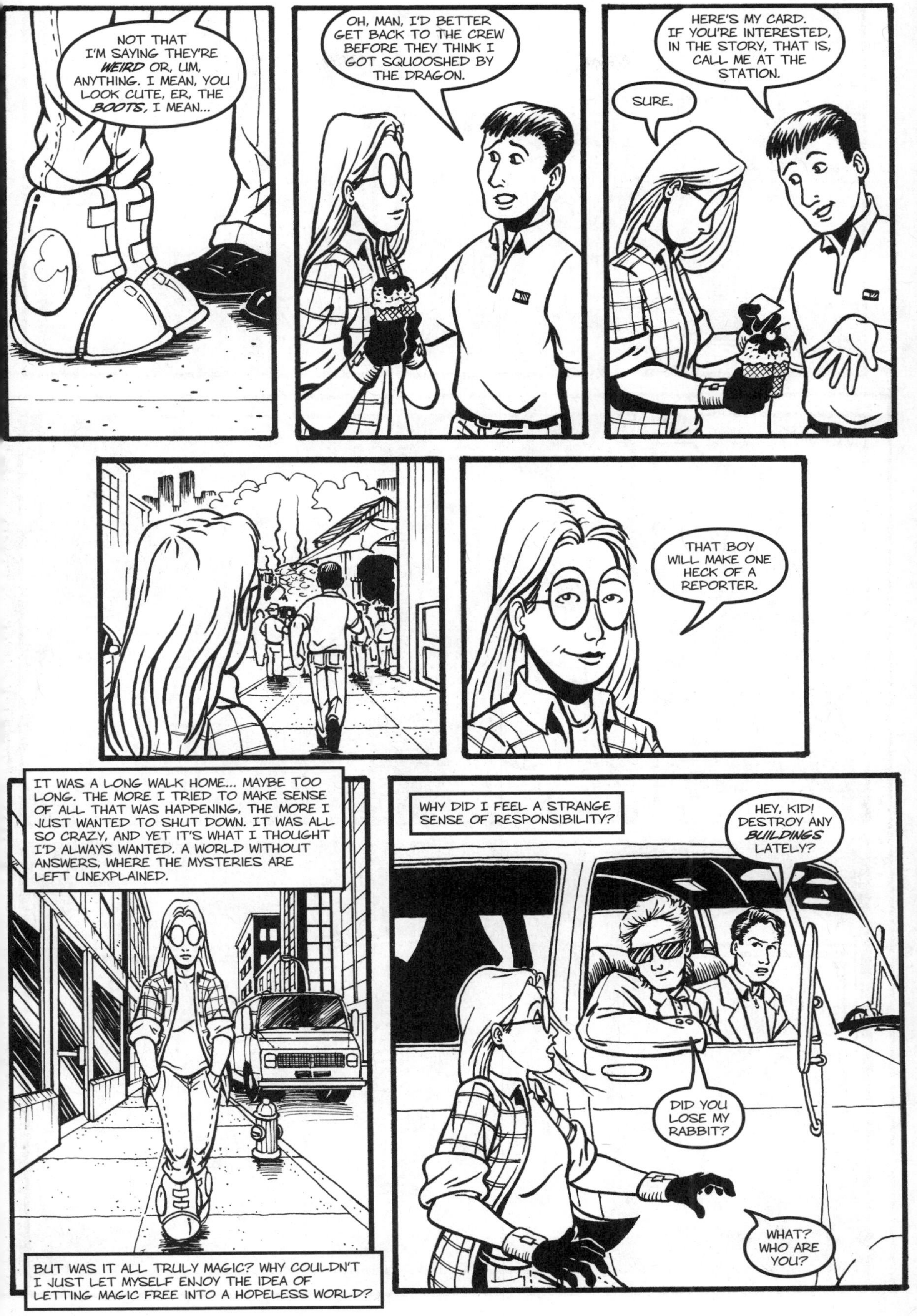
NOT THAT I'M SAYING THEY'RE *WEIRD* OR, UM, ANYTHING. I MEAN, YOU LOOK CUTE, ER, THE *BOOTS,* I MEAN...
OH, MAN, I'D BETTER GET BACK TO THE CREW BEFORE THEY THINK I GOT SQUOOSHED BY THE DRAGON.
HERE'S MY CARD. IF YOU'RE INTERESTED, IN THE STORY, THAT IS, CALL ME AT THE STATION.
SURE.
THAT BOY WILL MAKE ONE HECK OF A REPORTER.
IT WAS A LONG WALK HOME... MAYBE TOO LONG. THE MORE I TRIED TO MAKE SENSE OF ALL THAT WAS HAPPENING, THE MORE I JUST WANTED TO SHUT DOWN. IT WAS ALL SO CRAZY, AND YET IT'S WHAT I THOUGHT I'D ALWAYS WANTED. A WORLD WITHOUT ANSWERS, WHERE THE MYSTERIES ARE LEFT UNEXPLAINED.
BUT WAS IT ALL TRULY MAGIC? WHY COULDN'T I JUST LET MYSELF ENJOY THE IDEA OF LETTING MAGIC FREE INTO A HOPELESS WORLD?
WHY DID I FEEL A STRANGE SENSE OF RESPONSIBILITY?
HEY, KID! DESTROY ANY *BUILDINGS* LATELY?
DID YOU LOSE MY RABBIT?
WHAT? WHO ARE YOU?

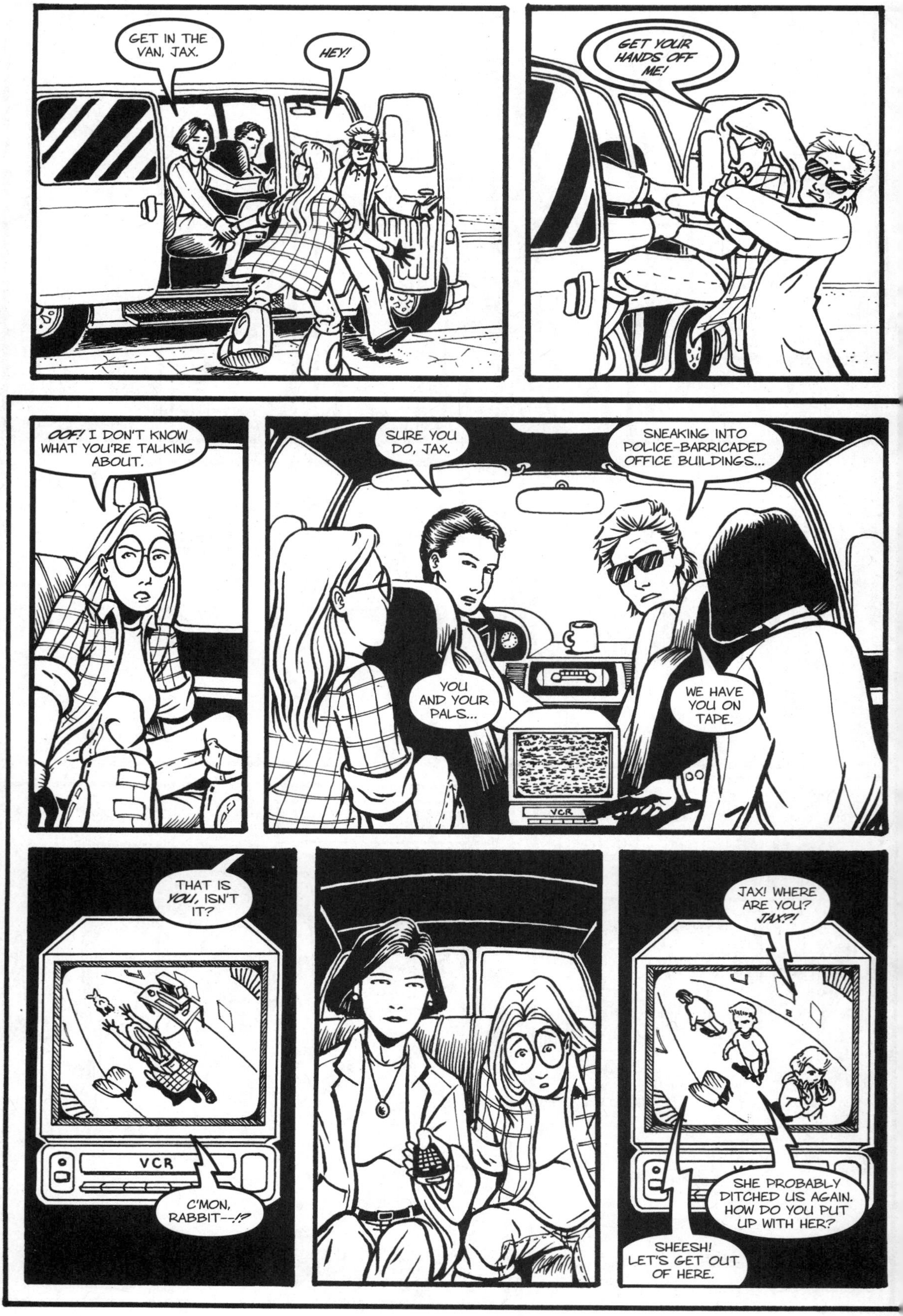
GET IN THE VAN, JAX.
HEY!
GET YOUR HANDS OFF ME!
OOF! I DON'T KNOW WHAT YOU'RE TALKING ABOUT.
SURE YOU DO, JAX.
SNEAKING INTO POLICE-BARRICADED OFFICE BUILDINGS...
YOU AND YOUR PALS...
WE HAVE YOU ON TAPE.
VCR
THAT IS YOU, ISN'T IT?
VCR
C'MON, RABBIT--!?
JAX! WHERE ARE YOU? JAX?!
SHE PROBABLY DITCHED US AGAIN. HOW DO YOU PUT UP WITH HER?
SHEESH! LET'S GET OUT OF HERE.

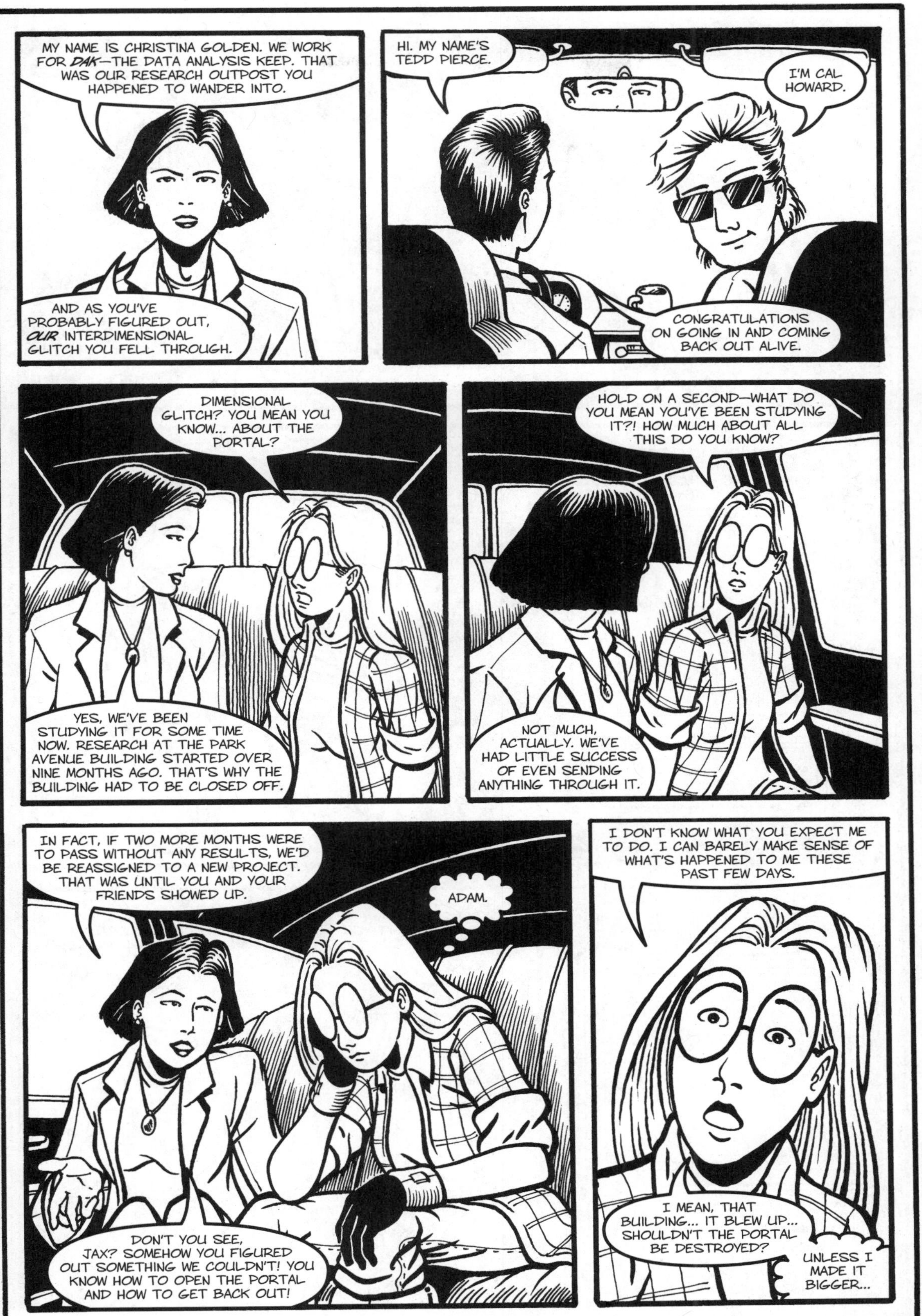
MY NAME IS CHRISTINA GOLDEN. WE WORK FOR *DAK*—THE DATA ANALYSIS KEEP. THAT WAS OUR RESEARCH OUTPOST YOU HAPPENED TO WANDER INTO.
AND AS YOU'VE PROBABLY FIGURED OUT, *OUR* INTERDIMENSIONAL GLITCH YOU FELL THROUGH.
HI. MY NAME'S TEDD PIERCE.
I'M CAL HOWARD.
CONGRATULATIONS ON GOING IN AND COMING BACK OUT ALIVE.
DIMENSIONAL GLITCH? YOU MEAN YOU KNOW... ABOUT THE PORTAL?
YES, WE'VE BEEN STUDYING IT FOR SOME TIME NOW. RESEARCH AT THE PARK AVENUE BUILDING STARTED OVER NINE MONTHS AGO. THAT'S WHY THE BUILDING HAD TO BE CLOSED OFF.
HOLD ON A SECOND—WHAT DO YOU MEAN YOU'VE BEEN STUDYING IT?! HOW MUCH ABOUT ALL THIS DO YOU KNOW?
NOT MUCH, ACTUALLY. WE'VE HAD LITTLE SUCCESS OF EVEN SENDING ANYTHING THROUGH IT.
IN FACT, IF TWO MORE MONTHS WERE TO PASS WITHOUT ANY RESULTS, WE'D BE REASSIGNED TO A NEW PROJECT. THAT WAS UNTIL YOU AND YOUR FRIENDS SHOWED UP.
ADAM.
DON'T YOU SEE, JAX? SOMEHOW YOU FIGURED OUT SOMETHING WE COULDN'T! YOU KNOW HOW TO OPEN THE PORTAL AND HOW TO GET BACK OUT!
I DON'T KNOW WHAT YOU EXPECT ME TO DO. I CAN BARELY MAKE SENSE OF WHAT'S HAPPENED TO ME THESE PAST FEW DAYS.
I MEAN, THAT BUILDING... IT BLEW UP... SHOULDN'T THE PORTAL BE DESTROYED?
UNLESS I MADE IT BIGGER...

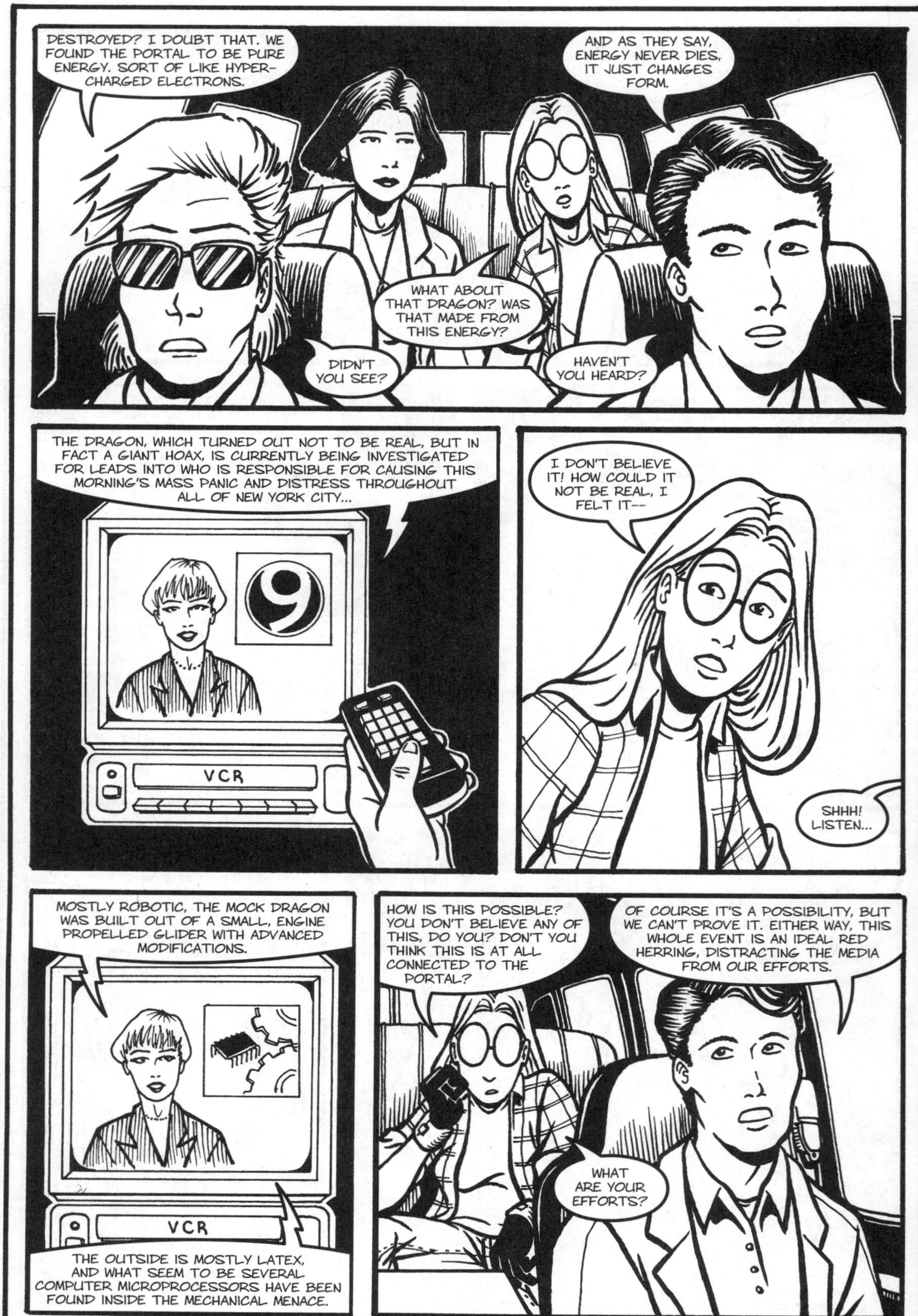
DESTROYED? I DOUBT THAT. WE FOUND THE PORTAL TO BE PURE ENERGY. SORT OF LIKE HYPER-CHARGED ELECTRONS.
AND AS THEY SAY, ENERGY NEVER DIES, IT JUST CHANGES FORM.
WHAT ABOUT THAT DRAGON? WAS THAT MADE FROM THIS ENERGY?
DIDN'T YOU SEE?
HAVEN'T YOU HEARD?
THE DRAGON, WHICH TURNED OUT NOT TO BE REAL, BUT IN FACT A GIANT HOAX, IS CURRENTLY BEING INVESTIGATED FOR LEADS INTO WHO IS RESPONSIBLE FOR CAUSING THIS MORNING'S MASS PANIC AND DISTRESS THROUGHOUT ALL OF NEW YORK CITY...
9
VCR
I DON'T BELIEVE IT! HOW COULD IT NOT BE REAL, I FELT IT--
SHHH! LISTEN...
MOSTLY ROBOTIC, THE MOCK DRAGON WAS BUILT OUT OF A SMALL, ENGINE PROPELLED GLIDER WITH ADVANCED MODIFICATIONS.
VCR
THE OUTSIDE IS MOSTLY LATEX, AND WHAT SEEM TO BE SEVERAL COMPUTER MICROPROCESSORS HAVE BEEN FOUND INSIDE THE MECHANICAL MENACE.
HOW IS THIS POSSIBLE? YOU DON'T BELIEVE ANY OF THIS, DO YOU? DON'T YOU THINK THIS IS AT ALL CONNECTED TO THE PORTAL?
OF COURSE IT'S A POSSIBILITY, BUT WE CAN'T PROVE IT. EITHER WAY, THIS WHOLE EVENT IS AN IDEAL RED HERRING, DISTRACTING THE MEDIA FROM OUR EFFORTS.
WHAT ARE YOUR EFFORTS?

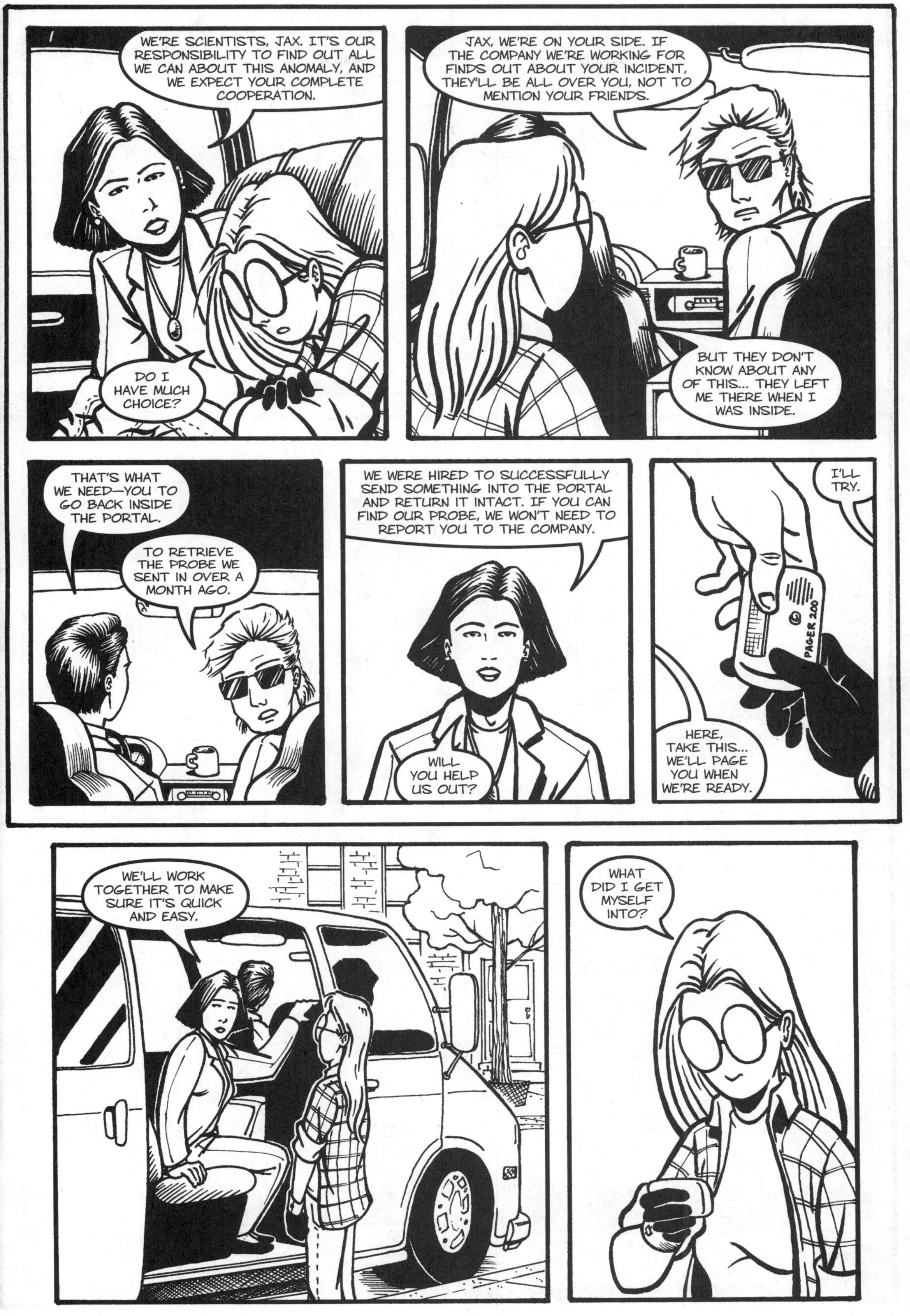
WE'RE SCIENTISTS, JAX. IT'S OUR RESPONSIBILITY TO FIND OUT ALL WE CAN ABOUT THIS ANOMALY, AND WE EXPECT YOUR COMPLETE COOPERATION.
DO I HAVE MUCH CHOICE?
JAX, WE'RE ON YOUR SIDE. IF THE COMPANY WE'RE WORKING FOR FINDS OUT ABOUT YOUR INCIDENT, THEY'LL BE ALL OVER YOU, NOT TO MENTION YOUR FRIENDS.
BUT THEY DON'T KNOW ABOUT ANY OF THIS... THEY LEFT ME THERE WHEN I WAS INSIDE.
THAT'S WHAT WE NEED—YOU TO GO BACK INSIDE THE PORTAL.
TO RETRIEVE THE PROBE WE SENT IN OVER A MONTH AGO.
WE WERE HIRED TO SUCCESSFULLY SEND SOMETHING INTO THE PORTAL AND RETURN IT INTACT. IF YOU CAN FIND OUR PROBE, WE WON'T NEED TO REPORT YOU TO THE COMPANY.
WILL YOU HELP US OUT?
I'LL TRY.
PAGER 200
HERE, TAKE THIS... WE'LL PAGE YOU WHEN WE'RE READY.
WE'LL WORK TOGETHER TO MAKE SURE IT'S QUICK AND EASY.
WHAT DID I GET MYSELF INTO?

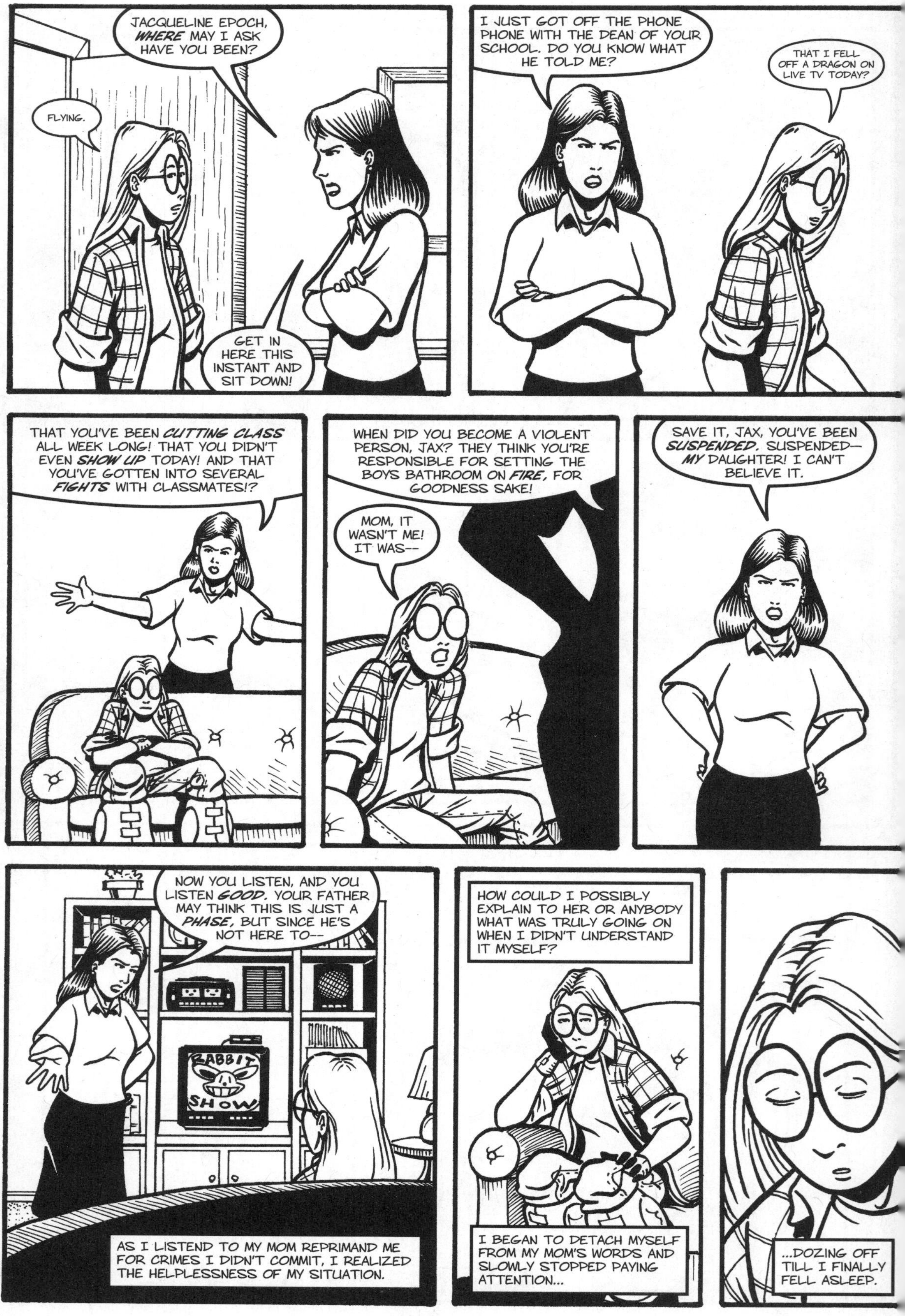
JACQUELINE EPOCH, WHERE MAY I ASK HAVE YOU BEEN?
FLYING.
GET IN HERE THIS INSTANT AND SIT DOWN!
I JUST GOT OFF THE PHONE PHONE WITH THE DEAN OF YOUR SCHOOL. DO YOU KNOW WHAT HE TOLD ME?
THAT I FELL OFF A DRAGON ON LIVE TV TODAY?
THAT YOU'VE BEEN CUTTING CLASS ALL WEEK LONG! THAT YOU DIDN'T EVEN SHOW UP TODAY! AND THAT YOU'VE GOTTEN INTO SEVERAL FIGHTS WITH CLASSMATES!?
WHEN DID YOU BECOME A VIOLENT PERSON, JAX? THEY THINK YOU'RE RESPONSIBLE FOR SETTING THE BOYS BATHROOM ON FIRE, FOR GOODNESS SAKE!
MOM, IT WASN'T ME! IT WAS--
SAVE IT, JAX, YOU'VE BEEN SUSPENDED. SUSPENDED— MY DAUGHTER! I CAN'T BELIEVE IT.
NOW YOU LISTEN, AND YOU LISTEN GOOD. YOUR FATHER MAY THINK THIS IS JUST A PHASE, BUT SINCE HE'S NOT HERE TO--
RABBIT SHOW
AS I LISTEND TO MY MOM REPRIMAND ME FOR CRIMES I DIDN'T COMMIT, I REALIZED THE HELPLESSNESS OF MY SITUATION.
HOW COULD I POSSIBLY EXPLAIN TO HER OR ANYBODY WHAT WAS TRULY GOING ON WHEN I DIDN'T UNDERSTAND IT MYSELF?
I BEGAN TO DETACH MYSELF FROM MY MOM'S WORDS AND SLOWLY STOPPED PAYING ATTENTION...
...DOZING OFF TILL I FINALLY FELL ASLEEP.

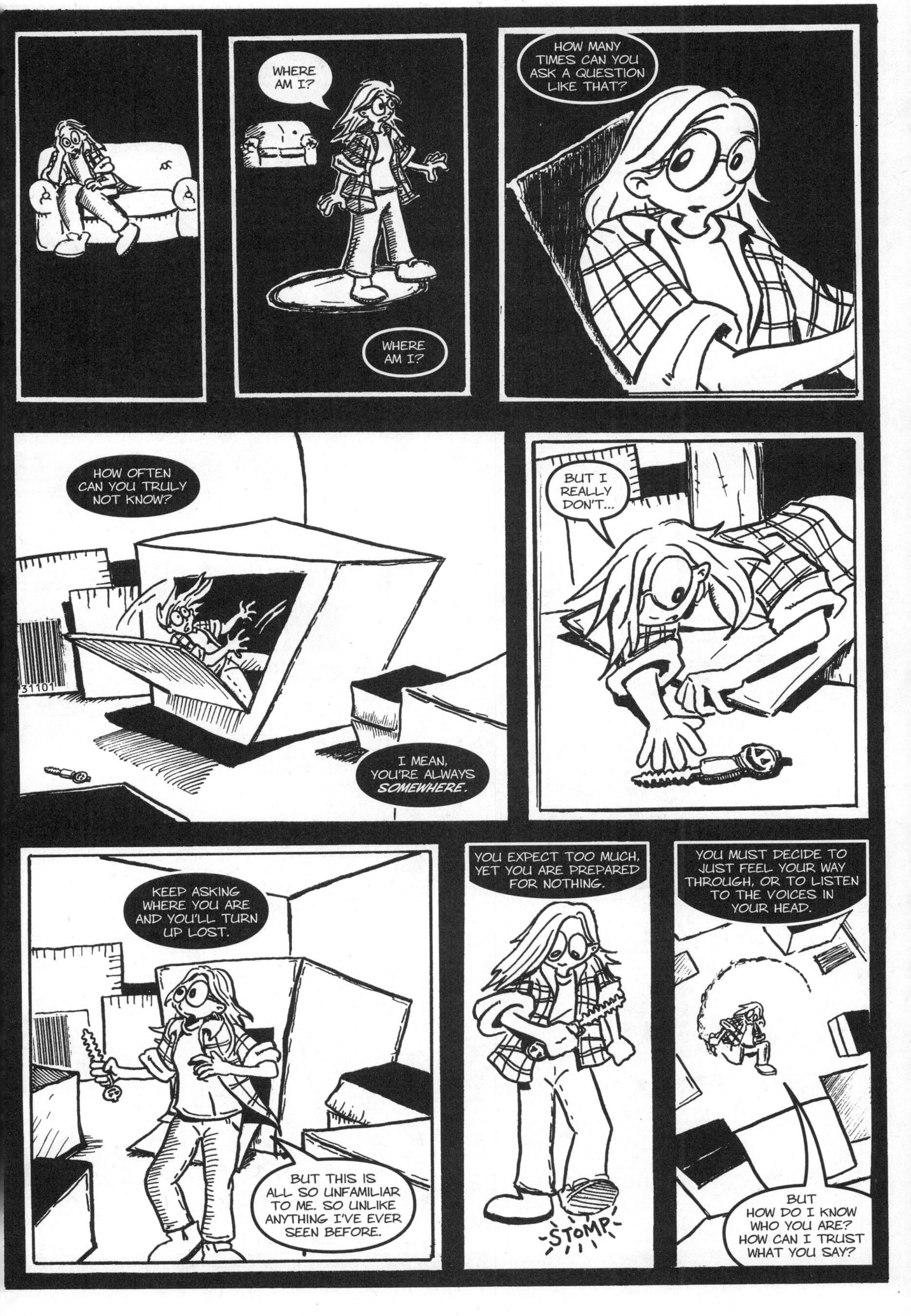
WHERE AM I?
WHERE AM I?
HOW MANY TIMES CAN YOU ASK A QUESTION LIKE THAT?
HOW OFTEN CAN YOU TRULY NOT KNOW?
I MEAN, YOU'RE ALWAYS *SOMEWHERE*.
BUT I REALLY DON'T...
KEEP ASKING WHERE YOU ARE AND YOU'LL TURN UP LOST.
BUT THIS IS ALL SO UNFAMILIAR TO ME. SO UNLIKE ANYTHING I'VE EVER SEEN BEFORE.
YOU EXPECT TOO MUCH, YET YOU ARE PREPARED FOR NOTHING.
STOMP
YOU MUST DECIDE TO JUST FEEL YOUR WAY THROUGH, OR TO LISTEN TO THE VOICES IN YOUR HEAD.
BUT HOW DO I KNOW WHO YOU ARE? HOW CAN I TRUST WHAT YOU SAY?

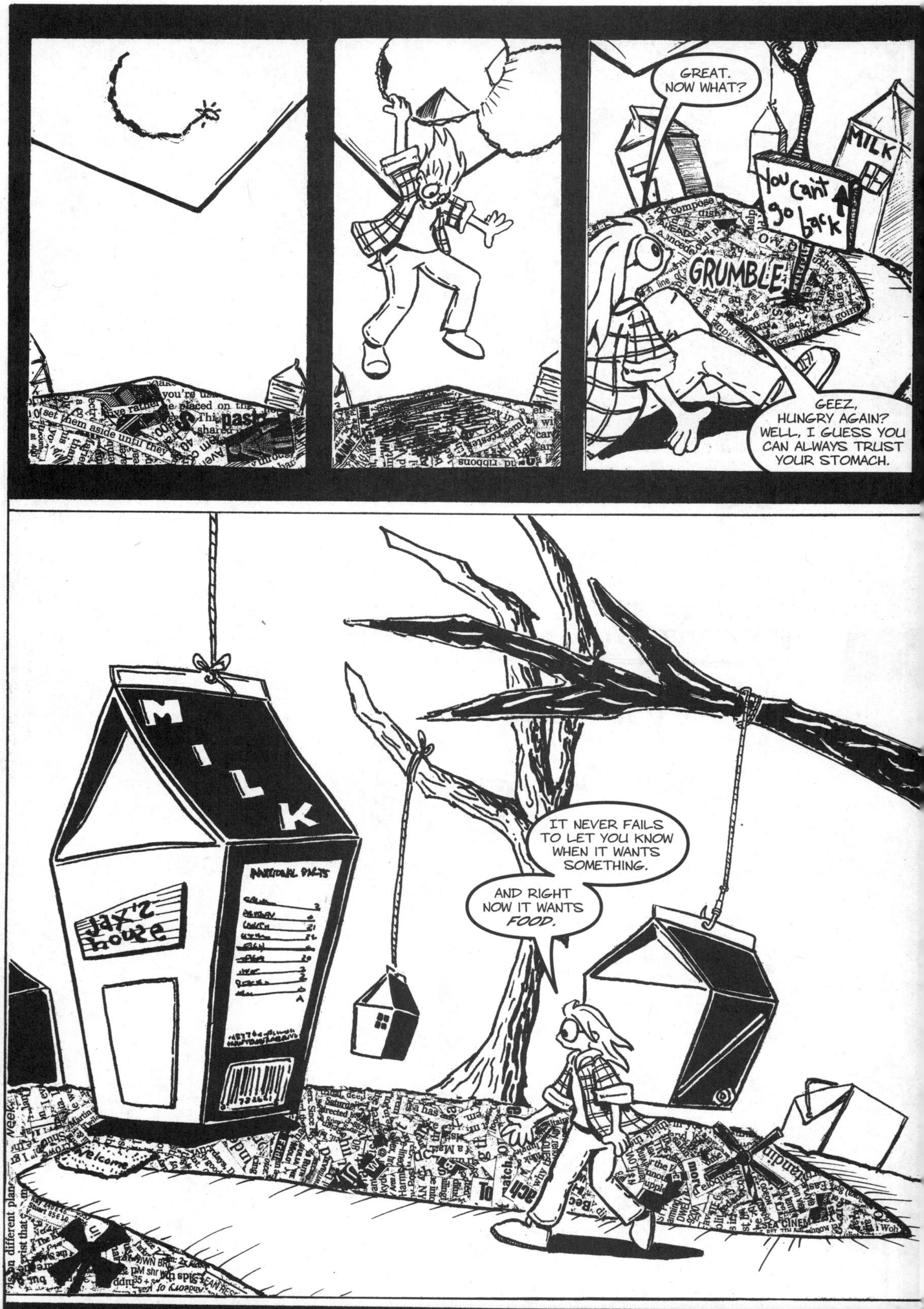
GREAT. NOW WHAT?
MILK
You can't go back
GRUMBLE
GEEZ, HUNGRY AGAIN? WELL, I GUESS YOU CAN ALWAYS TRUST YOUR STOMACH.
MILK
Jax's house
IT NEVER FAILS TO LET YOU KNOW WHEN IT WANTS SOMETHING.
AND RIGHT NOW IT WANTS *FOOD.*

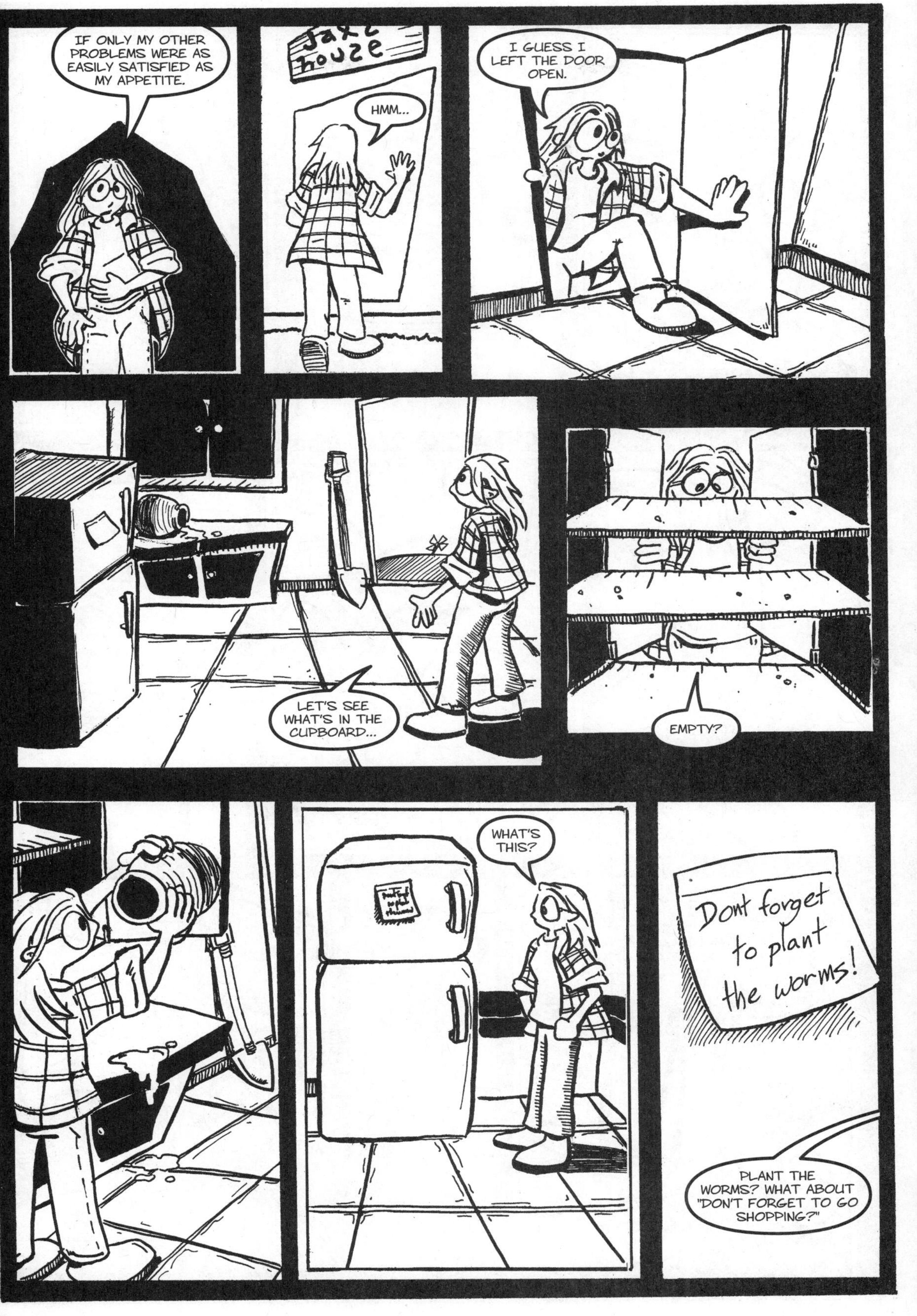
IF ONLY MY OTHER PROBLEMS WERE AS EASILY SATISFIED AS MY APPETITE.
HMM...
I GUESS I LEFT THE DOOR OPEN.
LET'S SEE WHAT'S IN THE CUPBOARD...
EMPTY?
WHAT'S THIS?
Dont forget to plant the worms!
PLANT THE WORMS? WHAT ABOUT "DON'T FORGET TO GO SHOPPING?"

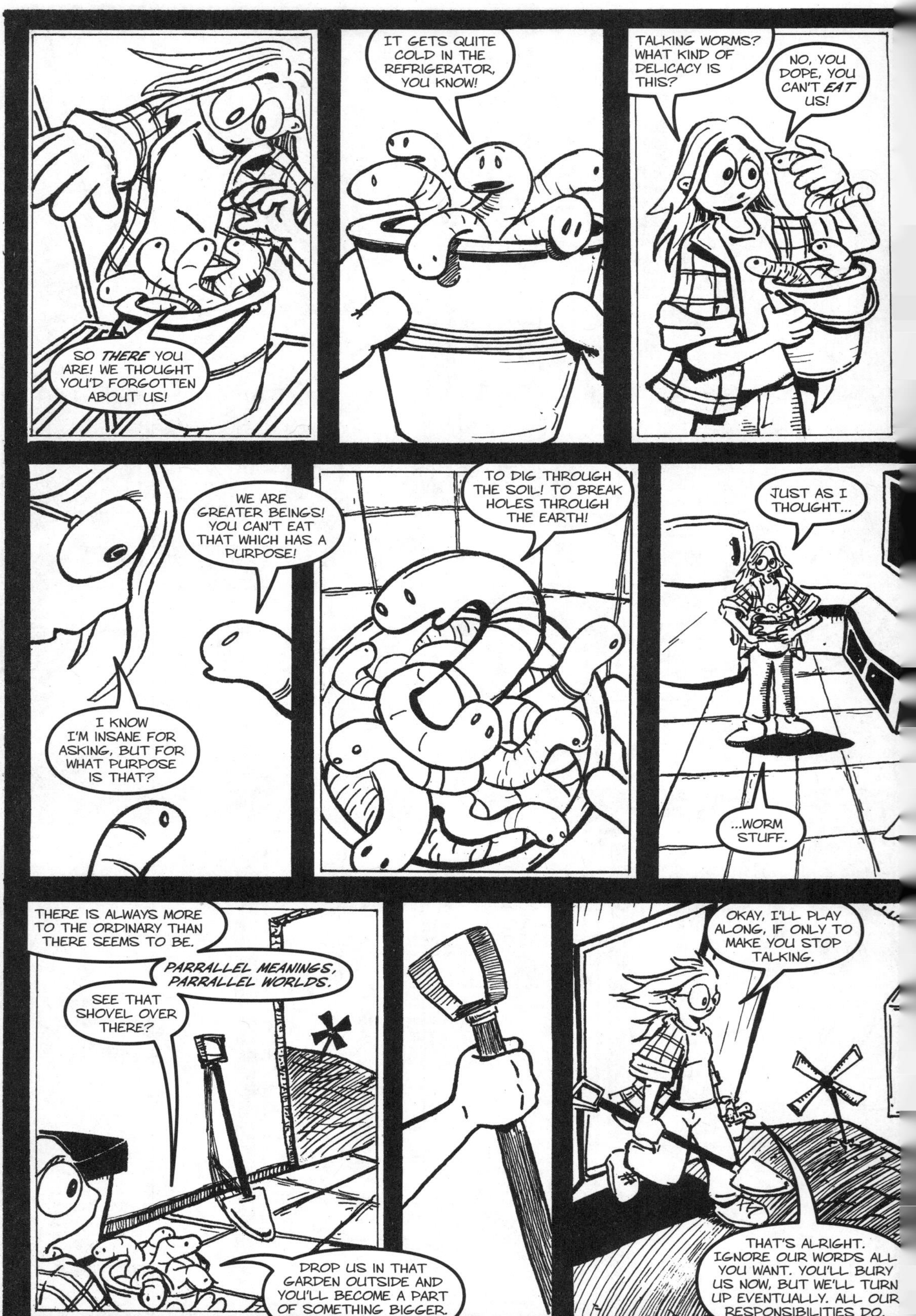
SO *THERE* YOU ARE! WE THOUGHT YOU'D FORGOTTEN ABOUT US!
IT GETS QUITE COLD IN THE REFRIGERATOR, YOU KNOW!
TALKING WORMS? WHAT KIND OF DELICACY IS THIS?
NO, YOU DOPE, YOU CAN'T *EAT* US!
WE ARE GREATER BEINGS! YOU CAN'T EAT THAT WHICH HAS A PURPOSE!
I KNOW I'M INSANE FOR ASKING, BUT FOR WHAT PURPOSE IS THAT?
TO DIG THROUGH THE SOIL! TO BREAK HOLES THROUGH THE EARTH!
JUST AS I THOUGHT...
...WORM STUFF.
THERE IS ALWAYS MORE TO THE ORDINARY THAN THERE SEEMS TO BE.
PARRALLEL MEANINGS, PARRALLEL WORLDS.
SEE THAT SHOVEL OVER THERE?
DROP US IN THAT GARDEN OUTSIDE AND YOU'LL BECOME A PART OF SOMETHING BIGGER.
OKAY, I'LL PLAY ALONG, IF ONLY TO MAKE YOU STOP TALKING.
THAT'S ALRIGHT. IGNORE OUR WORDS ALL YOU WANT. YOU'LL BURY US NOW, BUT WE'LL TURN UP EVENTUALLY. ALL OUR RESPONSIBILITIES DO.

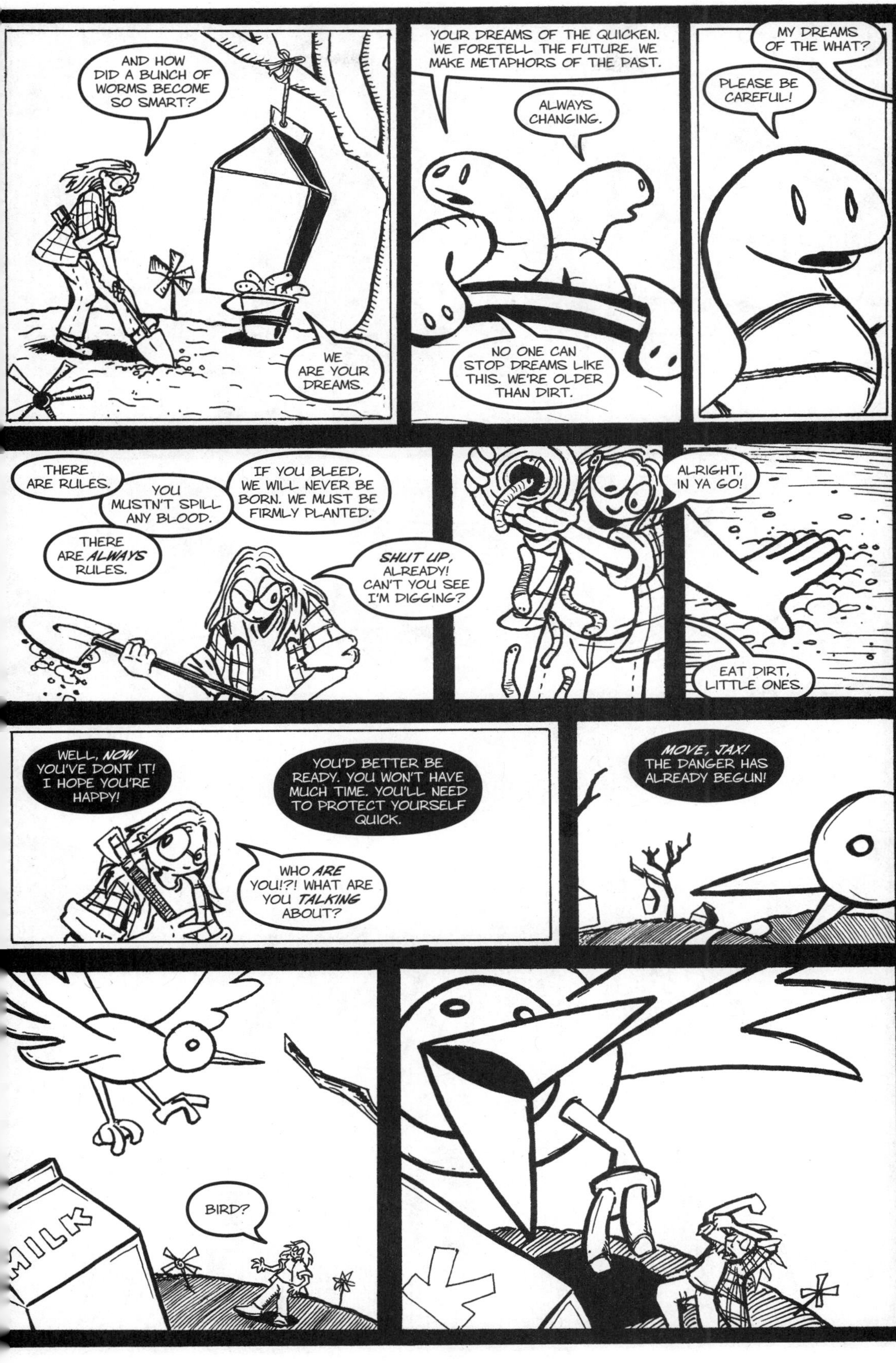
AND HOW DID A BUNCH OF WORMS BECOME SO SMART?
WE ARE YOUR DREAMS.
YOUR DREAMS OF THE QUICKEN. WE FORETELL THE FUTURE. WE MAKE METAPHORS OF THE PAST.
ALWAYS CHANGING.
NO ONE CAN STOP DREAMS LIKE THIS. WE'RE OLDER THAN DIRT.
MY DREAMS OF THE WHAT?
PLEASE BE CAREFUL!
THERE ARE RULES.
YOU MUSTN'T SPILL ANY BLOOD.
IF YOU BLEED, WE WILL NEVER BE BORN. WE MUST BE FIRMLY PLANTED.
THERE ARE *ALWAYS* RULES.
SHUT UP, ALREADY! CAN'T YOU SEE I'M DIGGING?
ALRIGHT, IN YA GO!
EAT DIRT, LITTLE ONES.
WELL, *NOW* YOU'VE DONT IT! I HOPE YOU'RE HAPPY!
YOU'D BETTER BE READY. YOU WON'T HAVE MUCH TIME. YOU'LL NEED TO PROTECT YOURSELF QUICK.
WHO *ARE* YOU!?! WHAT ARE YOU *TALKING* ABOUT?
MOVE, JAX! THE DANGER HAS ALREADY BEGUN!
MILK
BIRD?

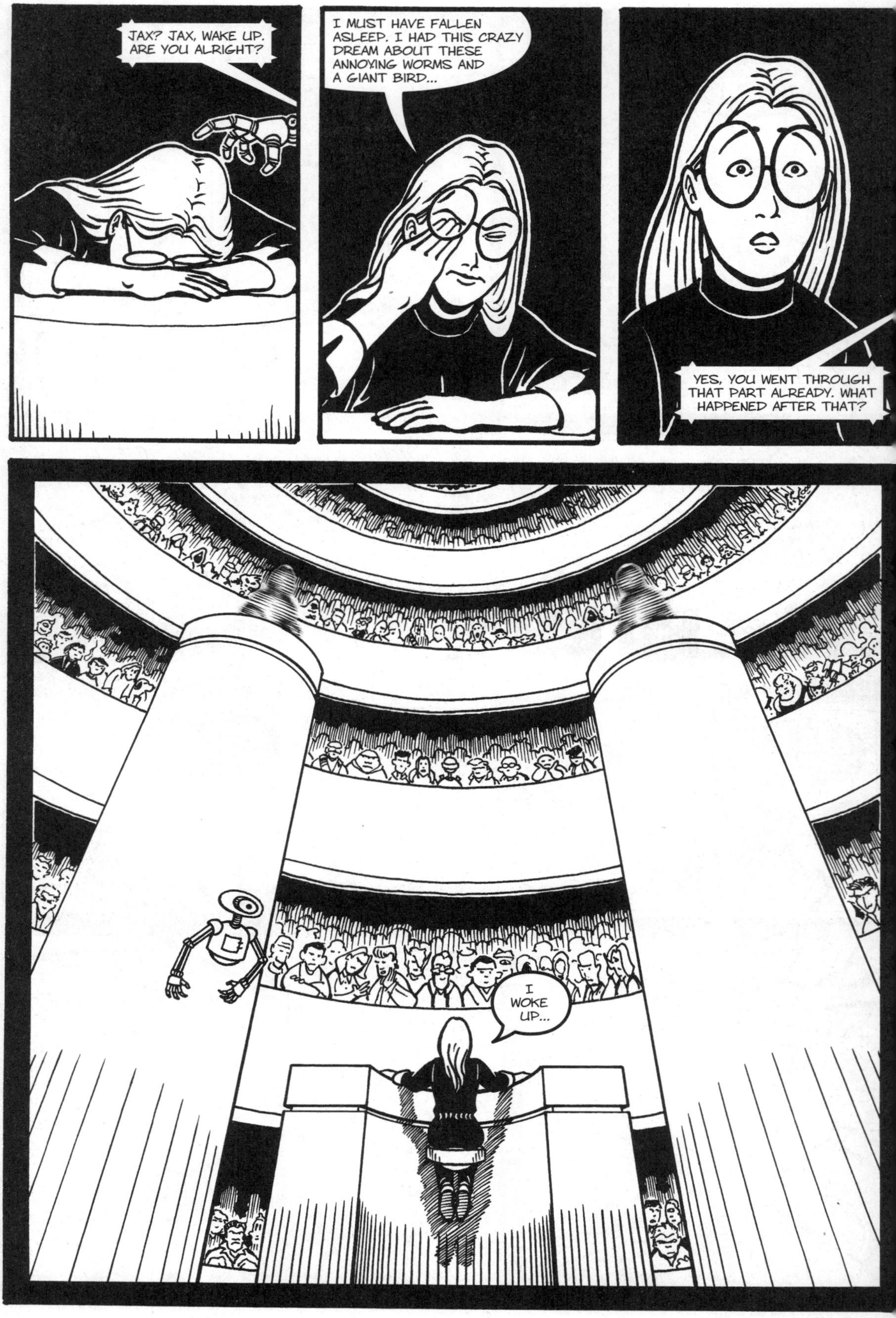
JAX? JAX, WAKE UP. ARE YOU ALRIGHT?
I MUST HAVE FALLEN ASLEEP. I HAD THIS CRAZY DREAM ABOUT THESE ANNOYING WORMS AND A GIANT BIRD...
YES, YOU WENT THROUGH THAT PART ALREADY. WHAT HAPPENED AFTER THAT?
I WOKE UP...

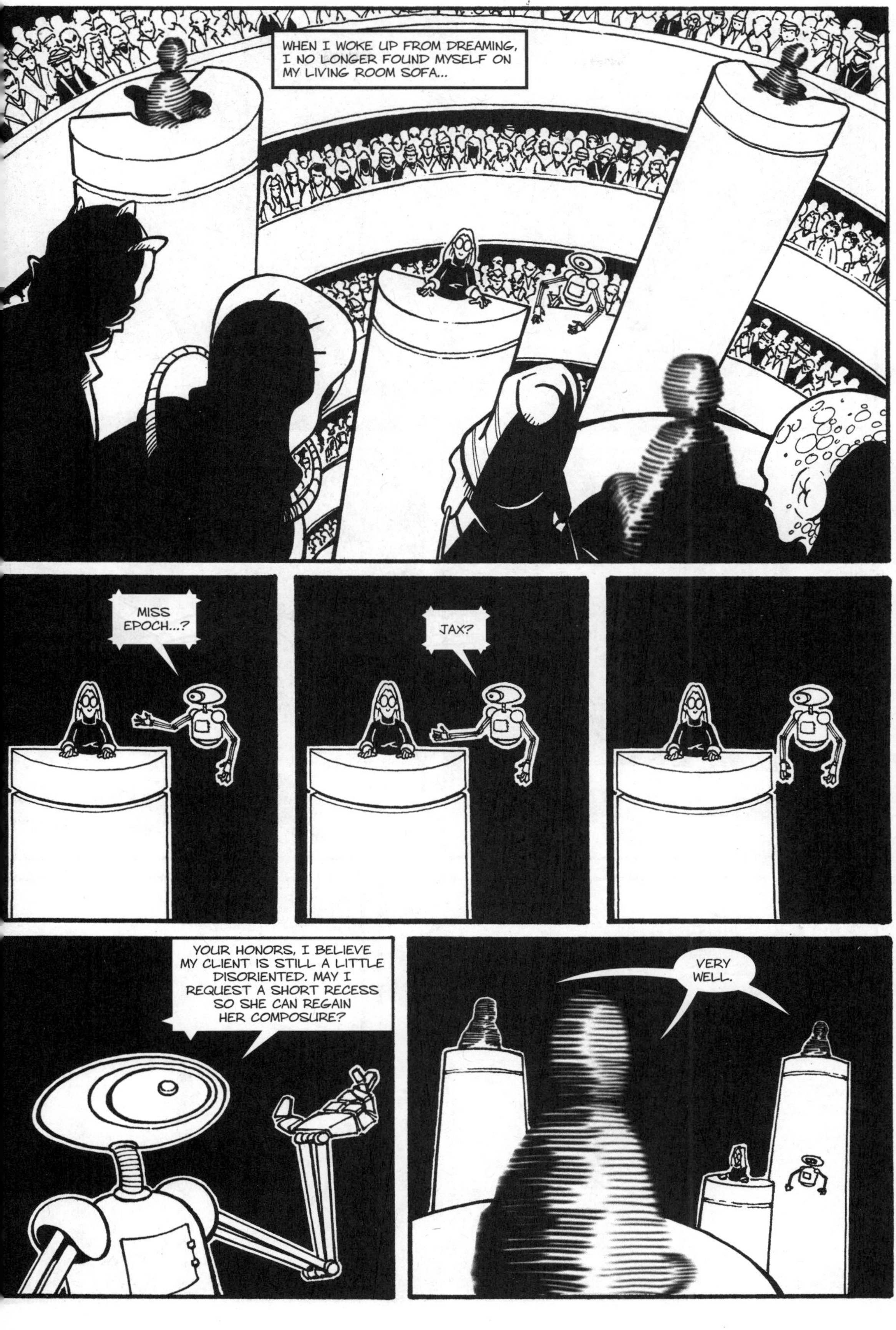
WHEN I WOKE UP FROM DREAMING, I NO LONGER FOUND MYSELF ON MY LIVING ROOM SOFA...
MISS EPOCH...?
JAX?
YOUR HONORS, I BELIEVE MY CLIENT IS STILL A LITTLE DISORIENTED. MAY I REQUEST A SHORT RECESS SO SHE CAN REGAIN HER COMPOSURE?
VERY WELL.

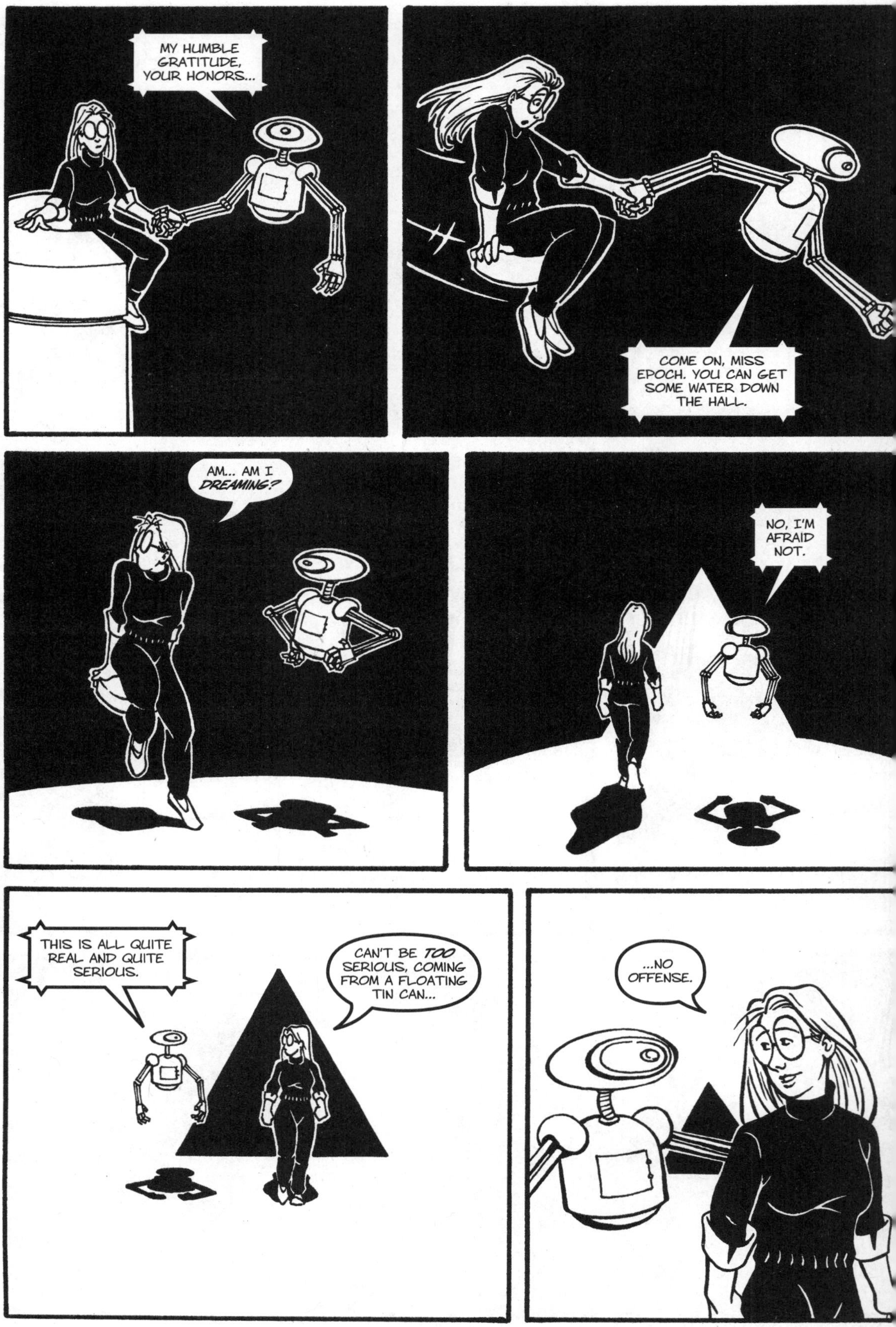
MY HUMBLE GRATITUDE, YOUR HONORS...
COME ON, MISS EPOCH. YOU CAN GET SOME WATER DOWN THE HALL.
AM... AM I *DREAMING?*
NO, I'M AFRAID NOT.
THIS IS ALL QUITE REAL AND QUITE SERIOUS.
CAN'T BE *TOO* SERIOUS, COMING FROM A FLOATING TIN CAN...
...NO OFFENSE.

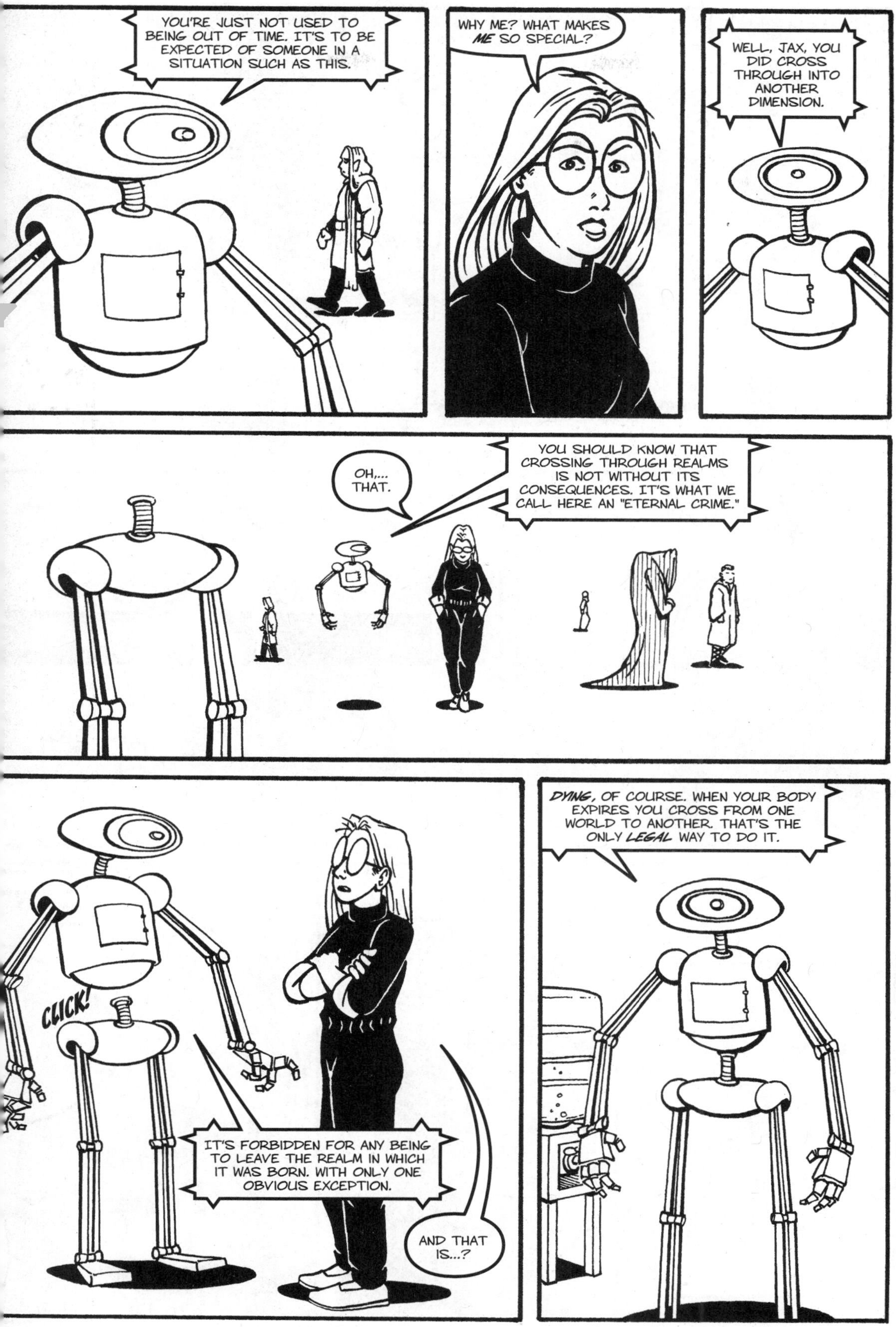
YOU'RE JUST NOT USED TO BEING OUT OF TIME. IT'S TO BE EXPECTED OF SOMEONE IN A SITUATION SUCH AS THIS.
WHY ME? WHAT MAKES *ME* SO SPECIAL?
WELL, JAX, YOU DID CROSS THROUGH INTO ANOTHER DIMENSION.
OH,... THAT.
YOU SHOULD KNOW THAT CROSSING THROUGH REALMS IS NOT WITHOUT ITS CONSEQUENCES. IT'S WHAT WE CALL HERE AN "ETERNAL CRIME."
CLICK!
IT'S FORBIDDEN FOR ANY BEING TO LEAVE THE REALM IN WHICH IT WAS BORN. WITH ONLY ONE OBVIOUS EXCEPTION.
AND THAT IS...?
DYING, OF COURSE. WHEN YOUR BODY EXPIRES YOU CROSS FROM ONE WORLD TO ANOTHER. THAT'S THE ONLY *LEGAL* WAY TO DO IT.

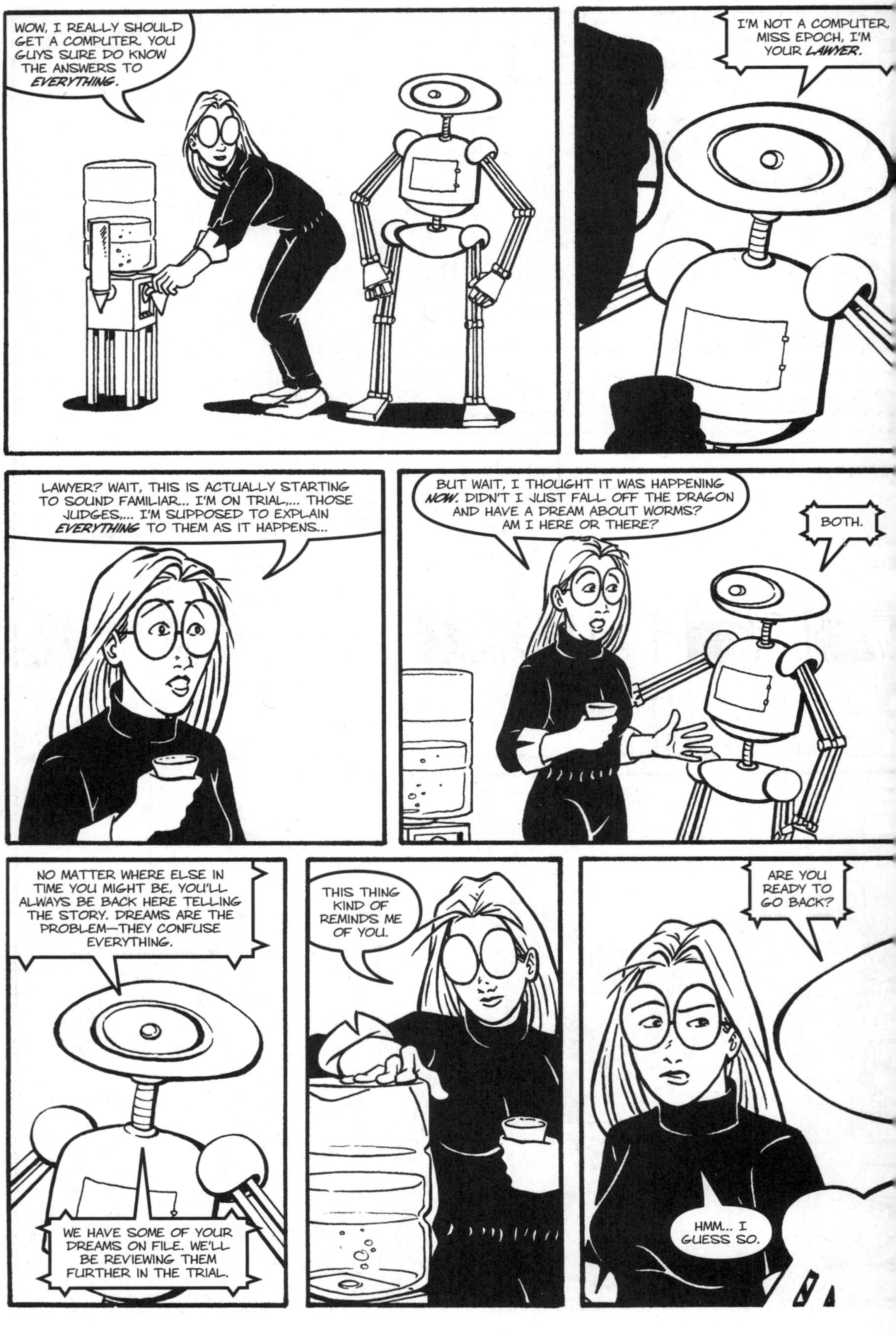
WOW, I REALLY SHOULD GET A COMPUTER. YOU GUYS SURE DO KNOW THE ANSWERS TO *EVERYTHING*.
I'M NOT A COMPUTER, MISS EPOCH, I'M YOUR *LAWYER*.
LAWYER? WAIT, THIS IS ACTUALLY STARTING TO SOUND FAMILIAR... I'M ON TRIAL,... THOSE JUDGES,... I'M SUPPOSED TO EXPLAIN *EVERYTHING* TO THEM AS IT HAPPENS...
BUT WAIT, I THOUGHT IT WAS HAPPENING *NOW*. DIDN'T I JUST FALL OFF THE DRAGON AND HAVE A DREAM ABOUT WORMS? AM I HERE OR THERE?
BOTH.
NO MATTER WHERE ELSE IN TIME YOU MIGHT BE, YOU'LL ALWAYS BE BACK HERE TELLING THE STORY. DREAMS ARE THE PROBLEM—THEY CONFUSE EVERYTHING.
WE HAVE SOME OF YOUR DREAMS ON FILE. WE'LL BE REVIEWING THEM FURTHER IN THE TRIAL.
THIS THING KIND OF REMINDS ME OF YOU.
ARE YOU READY TO GO BACK?
HMM... I GUESS SO.

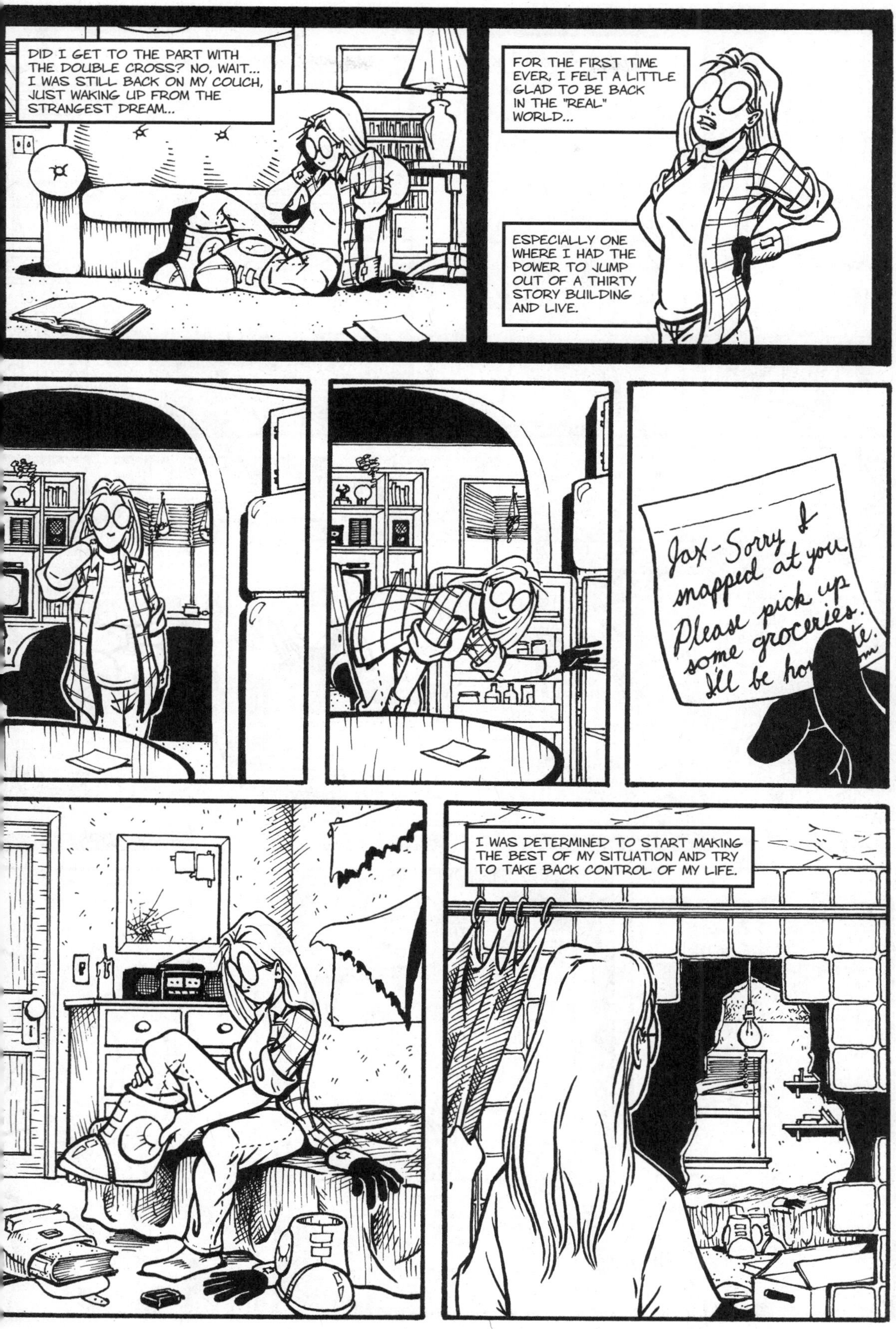
DID I GET TO THE PART WITH THE DOUBLE CROSS? NO, WAIT... I WAS STILL BACK ON MY COUCH, JUST WAKING UP FROM THE STRANGEST DREAM...
FOR THE FIRST TIME EVER, I FELT A LITTLE GLAD TO BE BACK IN THE "REAL" WORLD...
ESPECIALLY ONE WHERE I HAD THE POWER TO JUMP OUT OF A THIRTY STORY BUILDING AND LIVE.
Jax-Sorry I snapped at you. Please pick up some groceries. I'll be ho
I WAS DETERMINED TO START MAKING THE BEST OF MY SITUATION AND TRY TO TAKE BACK CONTROL OF MY LIFE.

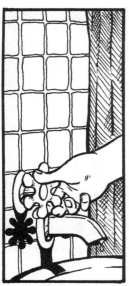

WITH ALL THESE RESOURCES AT MY FINGERTIPS, WHO KNEW *WHAT* I WAS CAPABLE OF!

IT'S TIME TO FIND OUT.

I NEEDED HELP, BUT I DIDN'T KNOW IF I COULD TRUST THE SCIENTISTS WHO CONFRONTED ME ABOUT THE PORTAL. WITH NOWHERE ELSE TO TURN, I DECIDED TO TAKE ADVANTAGE OF DOUG'S POSITION AT THE NEWS STATION.

ON AIR

ISN'T IT TRUE THAT A LOT OF THE COMPONENTS OF THE DRAGON WERE IN FACT MADE FROM PIECES OF A PERSONAL COMPUTER?

I COULD USE A NOTEBOOK...

HOW WOULD YOU EXPLAIN THIS PHENOMENA?

NEWS

PERSONALLY, I THINK IT WAS ALL A PUBLICITY STUNT BY THE MOVIE STUDIOS TO PROMOTE THEIR UPCOMING "DRAGONWORLD" MOVIE. AND MOST LIKELY THE SAME CASE AS WITH THE RECENT SKYSCRAPER DEMOLITION ON PARK AVENUE.

I COULD KEEP TRACK OF ALL I LEARN, VERY SCIENTIFIC...

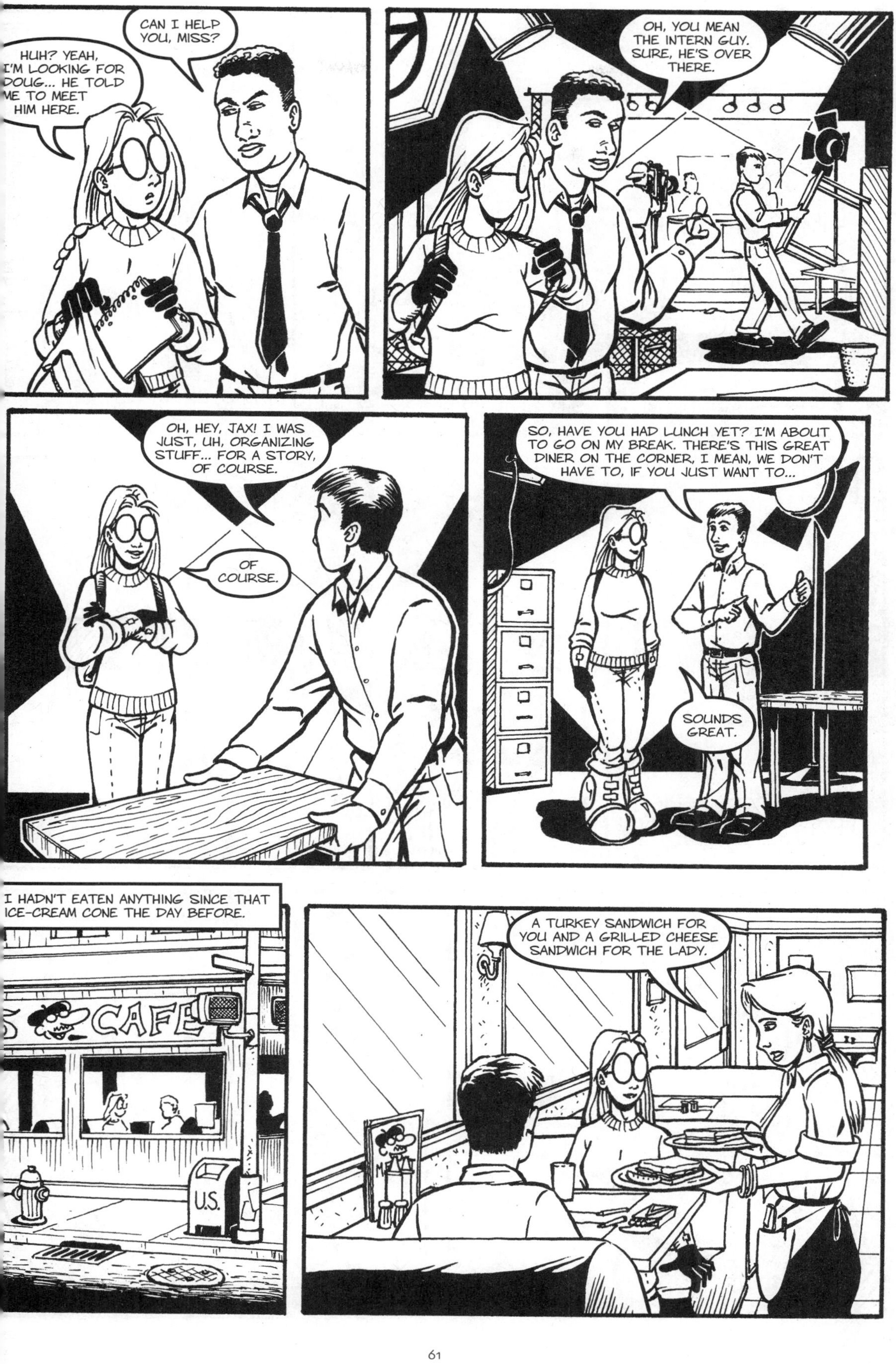
CAN I HELP YOU, MISS?
HUH? YEAH, I'M LOOKING FOR DOUG... HE TOLD ME TO MEET HIM HERE.
OH, YOU MEAN THE INTERN GUY. SURE, HE'S OVER THERE.
OH, HEY, JAX! I WAS JUST, UH, ORGANIZING STUFF... FOR A STORY, OF COURSE.
OF COURSE.
SO, HAVE YOU HAD LUNCH YET? I'M ABOUT TO GO ON MY BREAK. THERE'S THIS GREAT DINER ON THE CORNER, I MEAN, WE DON'T HAVE TO, IF YOU JUST WANT TO...
SOUNDS GREAT.
I HADN'T EATEN ANYTHING SINCE THAT ICE-CREAM CONE THE DAY BEFORE.
CAFE
U.S.
A TURKEY SANDWICH FOR YOU AND A GRILLED CHEESE SANDWICH FOR THE LADY.

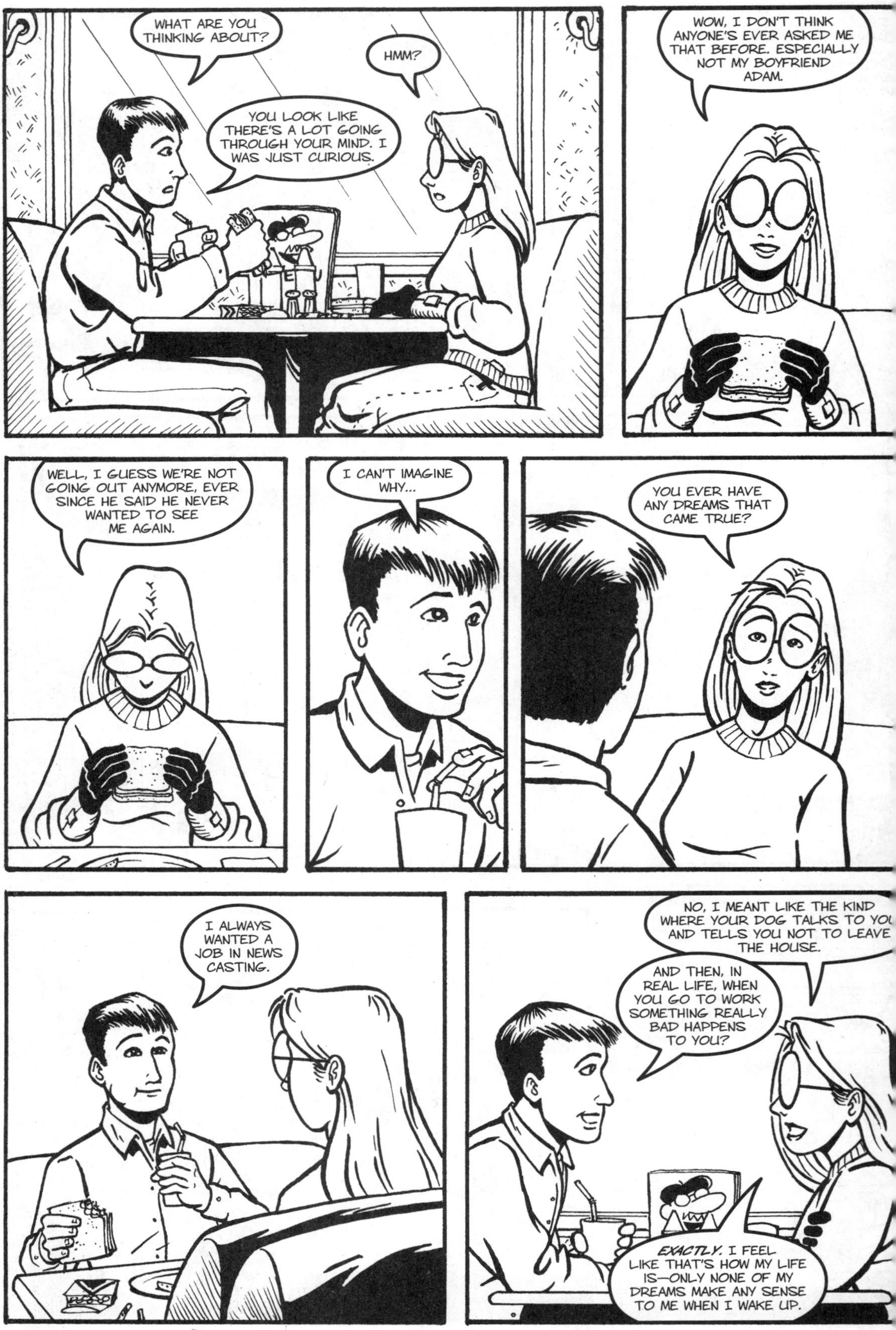
WHAT ARE YOU THINKING ABOUT?
HMM?
YOU LOOK LIKE THERE'S A LOT GOING THROUGH YOUR MIND. I WAS JUST CURIOUS.
WOW, I DON'T THINK ANYONE'S EVER ASKED ME THAT BEFORE. ESPECIALLY NOT MY BOYFRIEND ADAM.
WELL, I GUESS WE'RE NOT GOING OUT ANYMORE, EVER SINCE HE SAID HE NEVER WANTED TO SEE ME AGAIN.
I CAN'T IMAGINE WHY...
YOU EVER HAVE ANY DREAMS THAT CAME TRUE?
I ALWAYS WANTED A JOB IN NEWS CASTING.
NO, I MEANT LIKE THE KIND WHERE YOUR DOG TALKS TO YOU AND TELLS YOU NOT TO LEAVE THE HOUSE.
AND THEN, IN REAL LIFE, WHEN YOU GO TO WORK SOMETHING REALLY BAD HAPPENS TO YOU?
EXACTLY. I FEEL LIKE THAT'S HOW MY LIFE IS—ONLY NONE OF MY DREAMS MAKE ANY SENSE TO ME WHEN I WAKE UP.

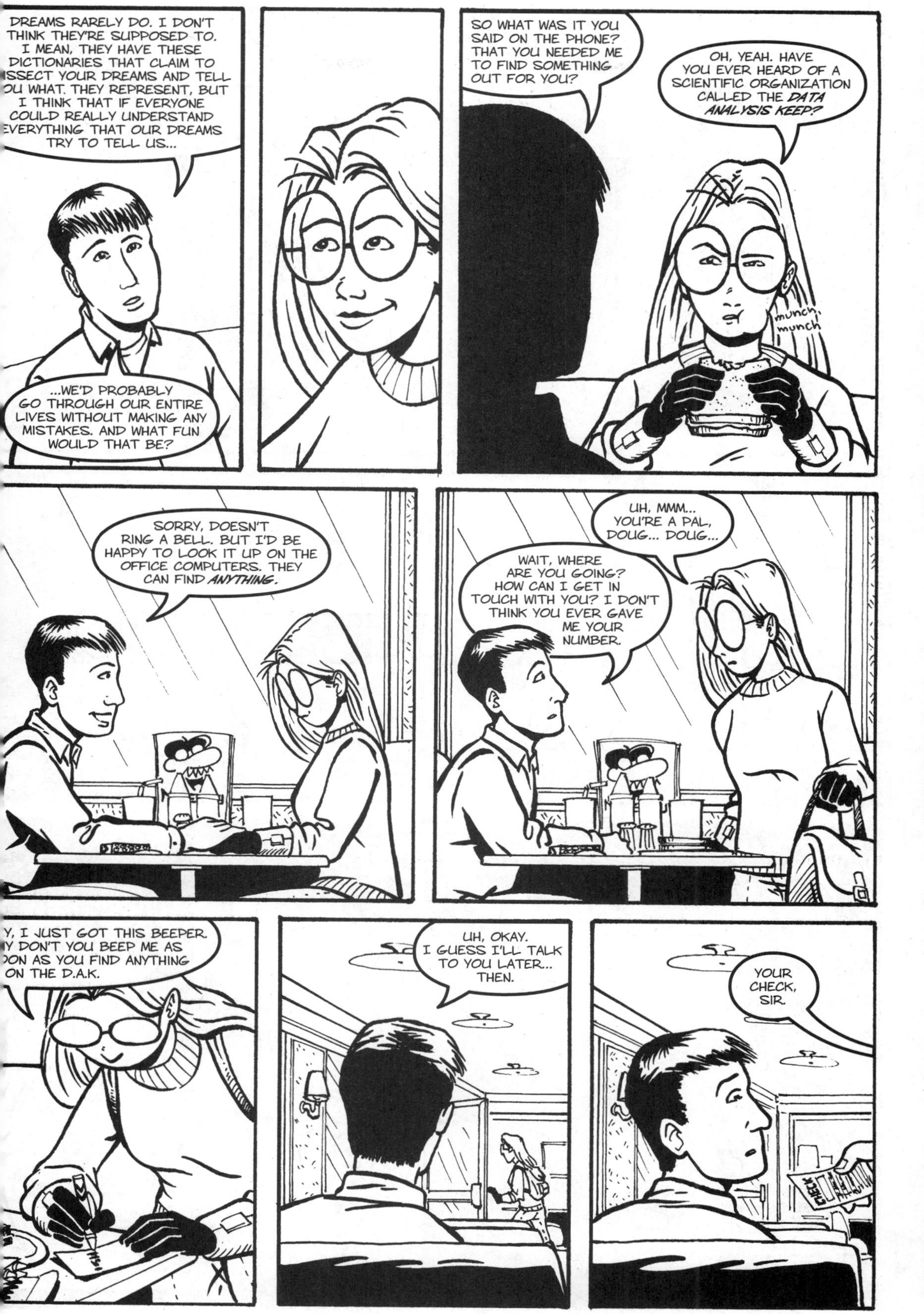
DREAMS RARELY DO. I DON'T THINK THEY'RE SUPPOSED TO. I MEAN, THEY HAVE THESE DICTIONARIES THAT CLAIM TO ISSECT YOUR DREAMS AND TELL OU WHAT. THEY REPRESENT, BUT I THINK THAT IF EVERYONE COULD REALLY UNDERSTAND EVERYTHING THAT OUR DREAMS TRY TO TELL US...
...WE'D PROBABLY GO THROUGH OUR ENTIRE LIVES WITHOUT MAKING ANY MISTAKES. AND WHAT FUN WOULD THAT BE?
SO WHAT WAS IT YOU SAID ON THE PHONE? THAT YOU NEEDED ME TO FIND SOMETHING OUT FOR YOU?
OH, YEAH. HAVE YOU EVER HEARD OF A SCIENTIFIC ORGANIZATION CALLED THE *DATA ANALYSIS KEEP?*
munch, munch
SORRY, DOESN'T RING A BELL. BUT I'D BE HAPPY TO LOOK IT UP ON THE OFFICE COMPUTERS. THEY CAN FIND *ANYTHING.*
UH, MMM... YOU'RE A PAL, DOUG... DOUG...
WAIT, WHERE ARE YOU GOING? HOW CAN I GET IN TOUCH WITH YOU? I DON'T THINK YOU EVER GAVE ME YOUR NUMBER.
Y, I JUST GOT THIS BEEPER. Y DON'T YOU BEEP ME AS OON AS YOU FIND ANYTHING ON THE D.A.K.
UH, OKAY. I GUESS I'LL TALK TO YOU LATER... THEN.
YOUR CHECK, SIR.
CHECK

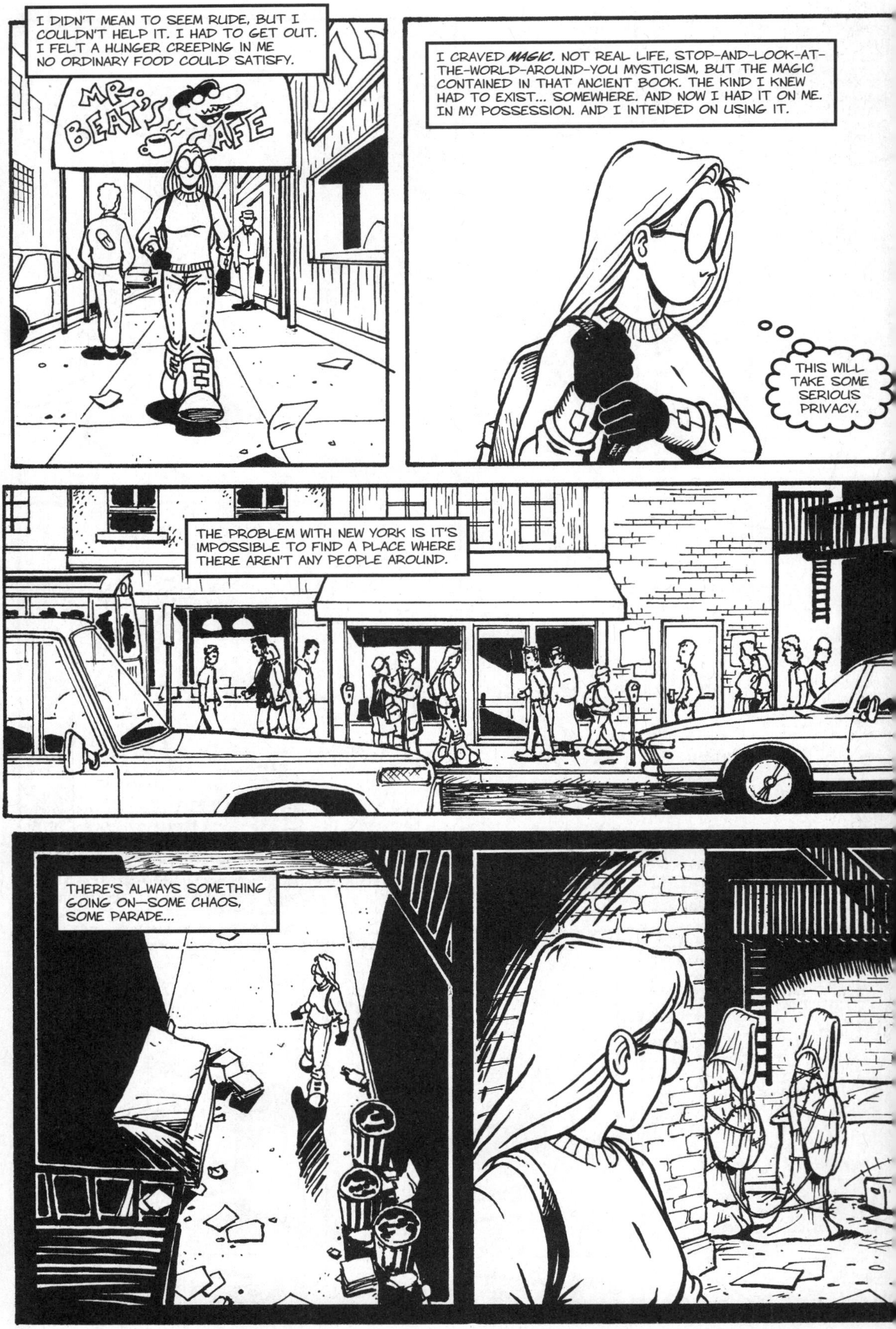
I DIDN'T MEAN TO SEEM RUDE, BUT I COULDN'T HELP IT. I HAD TO GET OUT. I FELT A HUNGER CREEPING IN ME NO ORDINARY FOOD COULD SATISFY.
MR. BEAT'S CAFE
I CRAVED *MAGIC.* NOT REAL LIFE, STOP-AND-LOOK-AT-THE-WORLD-AROUND-YOU MYSTICISM, BUT THE MAGIC CONTAINED IN THAT ANCIENT BOOK. THE KIND I KNEW HAD TO EXIST... SOMEWHERE. AND NOW I HAD IT ON ME. IN MY POSSESSION. AND I INTENDED ON USING IT.
THIS WILL TAKE SOME SERIOUS PRIVACY.
THE PROBLEM WITH NEW YORK IS IT'S IMPOSSIBLE TO FIND A PLACE WHERE THERE AREN'T ANY PEOPLE AROUND.
THERE'S ALWAYS SOMETHING GOING ON—SOME CHAOS, SOME PARADE...

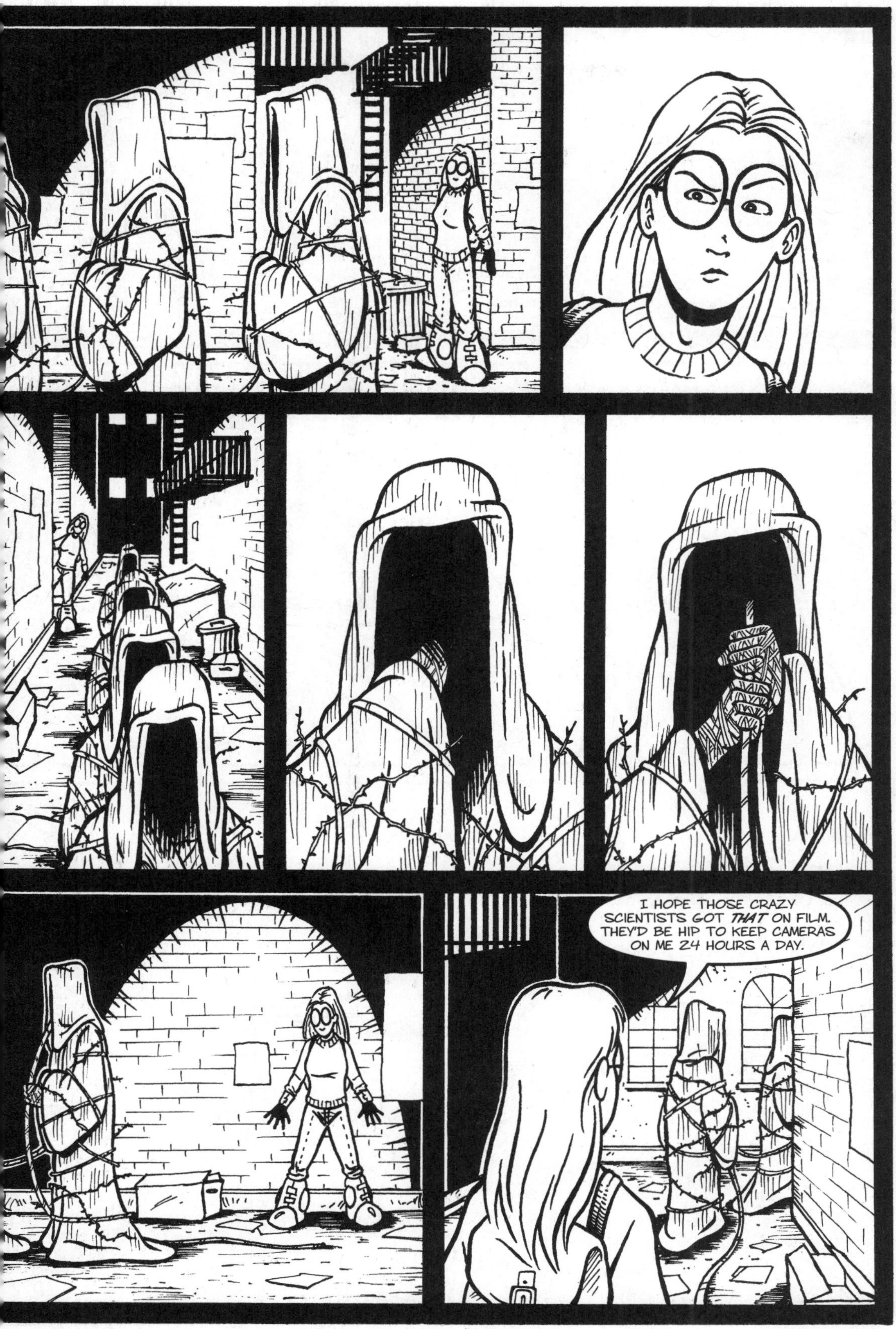
I HOPE THOSE CRAZY SCIENTISTS GOT *THAT* ON FILM. THEY'D BE HIP TO KEEP CAMERAS ON ME 24 HOURS A DAY.

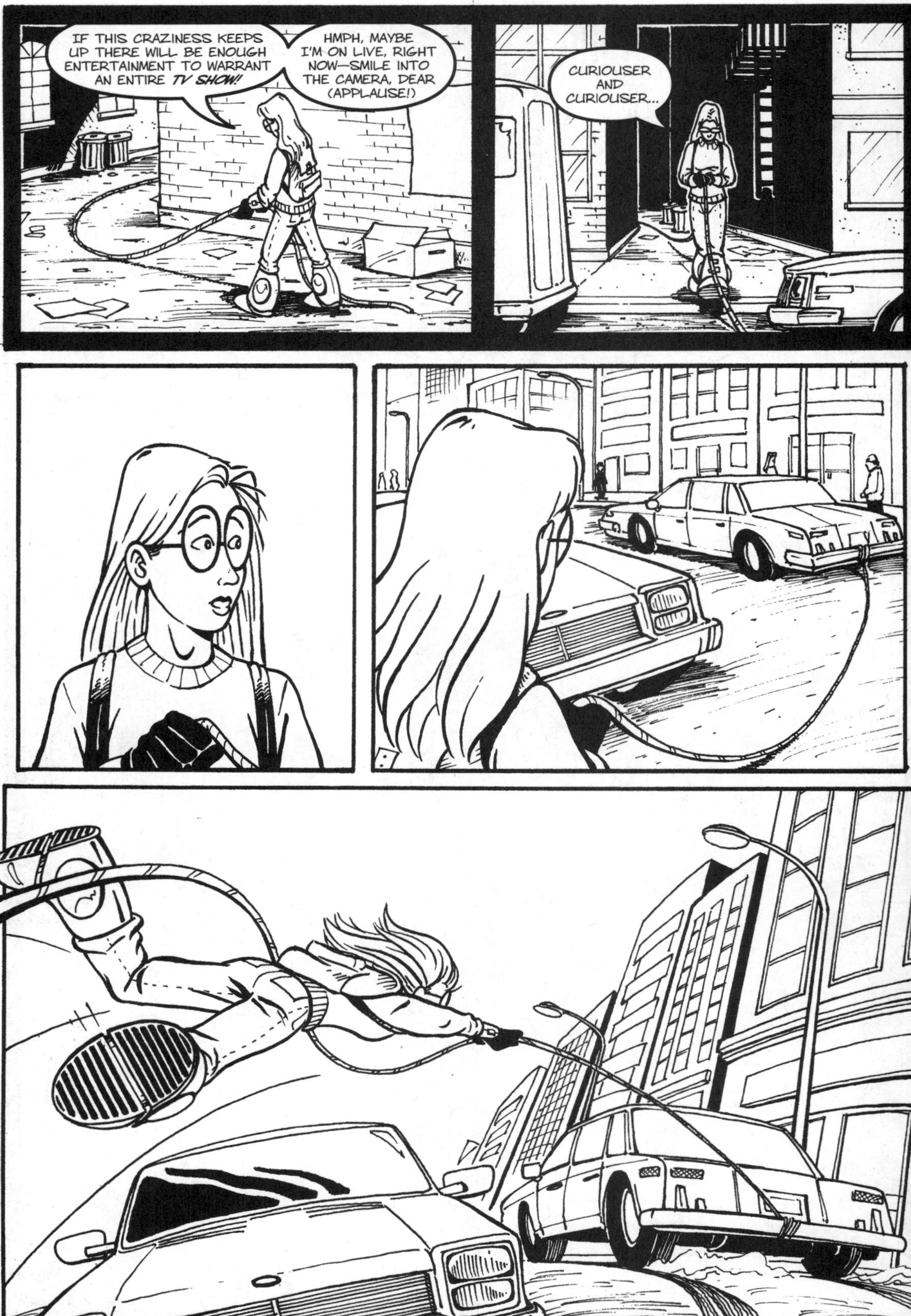
IF THIS CRAZINESS KEEPS UP THERE WILL BE ENOUGH ENTERTAINMENT TO WARRANT AN ENTIRE *TV SHOW!*
HMPH, MAYBE I'M ON LIVE, RIGHT NOW—SMILE INTO THE CAMERA, DEAR (APPLAUSE!)
CURIOUSER AND CURIOUSER...

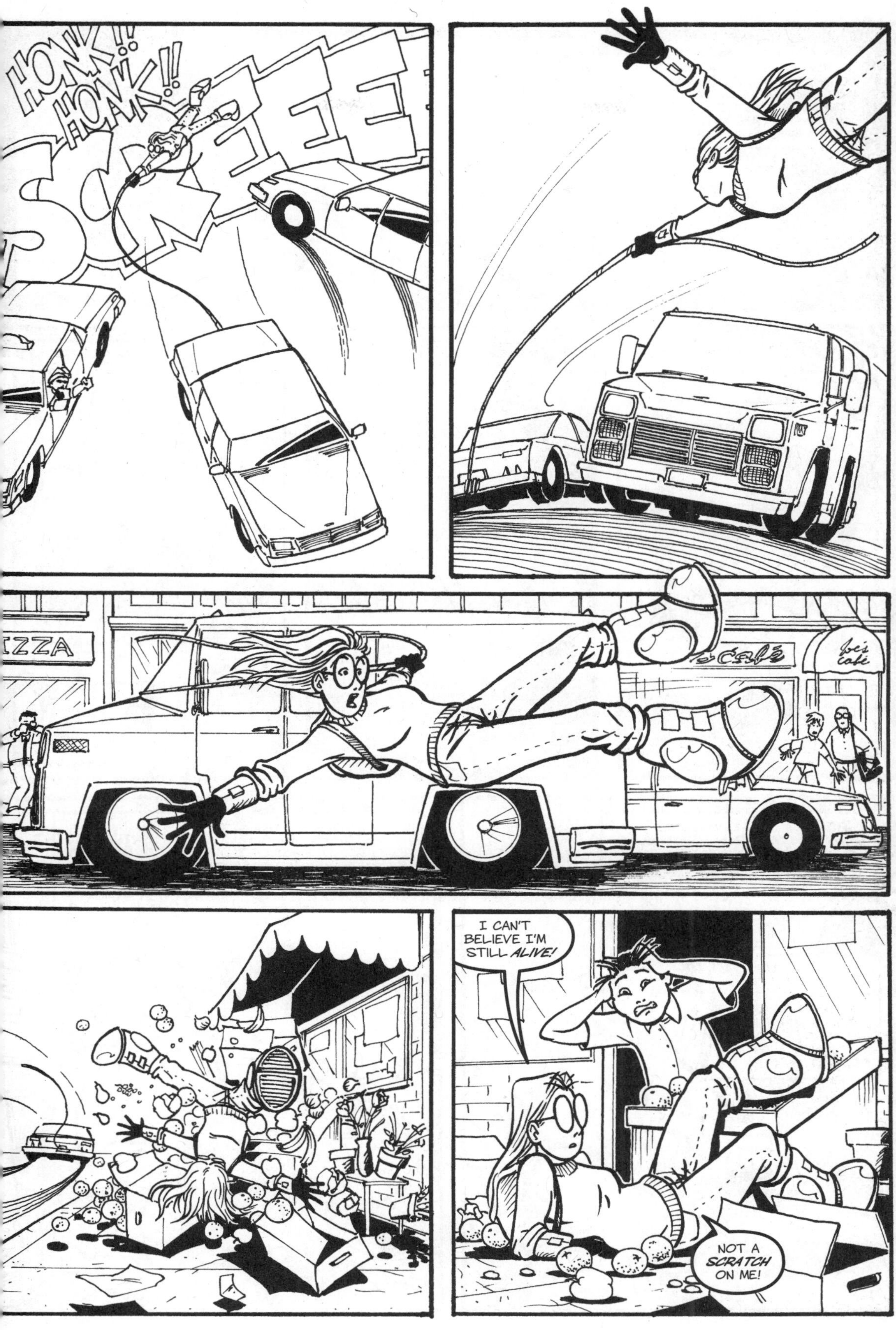
HONK!!
HONK!!
IZZA
I CAN'T BELIEVE I'M STILL *ALIVE!*
NOT A *SCRATCH* ON ME!

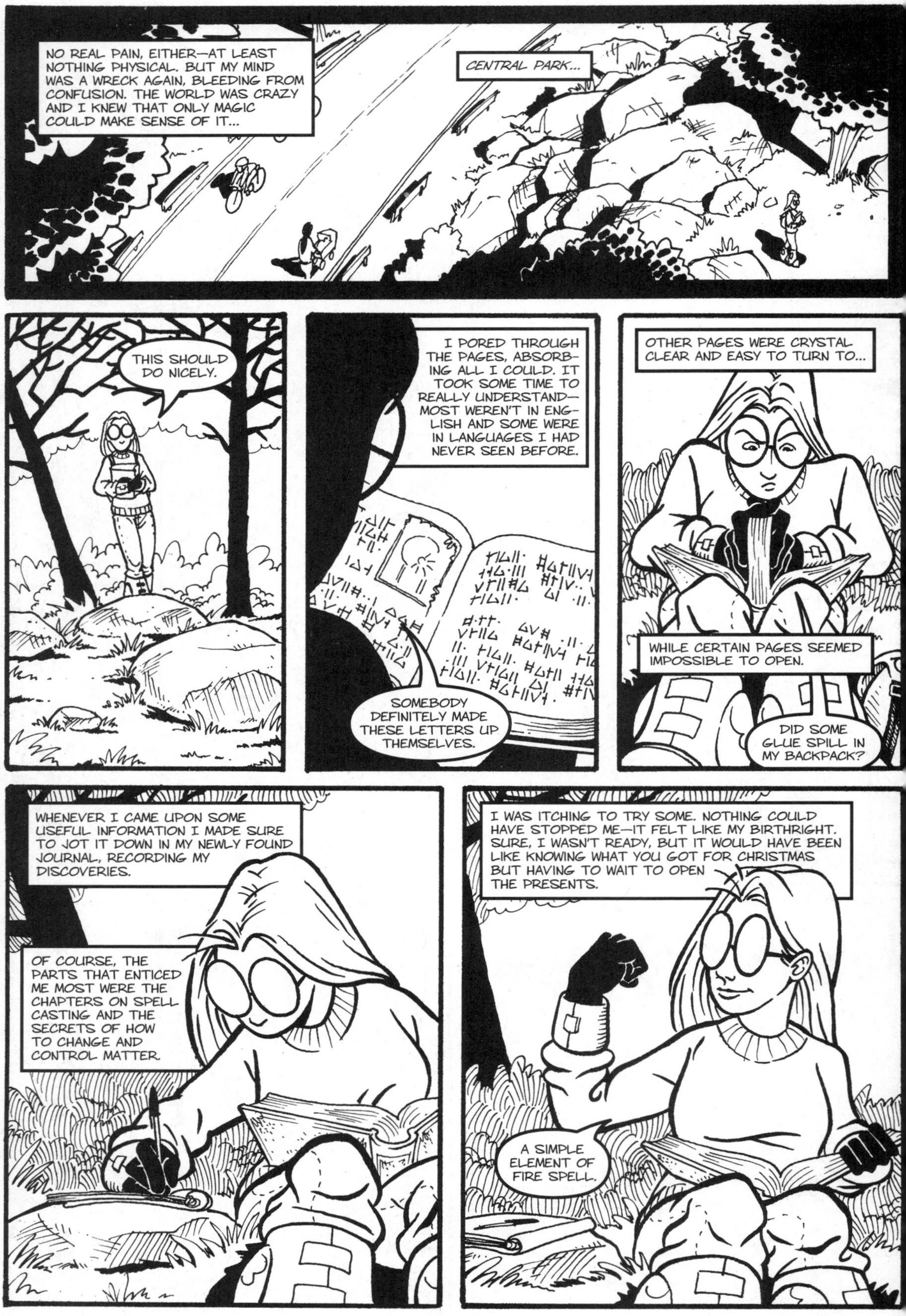
NO REAL PAIN, EITHER—AT LEAST NOTHING PHYSICAL. BUT MY MIND WAS A WRECK AGAIN, BLEEDING FROM CONFUSION. THE WORLD WAS CRAZY AND I KNEW THAT ONLY MAGIC COULD MAKE SENSE OF IT...
CENTRAL PARK...
THIS SHOULD DO NICELY.
I PORED THROUGH THE PAGES, ABSORBING ALL I COULD. IT TOOK SOME TIME TO REALLY UNDERSTAND—MOST WEREN'T IN ENGLISH AND SOME WERE IN LANGUAGES I HAD NEVER SEEN BEFORE.
SOMEBODY DEFINITELY MADE THESE LETTERS UP THEMSELVES.
OTHER PAGES WERE CRYSTAL CLEAR AND EASY TO TURN TO...
WHILE CERTAIN PAGES SEEMED IMPOSSIBLE TO OPEN.
DID SOME GLUE SPILL IN MY BACKPACK?
WHENEVER I CAME UPON SOME USEFUL INFORMATION I MADE SURE TO JOT IT DOWN IN MY NEWLY FOUND JOURNAL, RECORDING MY DISCOVERIES.
OF COURSE, THE PARTS THAT ENTICED ME MOST WERE THE CHAPTERS ON SPELL CASTING AND THE SECRETS OF HOW TO CHANGE AND CONTROL MATTER.
I WAS ITCHING TO TRY SOME. NOTHING COULD HAVE STOPPED ME—IT FELT LIKE MY BIRTHRIGHT. SURE, I WASN'T READY, BUT IT WOULD HAVE BEEN LIKE KNOWING WHAT YOU GOT FOR CHRISTMAS BUT HAVING TO WAIT TO OPEN THE PRESENTS.
A SIMPLE ELEMENT OF FIRE SPELL.

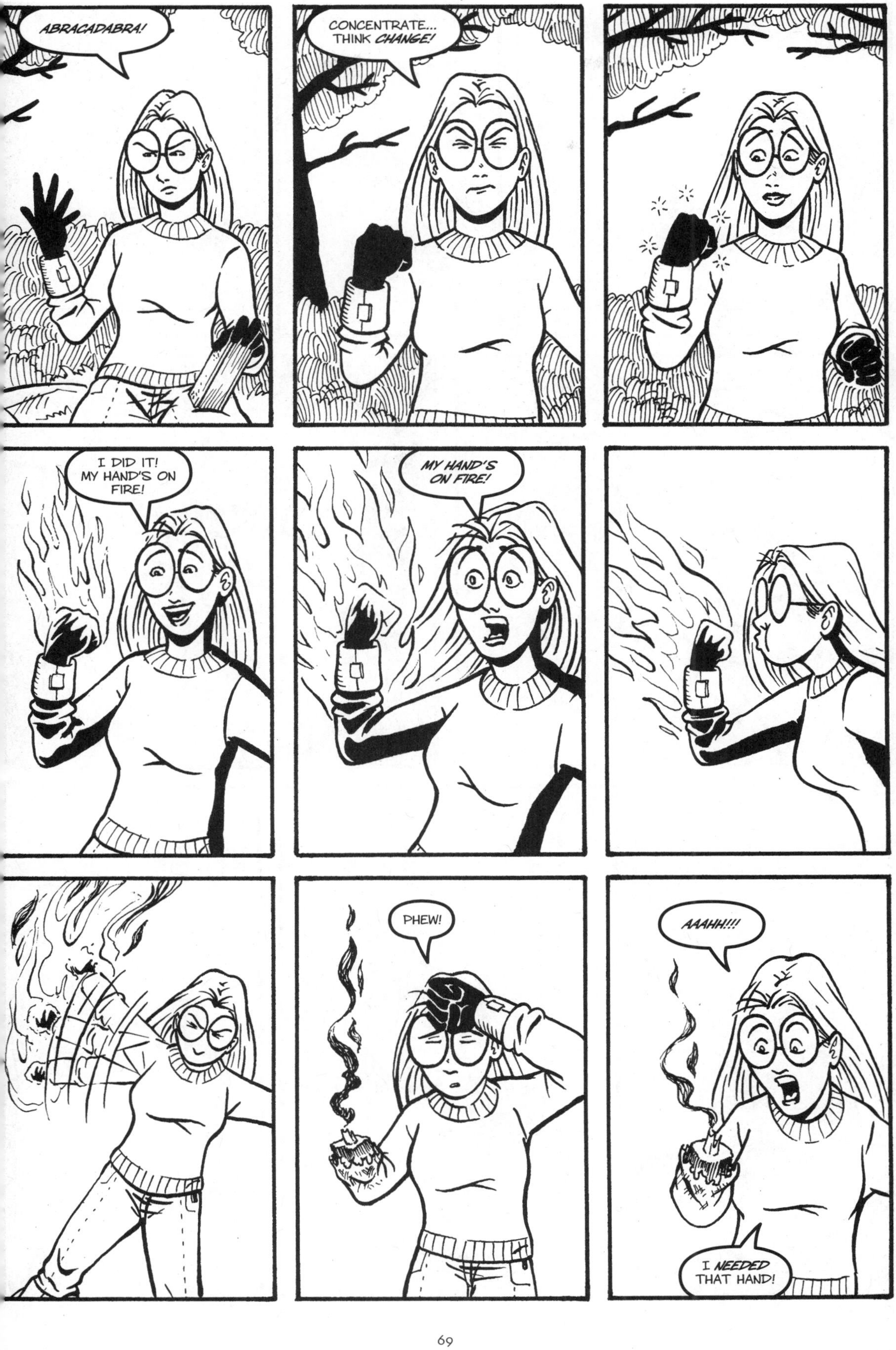
ABRACADABRA!
CONCENTRATE... THINK CHANGE!
I DID IT! MY HAND'S ON FIRE!
MY HAND'S ON FIRE!
PHEW!
AAAHH!!!
I NEEDED THAT HAND!

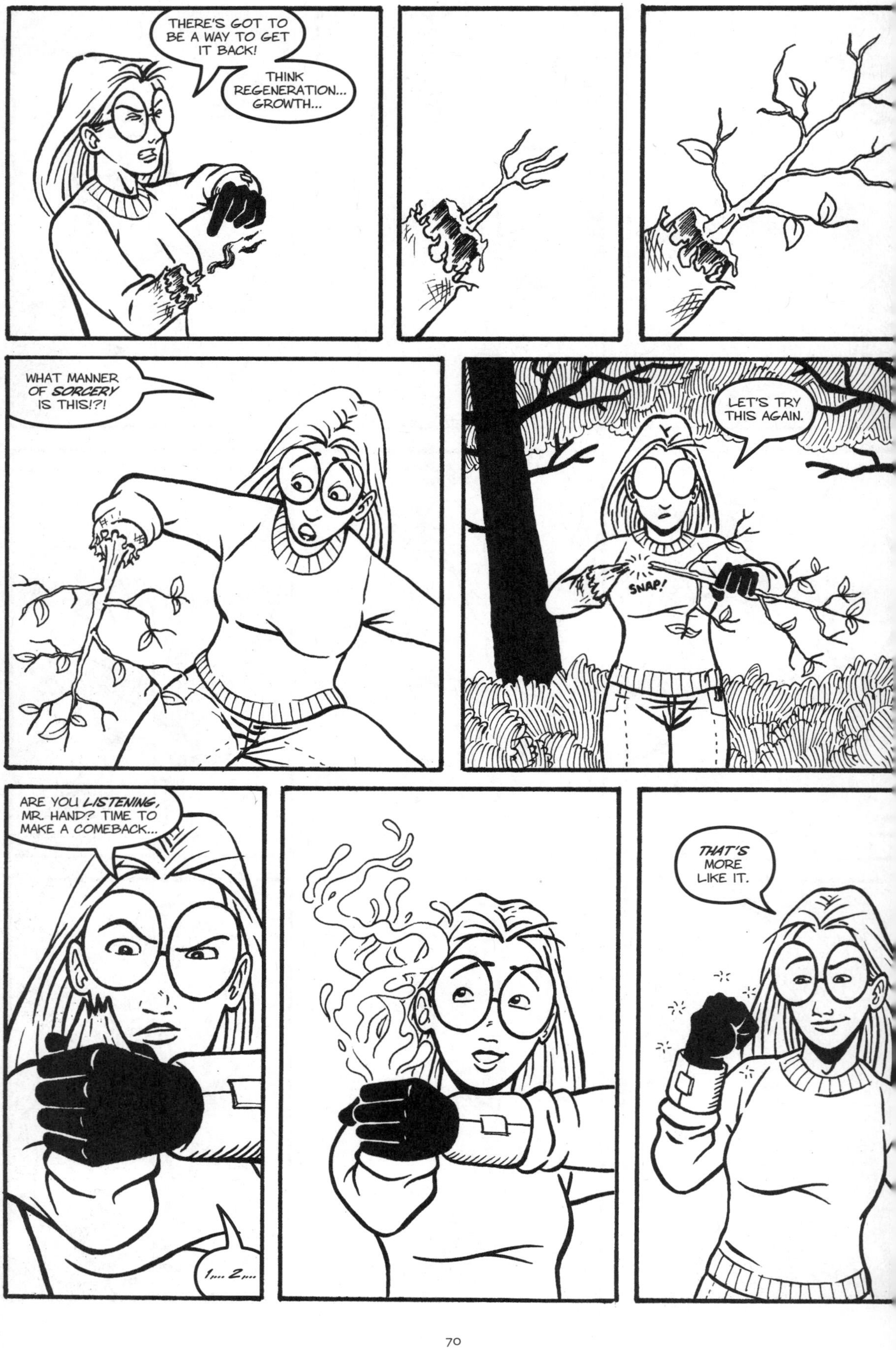
THERE'S GOT TO BE A WAY TO GET IT BACK!
THINK REGENERATION... GROWTH...
WHAT MANNER OF SORCERY IS THIS!?!
LET'S TRY THIS AGAIN.
SNAP!
ARE YOU LISTENING, MR. HAND? TIME TO MAKE A COMEBACK...
1,... 2,...
THAT'S MORE LIKE IT.

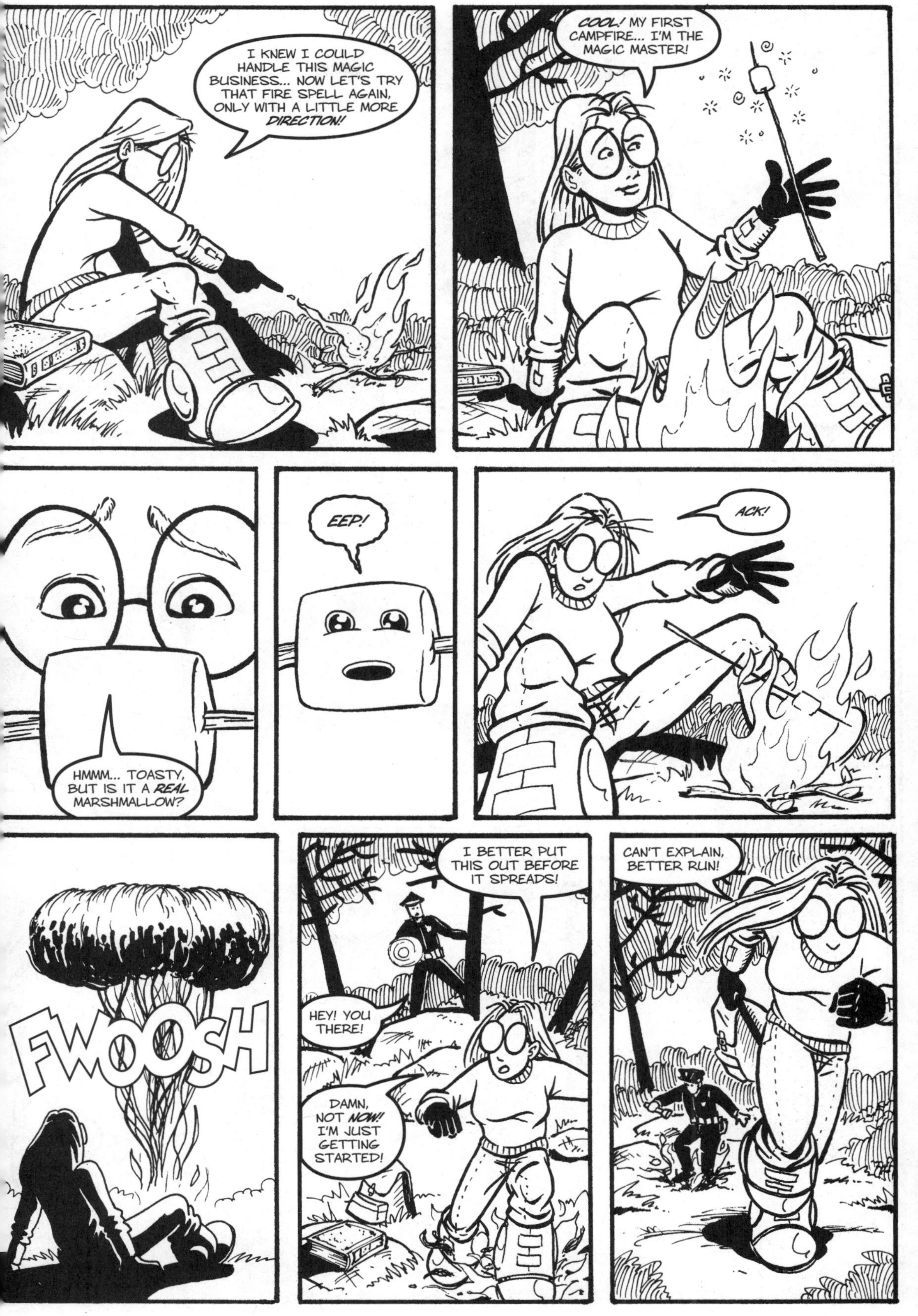

I KNEW I COULD HANDLE THIS MAGIC BUSINESS... NOW LET'S TRY THAT FIRE SPELL AGAIN, ONLY WITH A LITTLE MORE DIRECTION!
COOL! MY FIRST CAMPFIRE... I'M THE MAGIC MASTER!
HMMM... TOASTY, BUT IS IT A REAL MARSHMALLOW?
EEP!
ACK!
FWOOSH
I BETTER PUT THIS OUT BEFORE IT SPREADS!
HEY! YOU THERE!
DAMN, NOT NOW! I'M JUST GETTING STARTED!
CAN'T EXPLAIN, BETTER RUN!

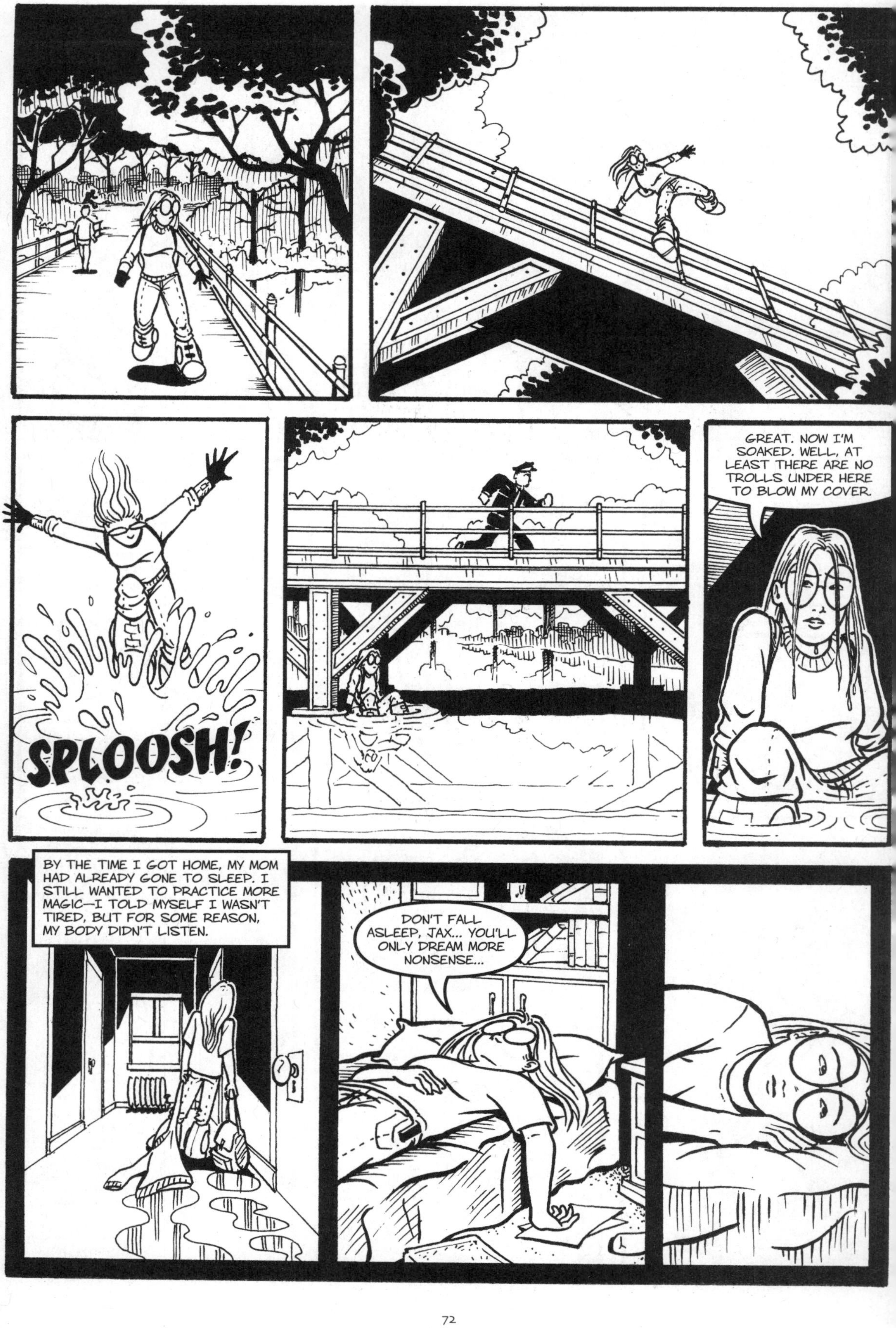
SPLOOSH!
GREAT. NOW I'M SOAKED. WELL, AT LEAST THERE ARE NO TROLLS UNDER HERE TO BLOW MY COVER.
BY THE TIME I GOT HOME, MY MOM HAD ALREADY GONE TO SLEEP. I STILL WANTED TO PRACTICE MORE MAGIC—I TOLD MYSELF I WASN'T TIRED, BUT FOR SOME REASON, MY BODY DIDN'T LISTEN.
DON'T FALL ASLEEP, JAX... YOU'LL ONLY DREAM MORE NONSENSE...

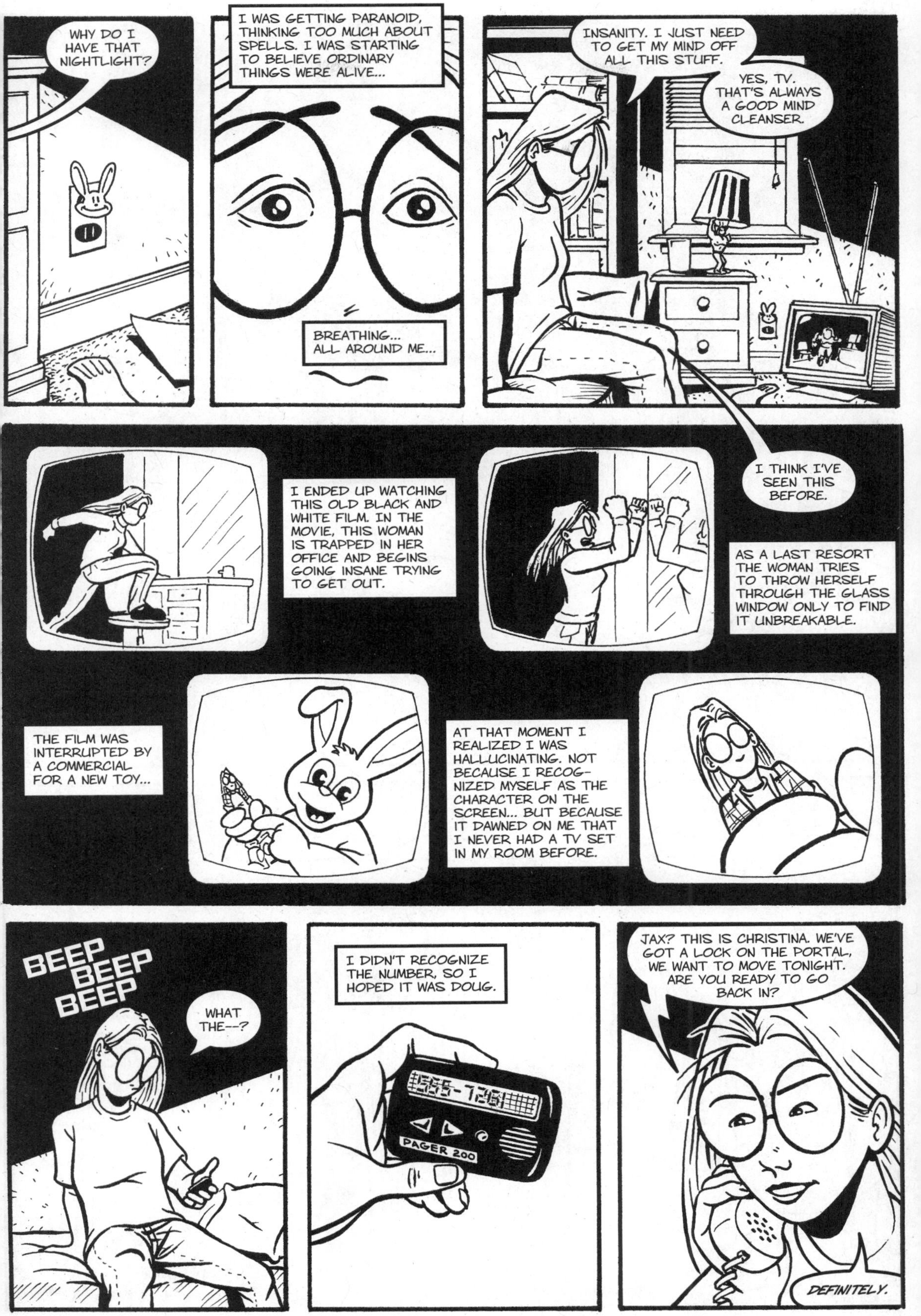

WHY DO I HAVE THAT NIGHTLIGHT?
I WAS GETTING PARANOID, THINKING TOO MUCH ABOUT SPELLS. I WAS STARTING TO BELIEVE ORDINARY THINGS WERE ALIVE...
BREATHING... ALL AROUND ME...
INSANITY. I JUST NEED TO GET MY MIND OFF ALL THIS STUFF.
YES, TV. THAT'S ALWAYS A GOOD MIND CLEANSER.
I ENDED UP WATCHING THIS OLD BLACK AND WHITE FILM. IN THE MOVIE, THIS WOMAN IS TRAPPED IN HER OFFICE AND BEGINS GOING INSANE TRYING TO GET OUT.
I THINK I'VE SEEN THIS BEFORE.
AS A LAST RESORT THE WOMAN TRIES TO THROW HERSELF THROUGH THE GLASS WINDOW ONLY TO FIND IT UNBREAKABLE.
THE FILM WAS INTERRUPTED BY A COMMERCIAL FOR A NEW TOY...
AT THAT MOMENT I REALIZED I WAS HALLUCINATING. NOT BECAUSE I RECOGNIZED MYSELF AS THE CHARACTER ON THE SCREEN... BUT BECAUSE IT DAWNED ON ME THAT I NEVER HAD A TV SET IN MY ROOM BEFORE.
BEEP BEEP BEEP
WHAT THE--?
I DIDN'T RECOGNIZE THE NUMBER, SO I HOPED IT WAS DOUG.
555-1261
PAGER 200
JAX? THIS IS CHRISTINA. WE'VE GOT A LOCK ON THE PORTAL, WE WANT TO MOVE TONIGHT. ARE YOU READY TO GO BACK IN?
DEFINITELY.

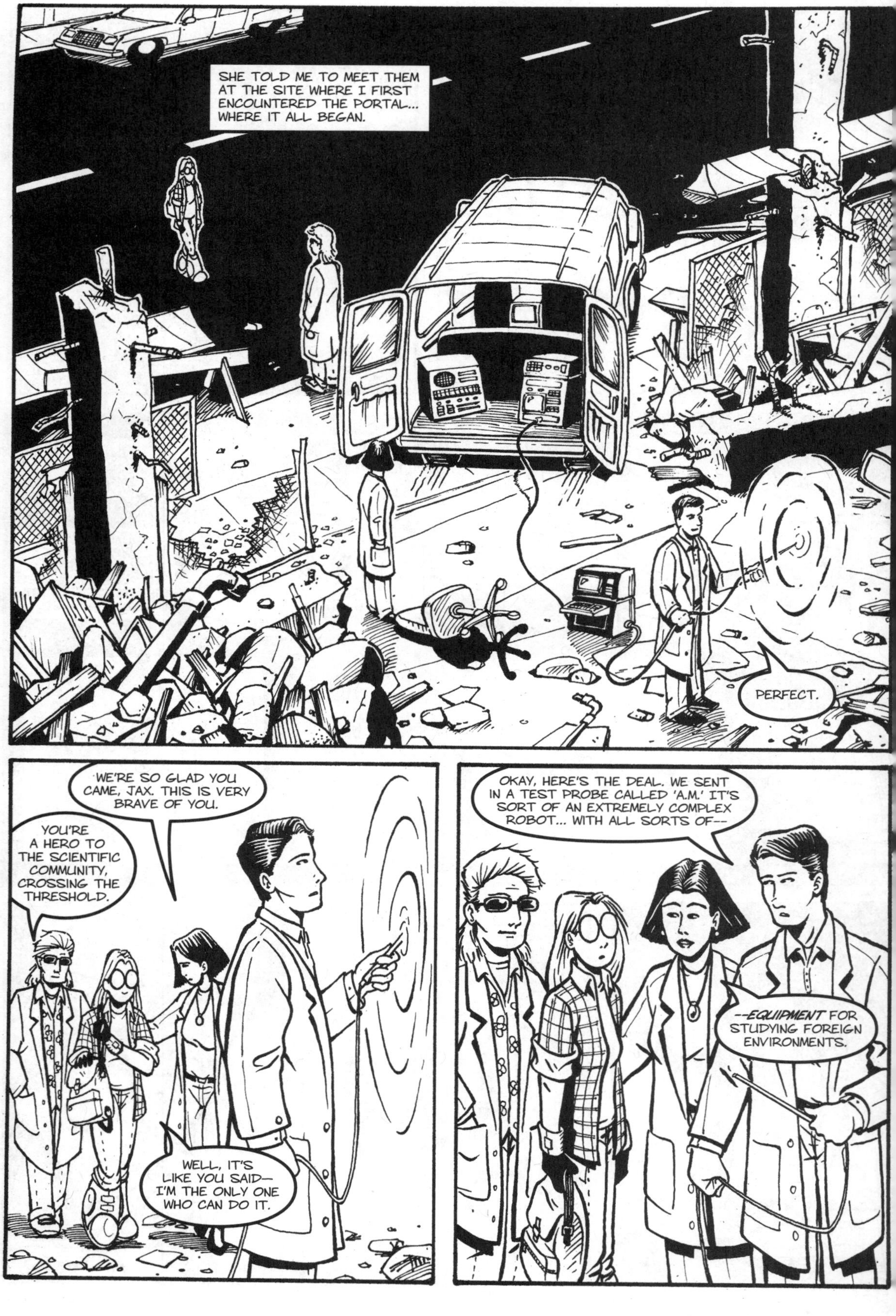
SHE TOLD ME TO MEET THEM AT THE SITE WHERE I FIRST ENCOUNTERED THE PORTAL... WHERE IT ALL BEGAN.
PERFECT.
WE'RE SO GLAD YOU CAME, JAX. THIS IS VERY BRAVE OF YOU.
YOU'RE A HERO TO THE SCIENTIFIC COMMUNITY, CROSSING THE THRESHOLD.
WELL, IT'S LIKE YOU SAID— I'M THE ONLY ONE WHO CAN DO IT.
OKAY, HERE'S THE DEAL. WE SENT IN A TEST PROBE CALLED 'A.M.' IT'S SORT OF AN EXTREMELY COMPLEX ROBOT... WITH ALL SORTS OF--
--*EQUIPMENT* FOR STUDYING FOREIGN ENVIRONMENTS.

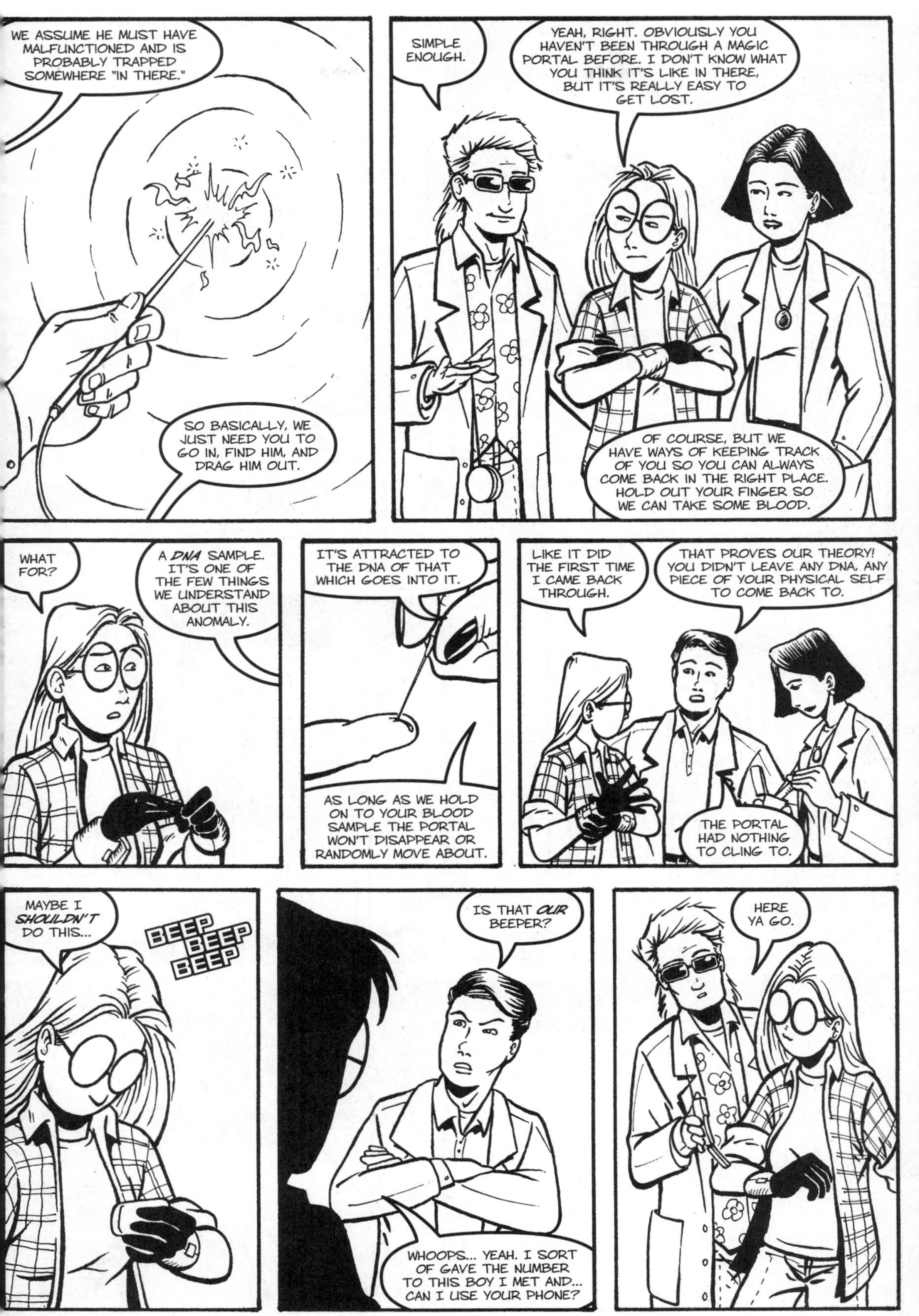
WE ASSUME HE MUST HAVE MALFUNCTIONED AND IS PROBABLY TRAPPED SOMEWHERE "IN THERE."
SO BASICALLY, WE JUST NEED YOU TO GO IN, FIND HIM, AND DRAG HIM OUT.
SIMPLE ENOUGH.
YEAH, RIGHT. OBVIOUSLY YOU HAVEN'T BEEN THROUGH A MAGIC PORTAL BEFORE. I DON'T KNOW WHAT YOU THINK IT'S LIKE IN THERE, BUT IT'S REALLY EASY TO GET LOST.
OF COURSE, BUT WE HAVE WAYS OF KEEPING TRACK OF YOU SO YOU CAN ALWAYS COME BACK IN THE RIGHT PLACE. HOLD OUT YOUR FINGER SO WE CAN TAKE SOME BLOOD.
WHAT FOR?
A *DNA* SAMPLE. IT'S ONE OF THE FEW THINGS WE UNDERSTAND ABOUT THIS ANOMALY.
IT'S ATTRACTED TO THE DNA OF THAT WHICH GOES INTO IT.
AS LONG AS WE HOLD ON TO YOUR BLOOD SAMPLE THE PORTAL WON'T DISAPPEAR OR RANDOMLY MOVE ABOUT.
LIKE IT DID THE FIRST TIME I CAME BACK THROUGH.
THAT PROVES OUR THEORY! YOU DIDN'T LEAVE ANY DNA, ANY PIECE OF YOUR PHYSICAL SELF TO COME BACK TO.
THE PORTAL HAD NOTHING TO CLING TO.
MAYBE I *SHOULDN'T* DO THIS...
BEEP BEEP BEEP
IS THAT *OUR* BEEPER?
WHOOPS... YEAH. I SORT OF GAVE THE NUMBER TO THIS BOY I MET AND... CAN I USE YOUR PHONE?
HERE YA GO.

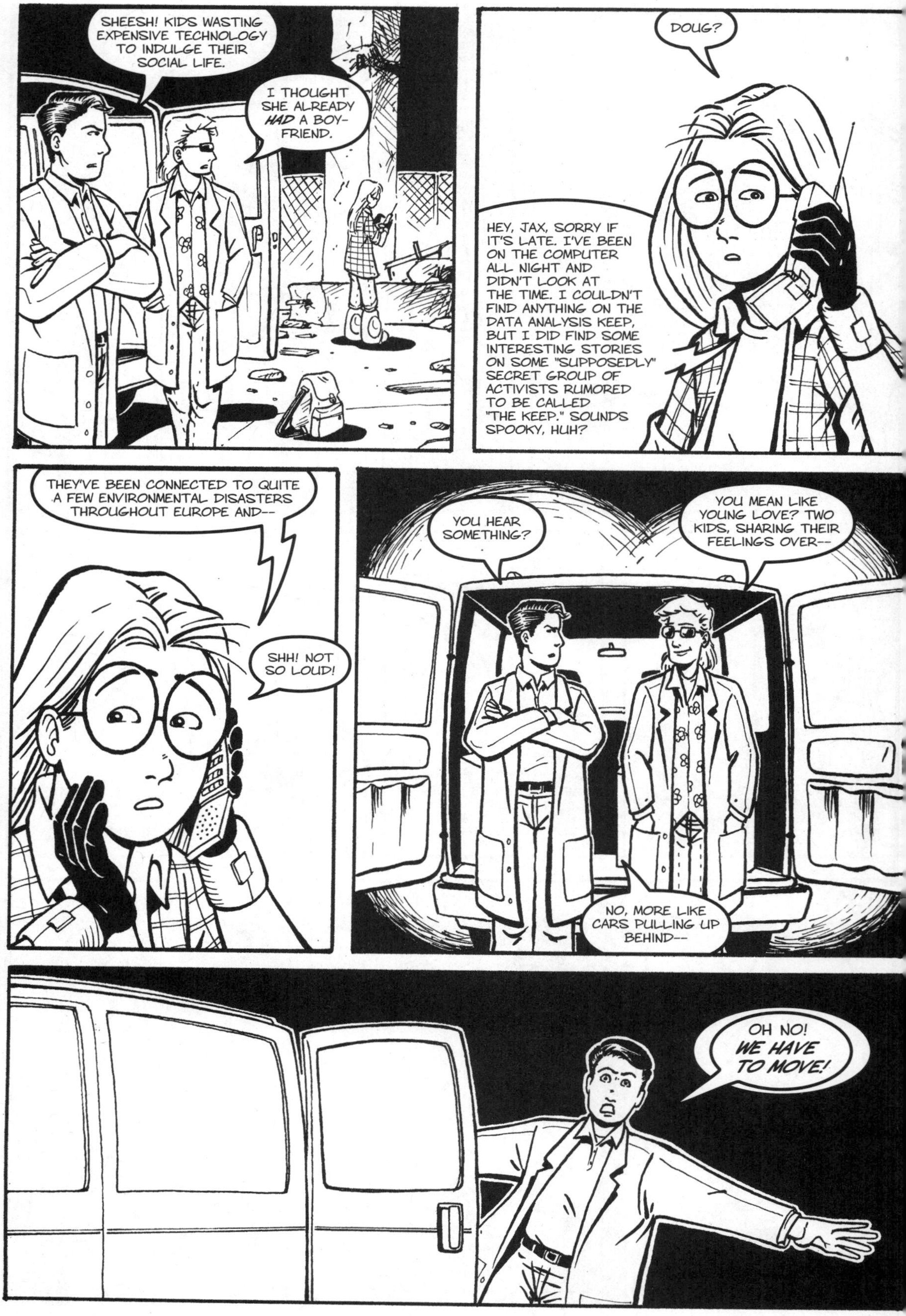
SHEESH! KIDS WASTING EXPENSIVE TECHNOLOGY TO INDULGE THEIR SOCIAL LIFE.
I THOUGHT SHE ALREADY HAD A BOY-FRIEND.
DOUG?
HEY, JAX, SORRY IF IT'S LATE. I'VE BEEN ON THE COMPUTER ALL NIGHT AND DIDN'T LOOK AT THE TIME. I COULDN'T FIND ANYTHING ON THE DATA ANALYSIS KEEP, BUT I DID FIND SOME INTERESTING STORIES ON SOME "SUPPOSEDLY" SECRET GROUP OF ACTIVISTS RUMORED TO BE CALLED "THE KEEP." SOUNDS SPOOKY, HUH?
THEY'VE BEEN CONNECTED TO QUITE A FEW ENVIRONMENTAL DISASTERS THROUGHOUT EUROPE AND--
SHH! NOT SO LOUD!
YOU HEAR SOMETHING?
YOU MEAN LIKE YOUNG LOVE? TWO KIDS, SHARING THEIR FEELINGS OVER--
NO, MORE LIKE CARS PULLING UP BEHIND--
OH NO! WE HAVE TO MOVE!

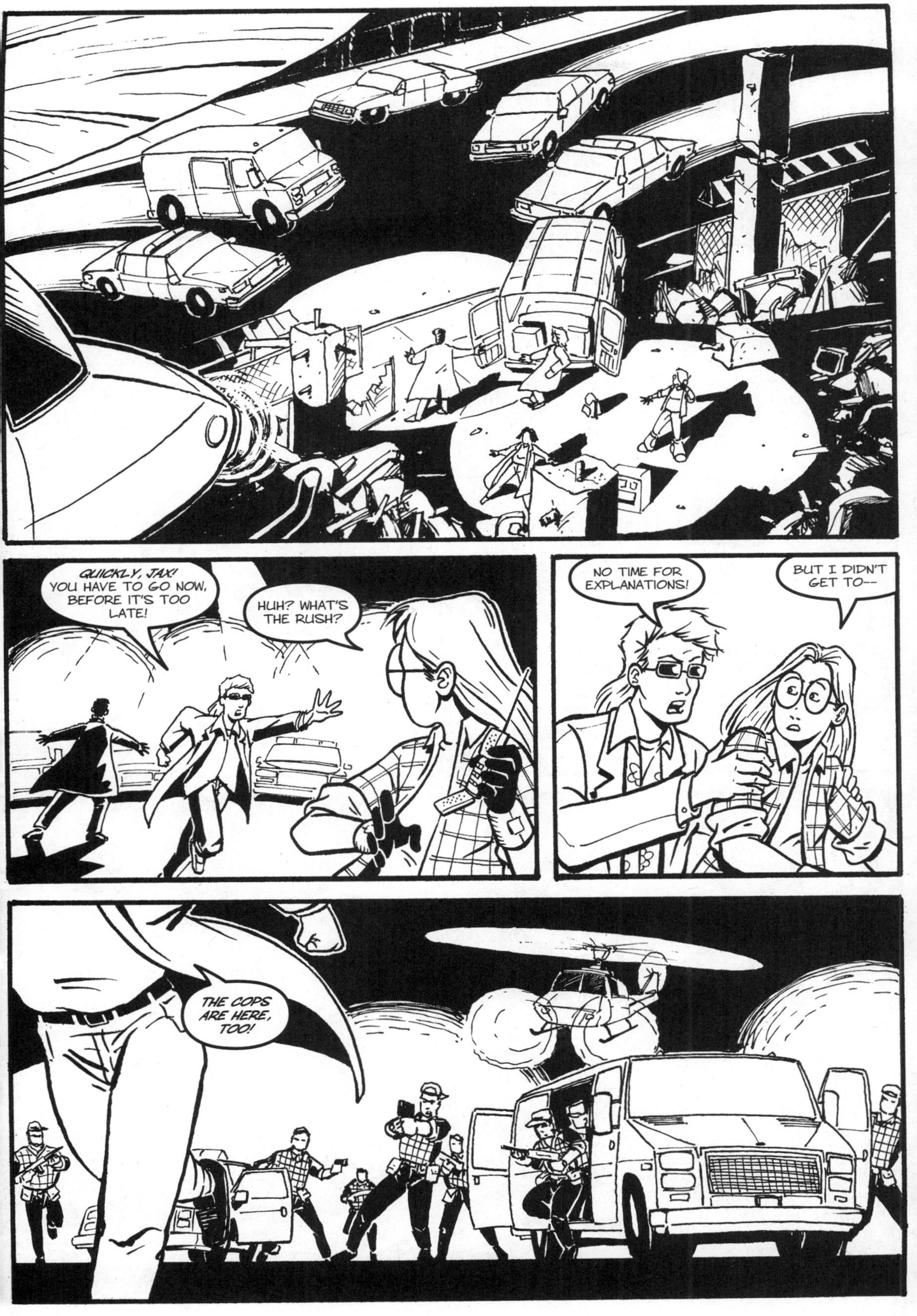
QUICKLY, JAX! YOU HAVE TO GO NOW, BEFORE IT'S TOO LATE!
HUH? WHAT'S THE RUSH?
NO TIME FOR EXPLANATIONS!
BUT I DIDN'T GET TO--
THE COPS ARE HERE, TOO!

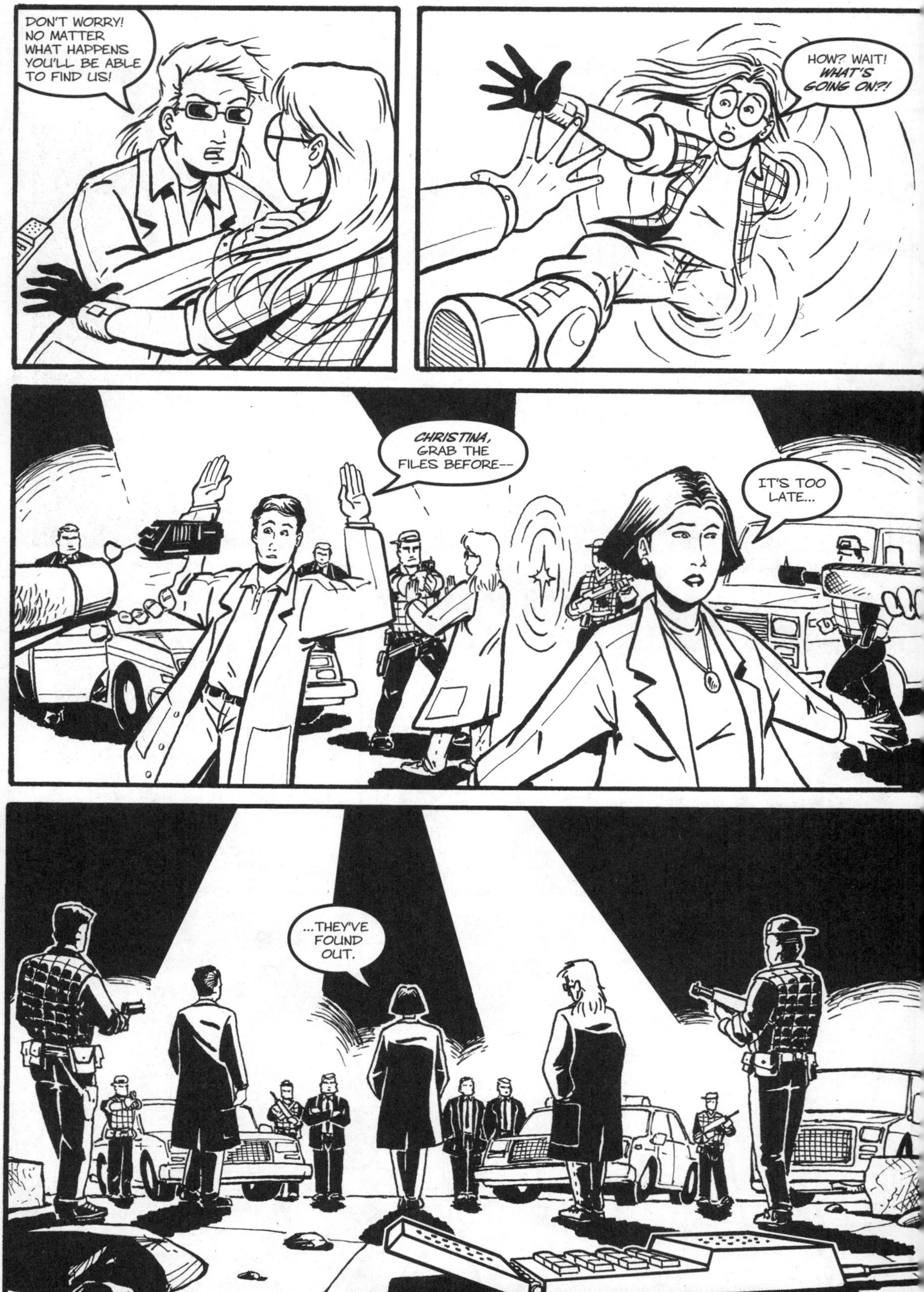
DON'T WORRY! NO MATTER WHAT HAPPENS YOU'LL BE ABLE TO FIND US!
HOW? WAIT! WHAT'S GOING ON?!
CHRISTINA, GRAB THE FILES BEFORE--
IT'S TOO LATE...
...THEY'VE FOUND OUT.

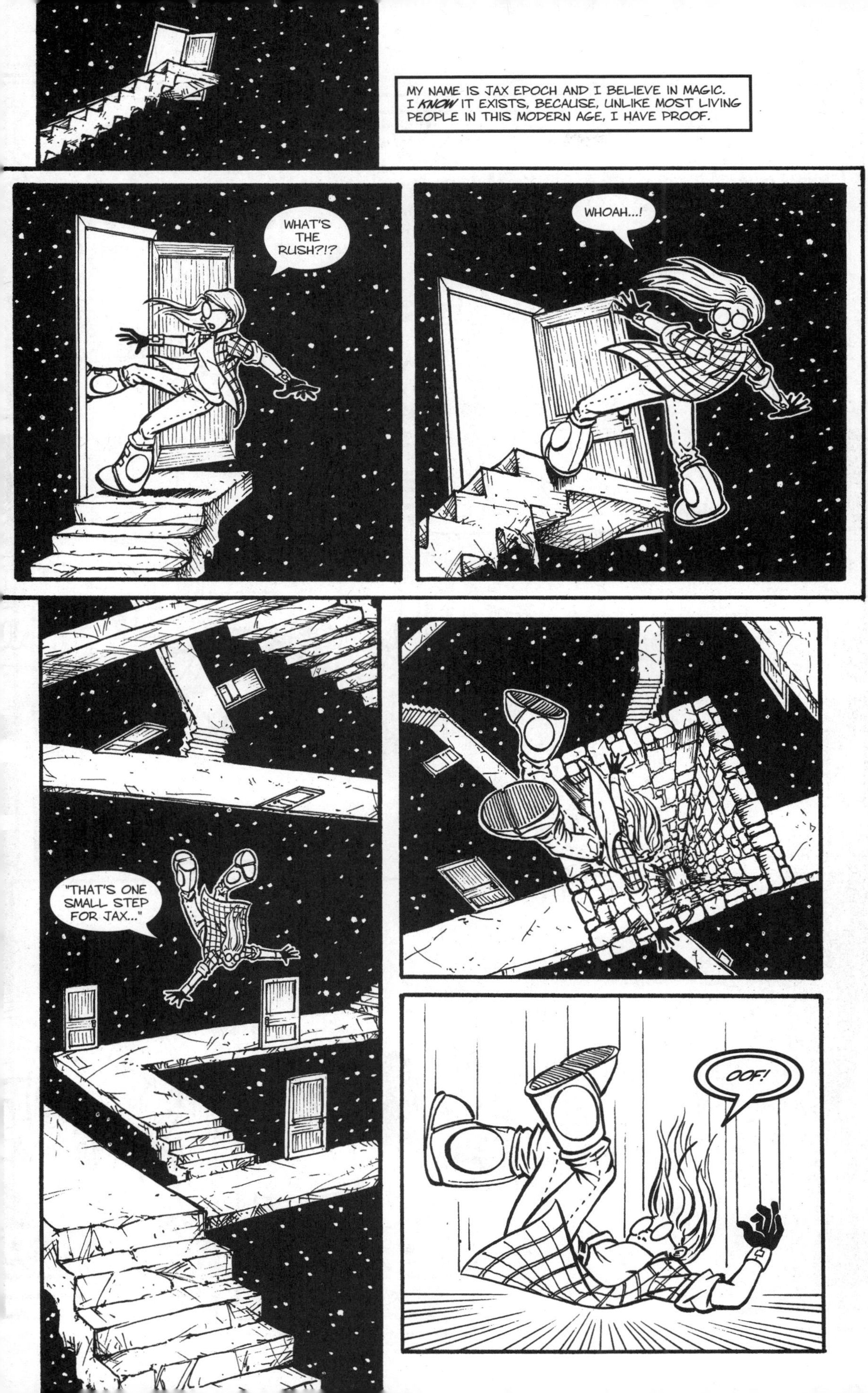
MY NAME IS JAX EPOCH AND I BELIEVE IN MAGIC. I KNOW IT EXISTS, BECAUSE, UNLIKE MOST LIVING PEOPLE IN THIS MODERN AGE, I HAVE PROOF.
WHAT'S THE RUSH?!?
WHOAH...!
"THAT'S ONE SMALL STEP FOR JAX..."
OOF!

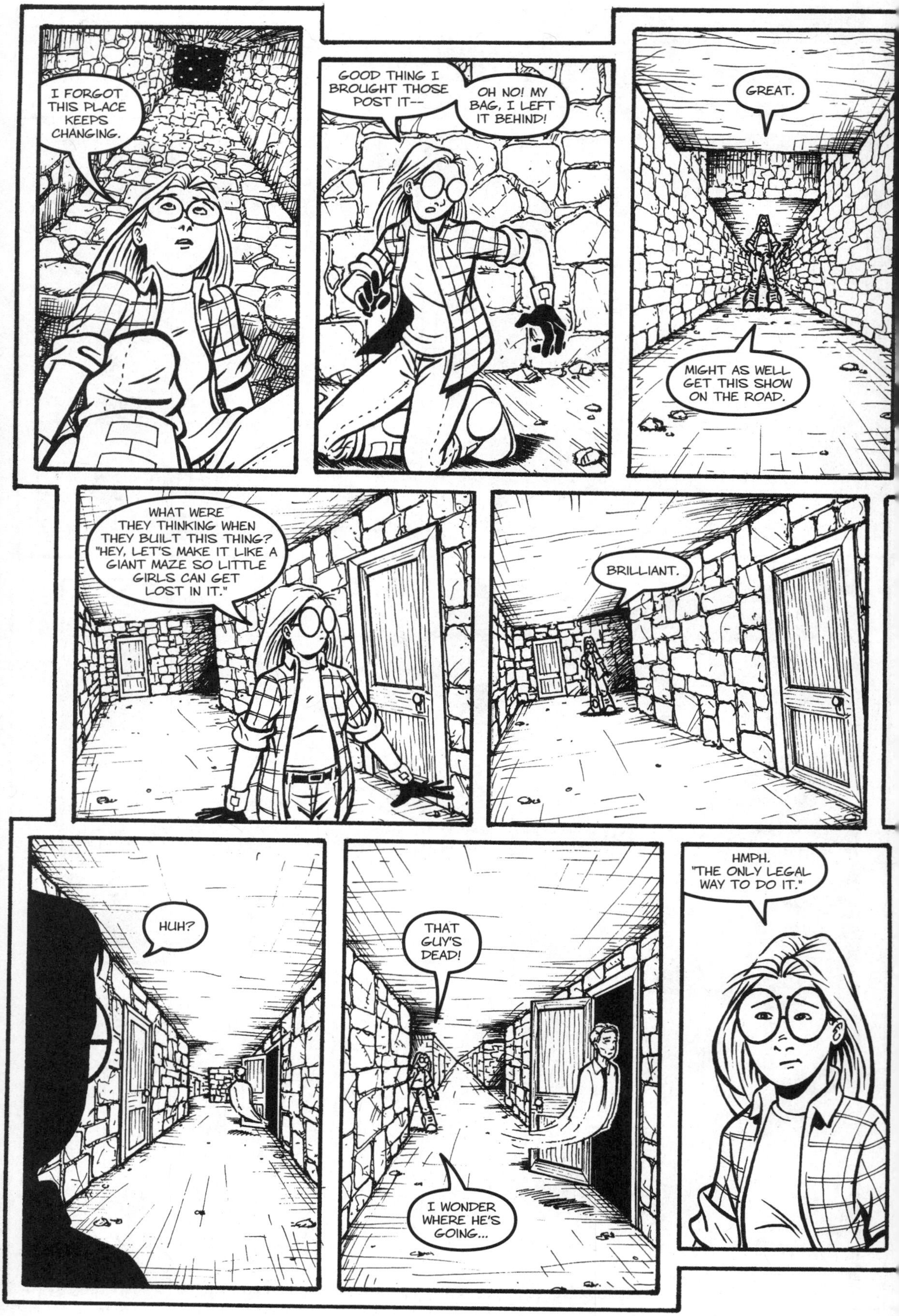
I FORGOT THIS PLACE KEEPS CHANGING.
GOOD THING I BROUGHT THOSE POST IT--
OH NO! MY BAG, I LEFT IT BEHIND!
GREAT.
MIGHT AS WELL GET THIS SHOW ON THE ROAD.
WHAT WERE THEY THINKING WHEN THEY BUILT THIS THING? "HEY, LET'S MAKE IT LIKE A GIANT MAZE SO LITTLE GIRLS CAN GET LOST IN IT."
BRILLIANT.
HUH?
THAT GUY'S DEAD!
I WONDER WHERE HE'S GOING...
HMPH. "THE ONLY LEGAL WAY TO DO IT."

HMM... ALL THESE DOORS...

I BEGAN TO REALIZE WHY THE SCIENTISTS WERE SO ANXIOUS TO HAVE ME GO BACK THROUGH THE PORTAL...

THERE'S SO MUCH TO DISCOVER, SO MANY THINGS TO SEE AND LEARN. INFINITE THINGS WE KNOW NOTHING ABOUT YET.

EENY, MEENY, MINY MOE...

THIS PORTAL COULD BE THE BEGINNING OF SOMETHING HUGE. I MEAN, HECK—IT ALREADY WAS!

CATCH A TIGER BY THE--

NOTHING COULD STOP ME.

YOU'RE NOT A GHOST, ARE YOU?

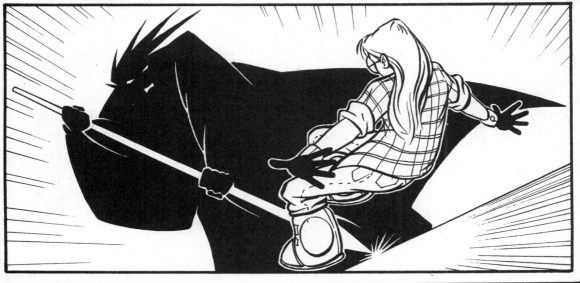

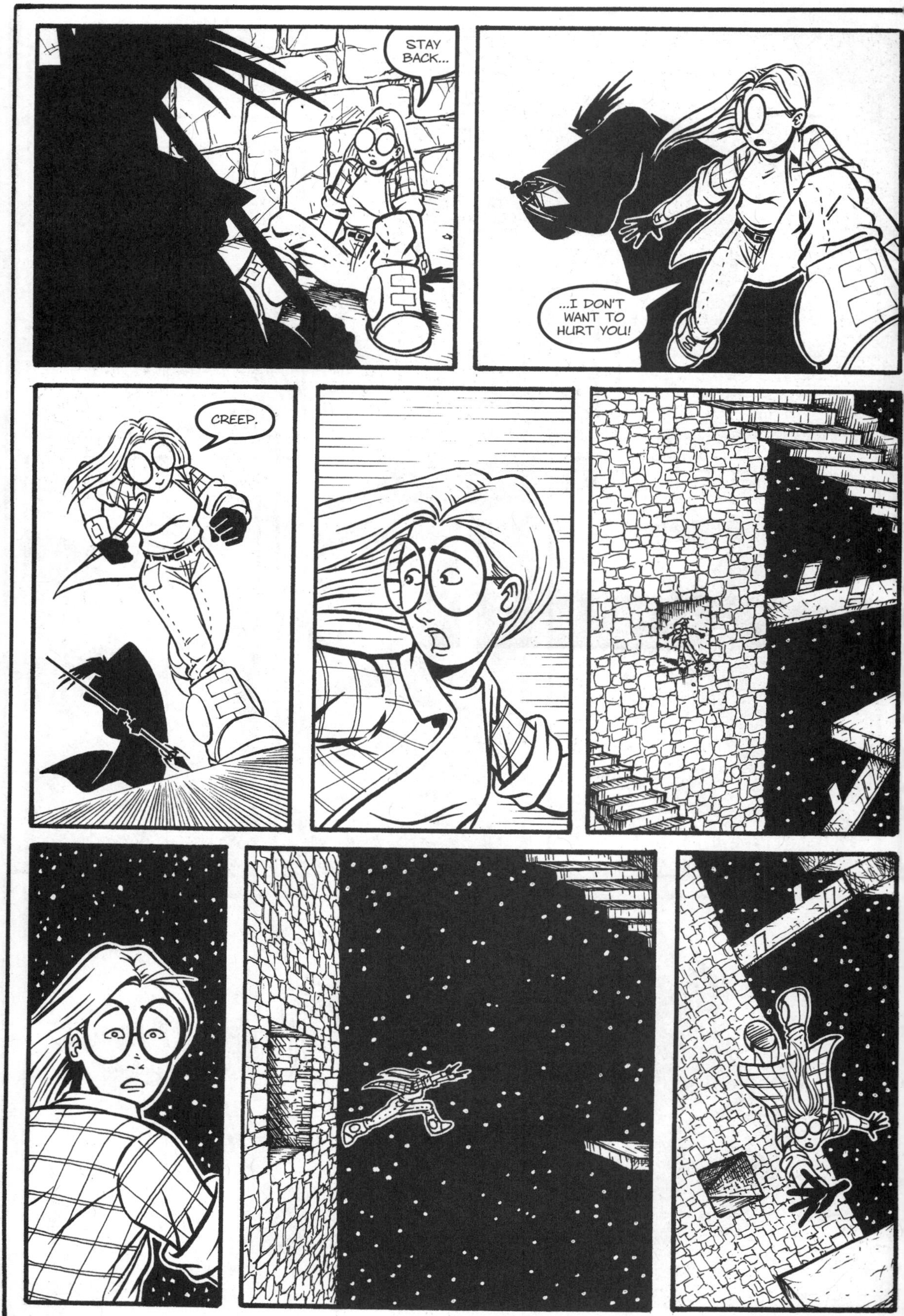
STAY BACK...
...I DON'T WANT TO HURT YOU!
CREEP.

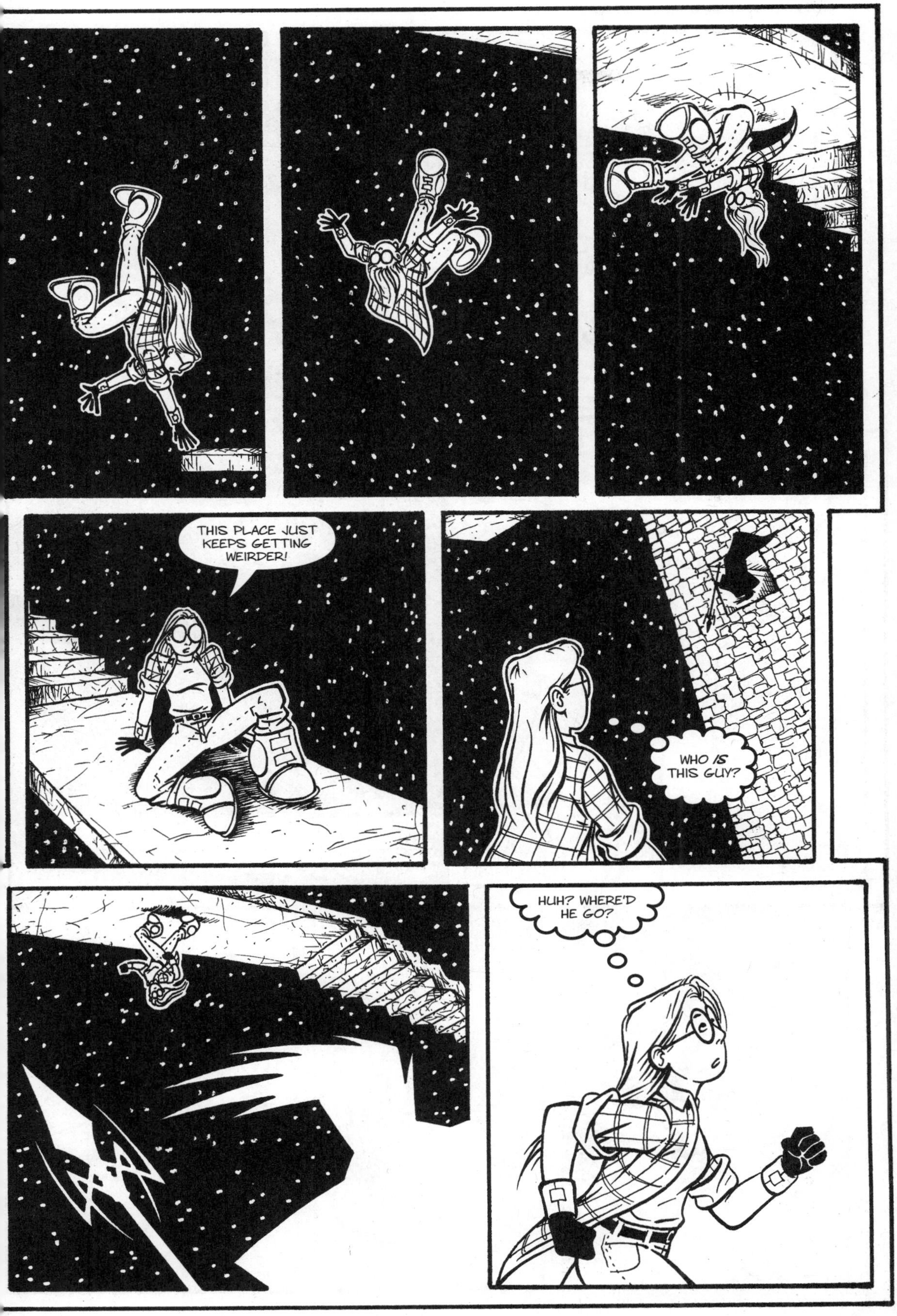
THIS PLACE JUST KEEPS GETTING WEIRDER!
WHO IS THIS GUY?
HUH? WHERE'D HE GO?

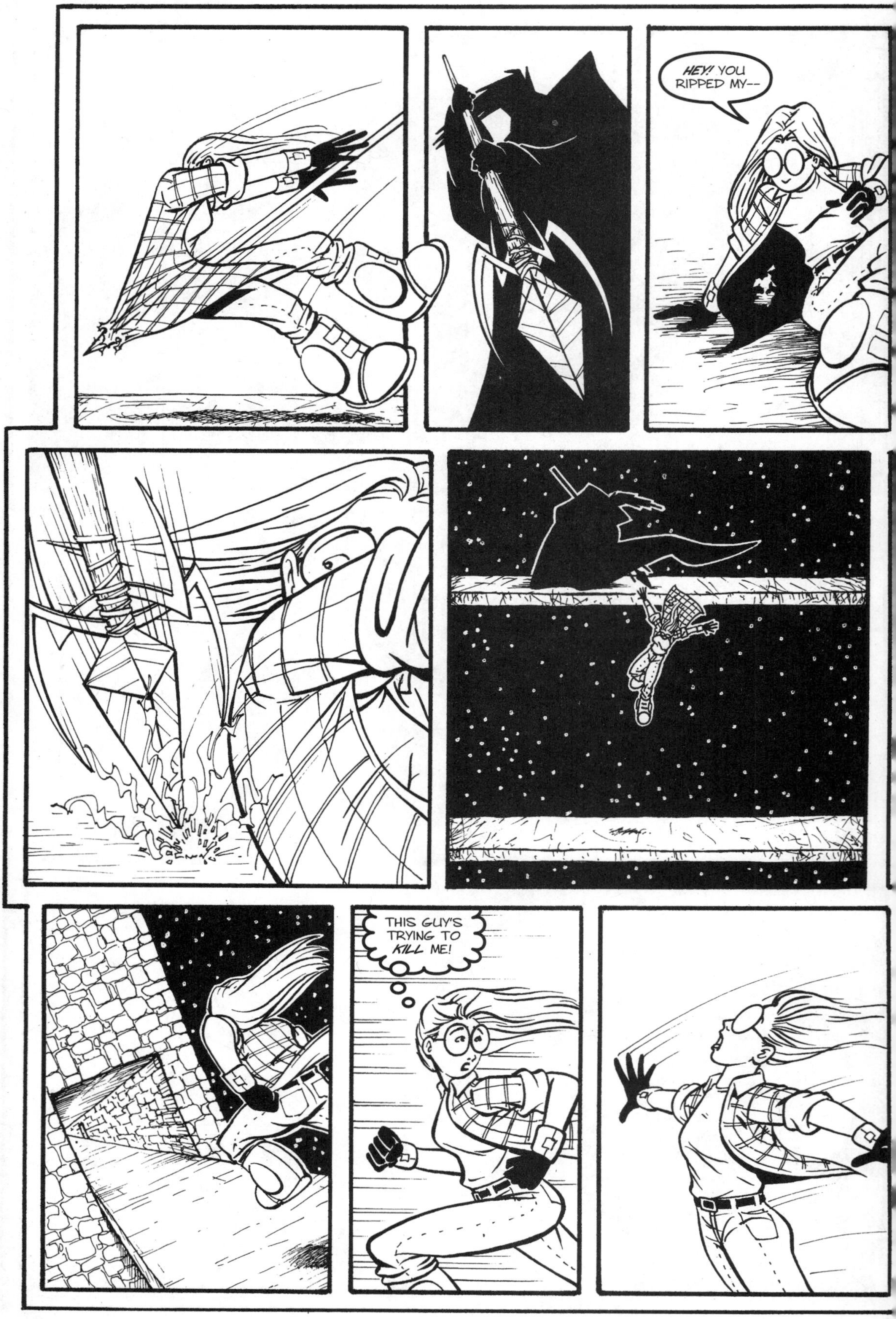
HEY! YOU RIPPED MY--
THIS GUY'S TRYING TO KILL ME!

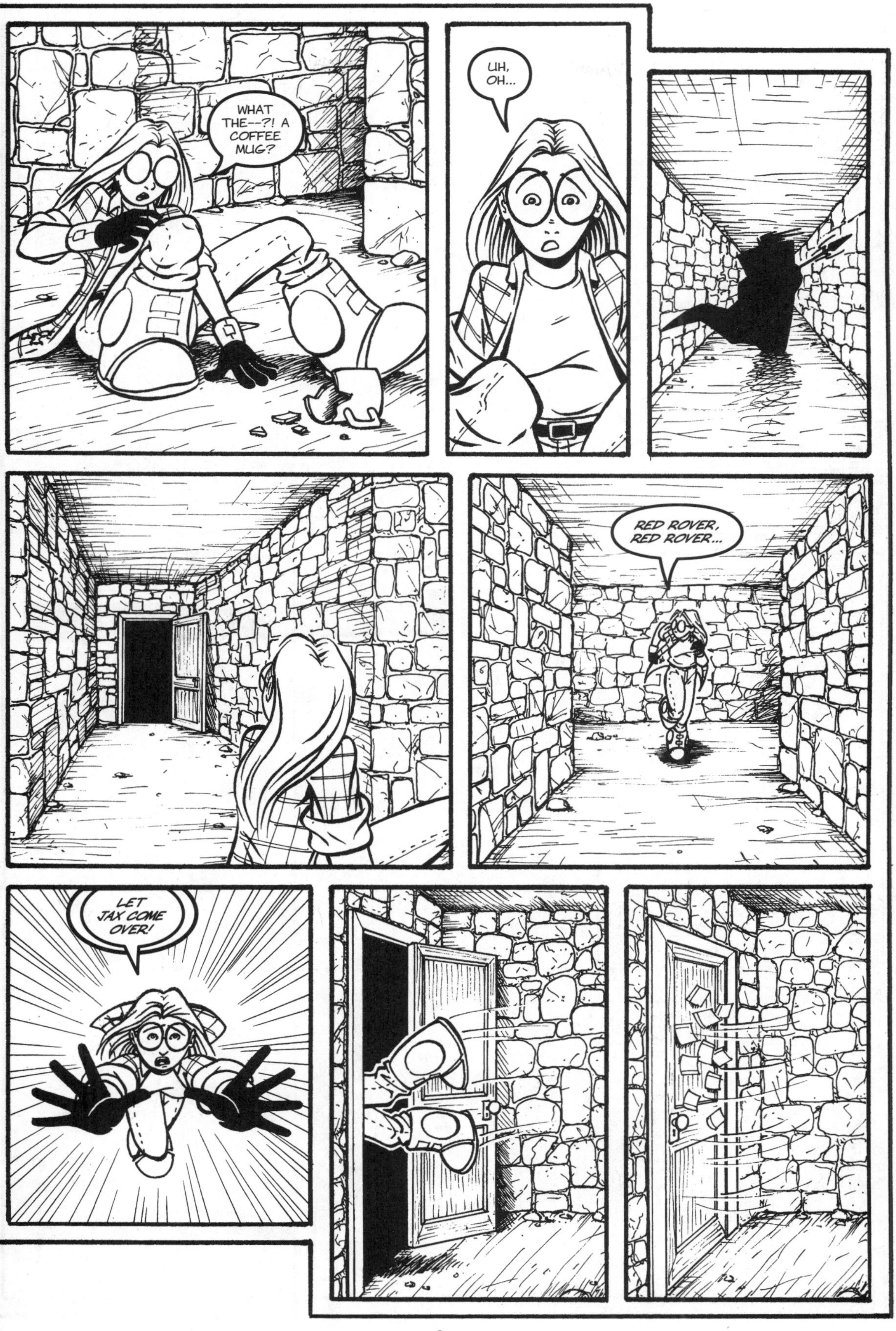
WHAT THE--?! A COFFEE MUG?
UH, OH...
RED ROVER, RED ROVER...
LET JAX COME OVER!

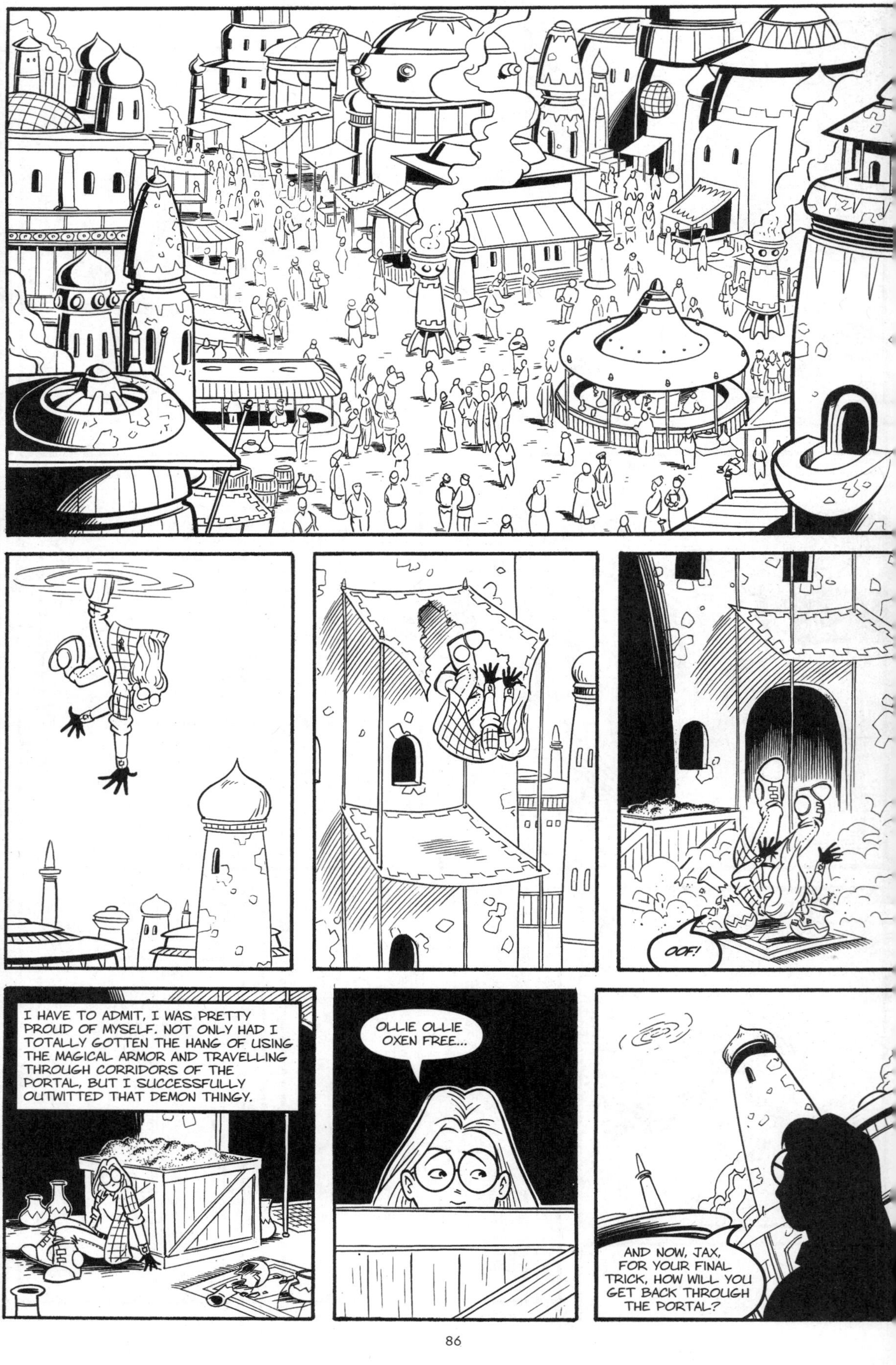
OOF!
I HAVE TO ADMIT, I WAS PRETTY PROUD OF MYSELF. NOT ONLY HAD I TOTALLY GOTTEN THE HANG OF USING THE MAGICAL ARMOR AND TRAVELLING THROUGH CORRIDORS OF THE PORTAL, BUT I SUCCESSFULLY OUTWITTED THAT DEMON THING.
OLLIE OLLIE OXEN FREE...
AND NOW, JAX, FOR YOUR FINAL TRICK, HOW WILL YOU GET BACK THROUGH THE PORTAL?

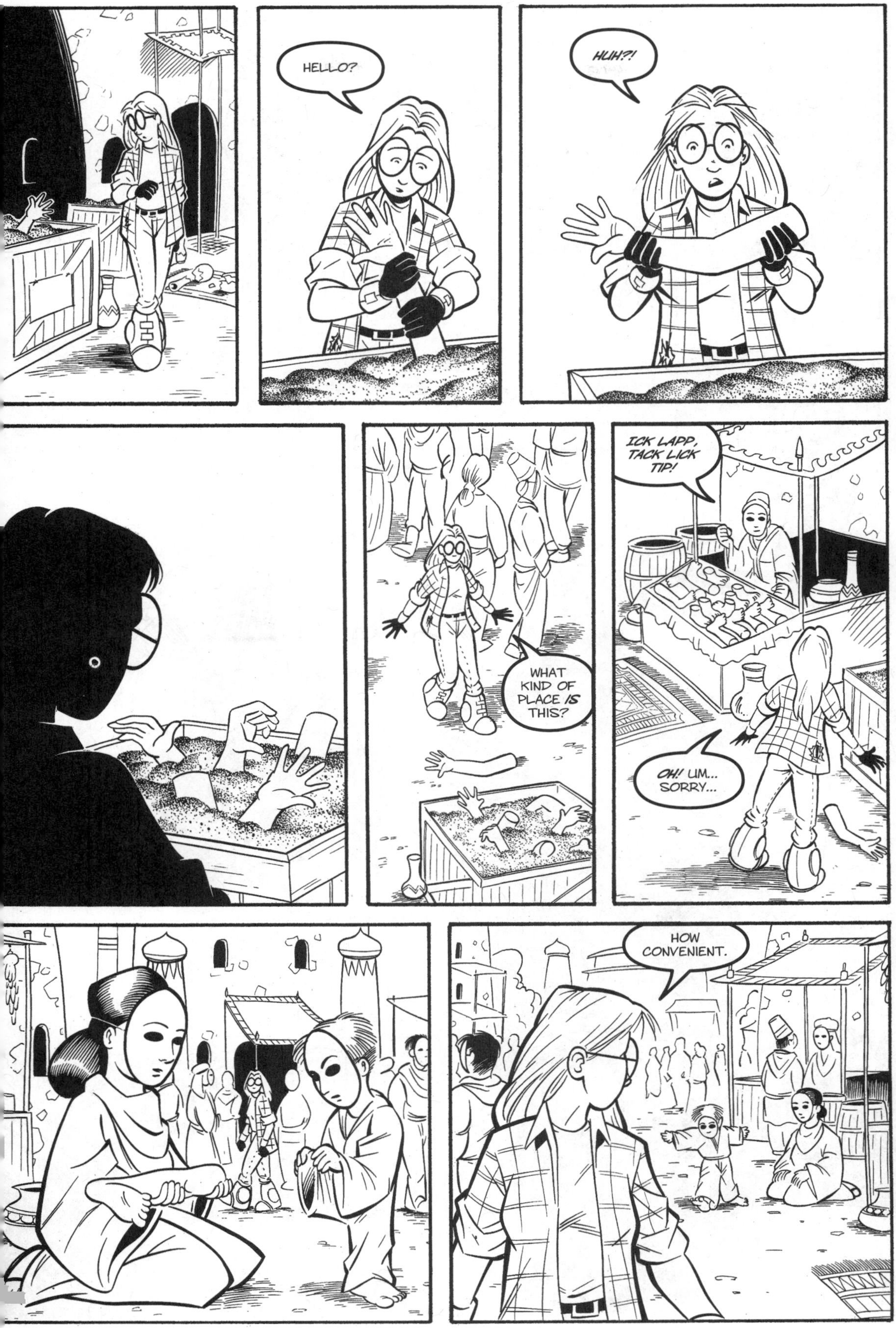
HELLO?
HUH?!
ICK LAPP, TACK LICK TIP!
WHAT KIND OF PLACE IS THIS?
OH! UM... SORRY...
HOW CONVENIENT.

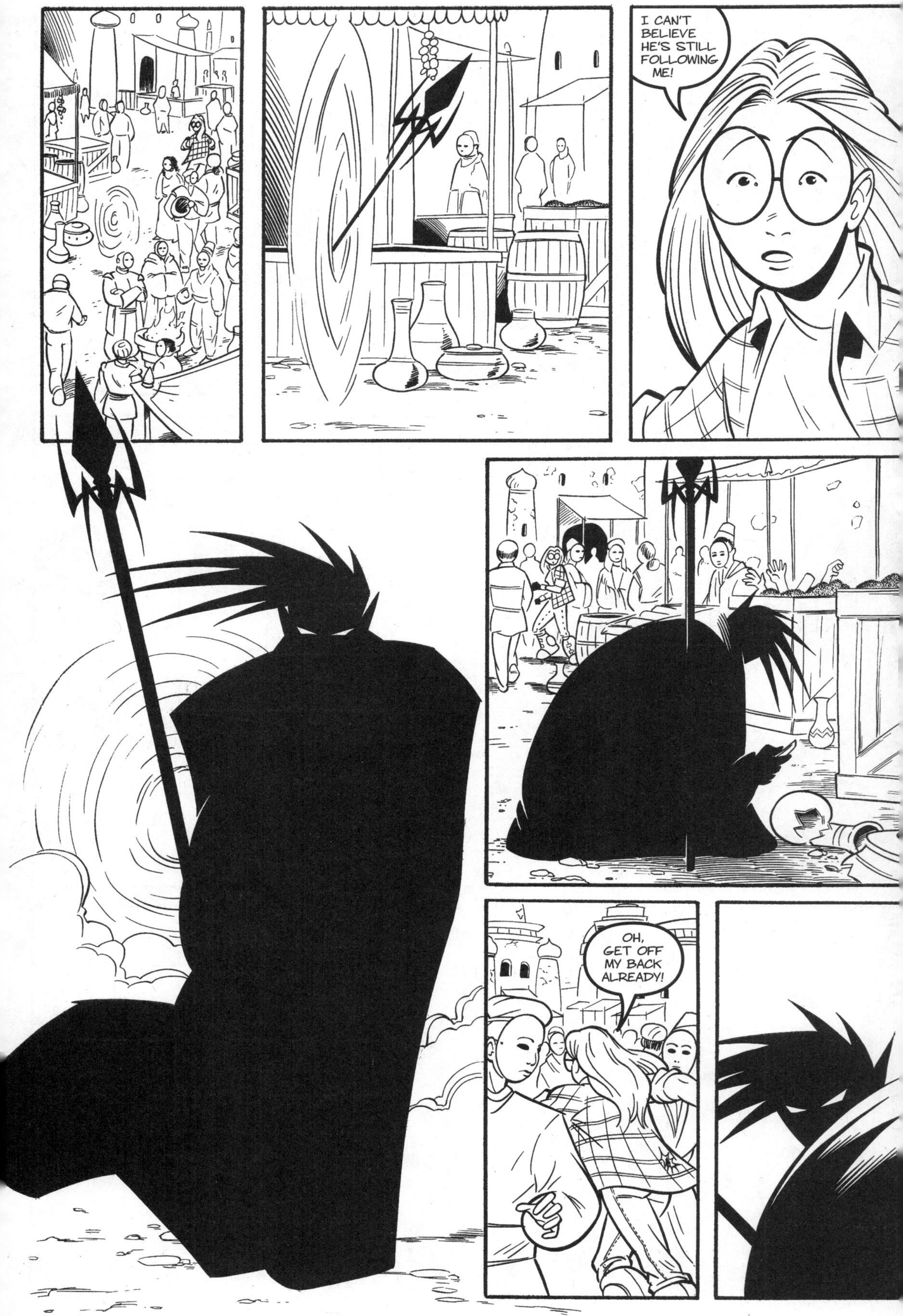
I CAN'T BELIEVE HE'S STILL FOLLOWING ME!
OH, GET OFF MY BACK ALREADY!

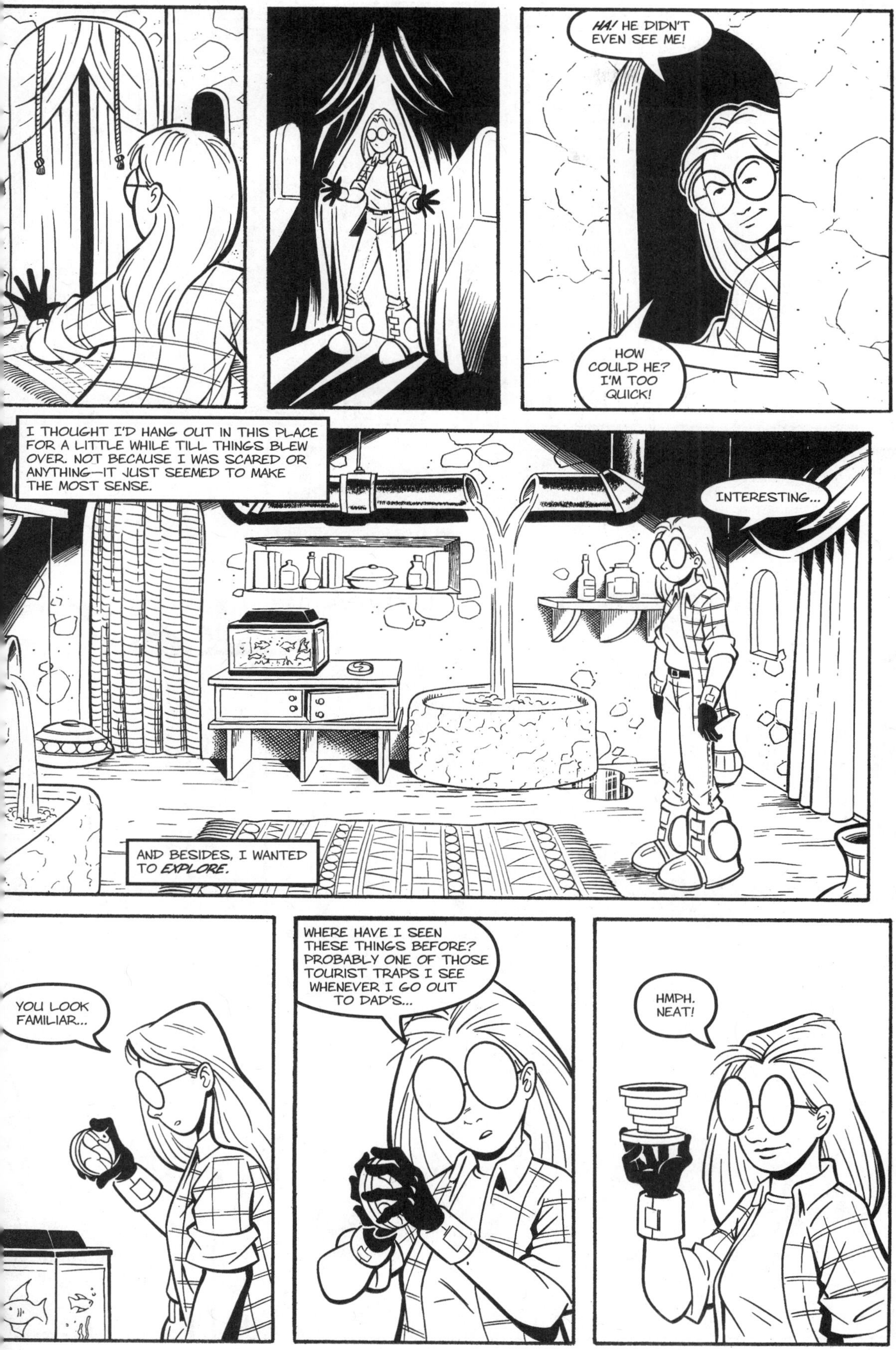
HA! HE DIDN'T EVEN SEE ME!
HOW COULD HE? I'M TOO QUICK!
I THOUGHT I'D HANG OUT IN THIS PLACE FOR A LITTLE WHILE TILL THINGS BLEW OVER. NOT BECAUSE I WAS SCARED OR ANYTHING—IT JUST SEEMED TO MAKE THE MOST SENSE.
INTERESTING...
AND BESIDES, I WANTED TO *EXPLORE.*
YOU LOOK FAMILIAR...
WHERE HAVE I SEEN THESE THINGS BEFORE? PROBABLY ONE OF THOSE TOURIST TRAPS I SEE WHENEVER I GO OUT TO DAD'S...
HMPH. NEAT!

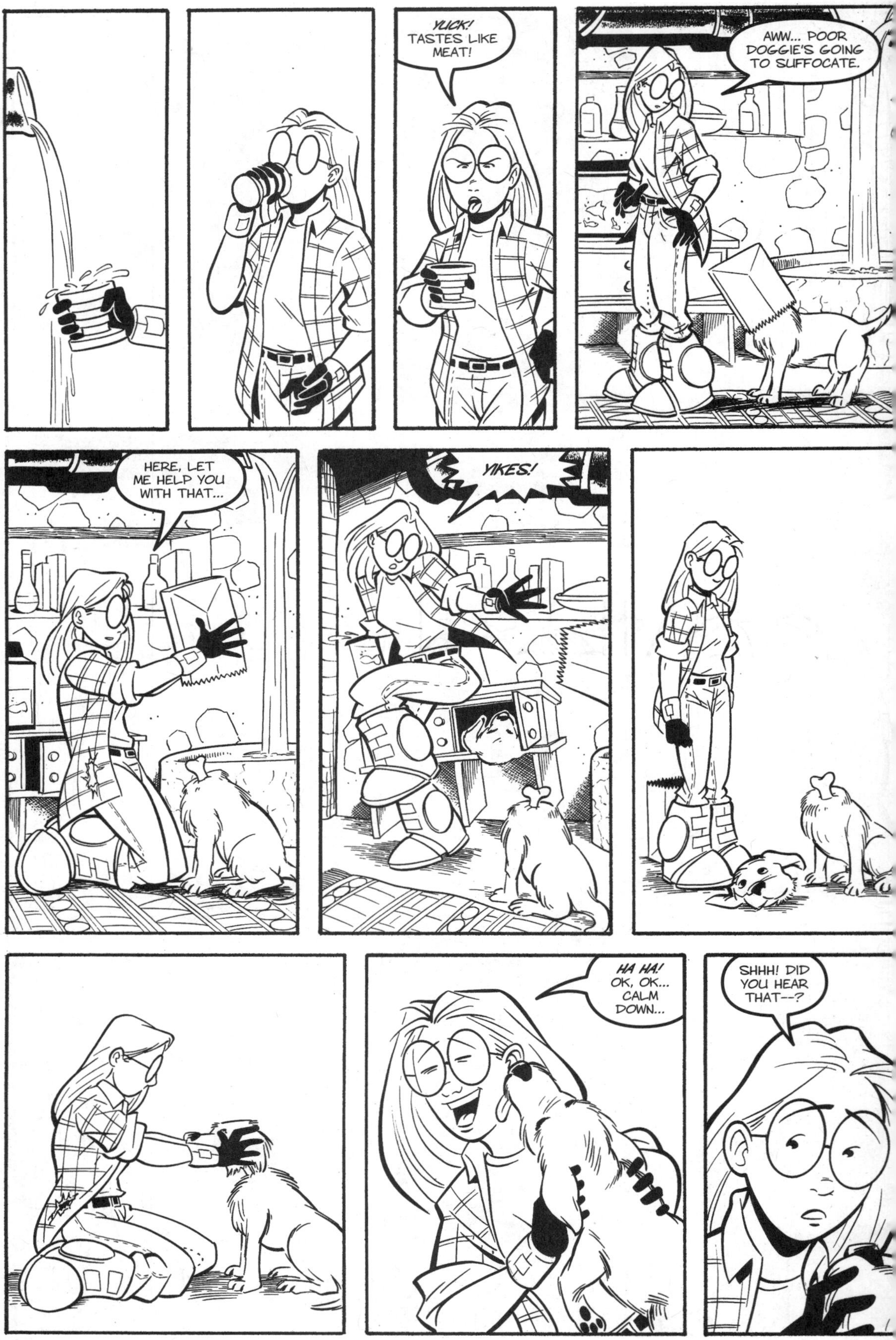
YUCK! TASTES LIKE MEAT!
AWW... POOR DOGGIE'S GOING TO SUFFOCATE.
HERE, LET ME HELP YOU WITH THAT...
YIKES!
HA HA! OK, OK... CALM DOWN...
SHHH! DID YOU HEAR THAT--?

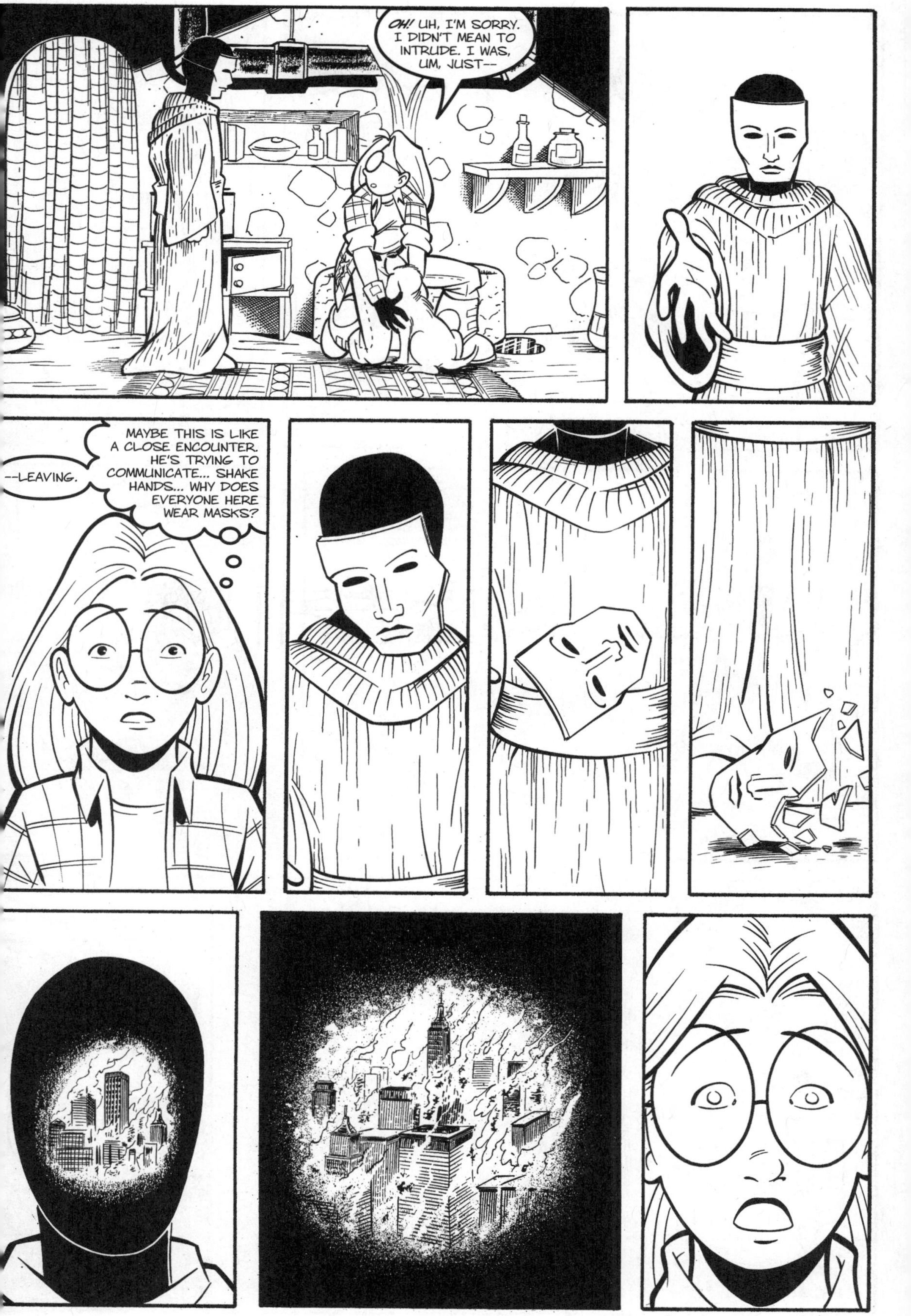
OH! UH, I'M SORRY. I DIDN'T MEAN TO INTRUDE. I WAS, UM, JUST--
--LEAVING.
MAYBE THIS IS LIKE A CLOSE ENCOUNTER. HE'S TRYING TO COMMUNICATE... SHAKE HANDS... WHY DOES EVERYONE HERE WEAR MASKS?

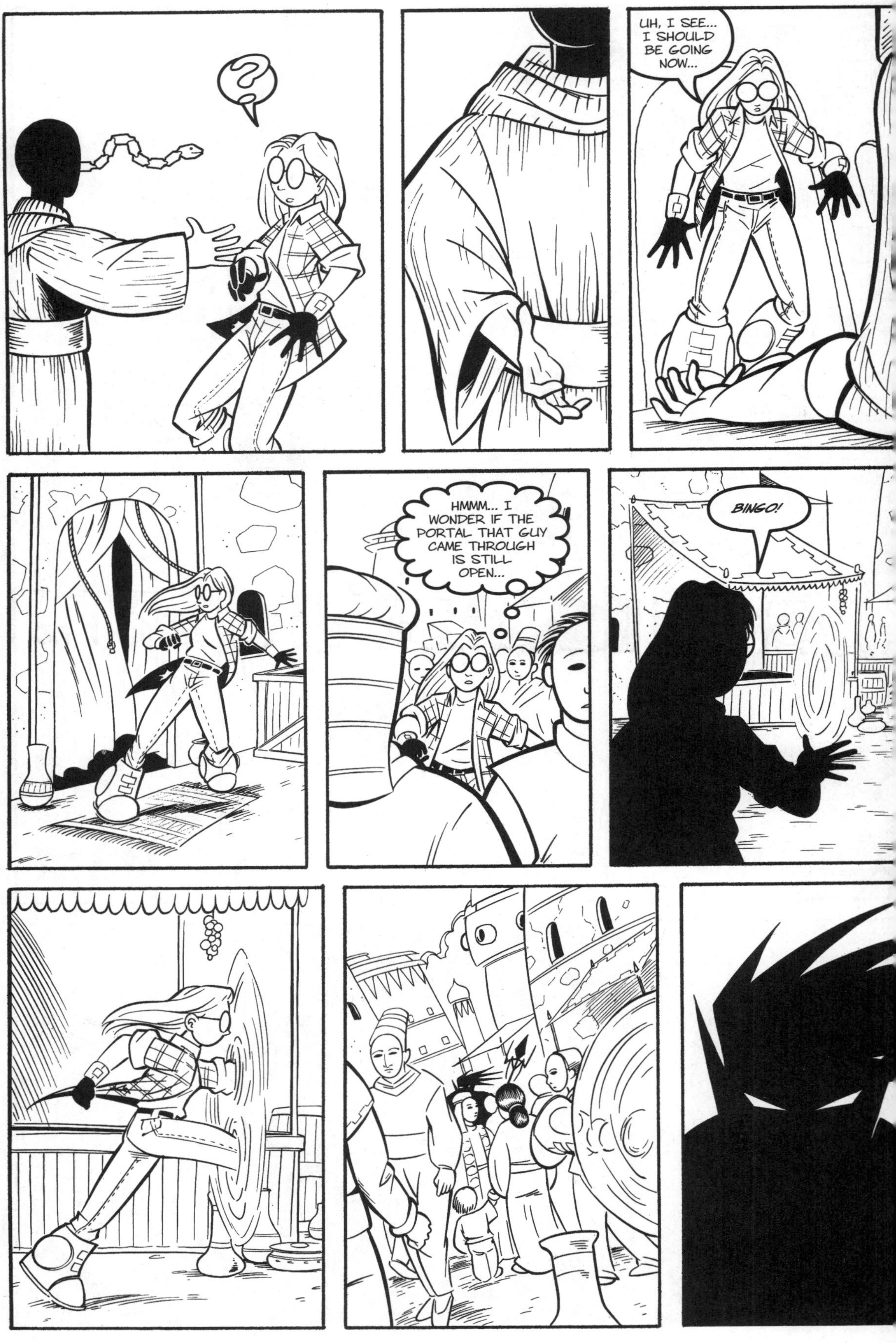
?
UH, I SEE... I SHOULD BE GOING NOW...
HMMM... I WONDER IF THE PORTAL THAT GUY CAME THROUGH IS STILL OPEN...
BINGO!

I HAVE *GOT* TO WORK ON MY LANDINGS.

HEY, WHAT HAVE WE HERE?

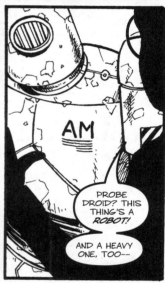

PROBE DROID? THIS THING'S A *ROBOT!*

AND A HEAVY ONE, TOO--

WHERE DO YOU THINK YOU'RE GOING WITH THAT?

WHO, ME?

I'M SORRY, THIS IS MY ROBOT. I JUST CAME TO GET IT BACK.

SHE'S TRYING TO STEAL IT!

YEAH! THAT'S NOT YOURS!

UM... YES IT IS.

IT WAS HERE, IT BELONGS TO US!

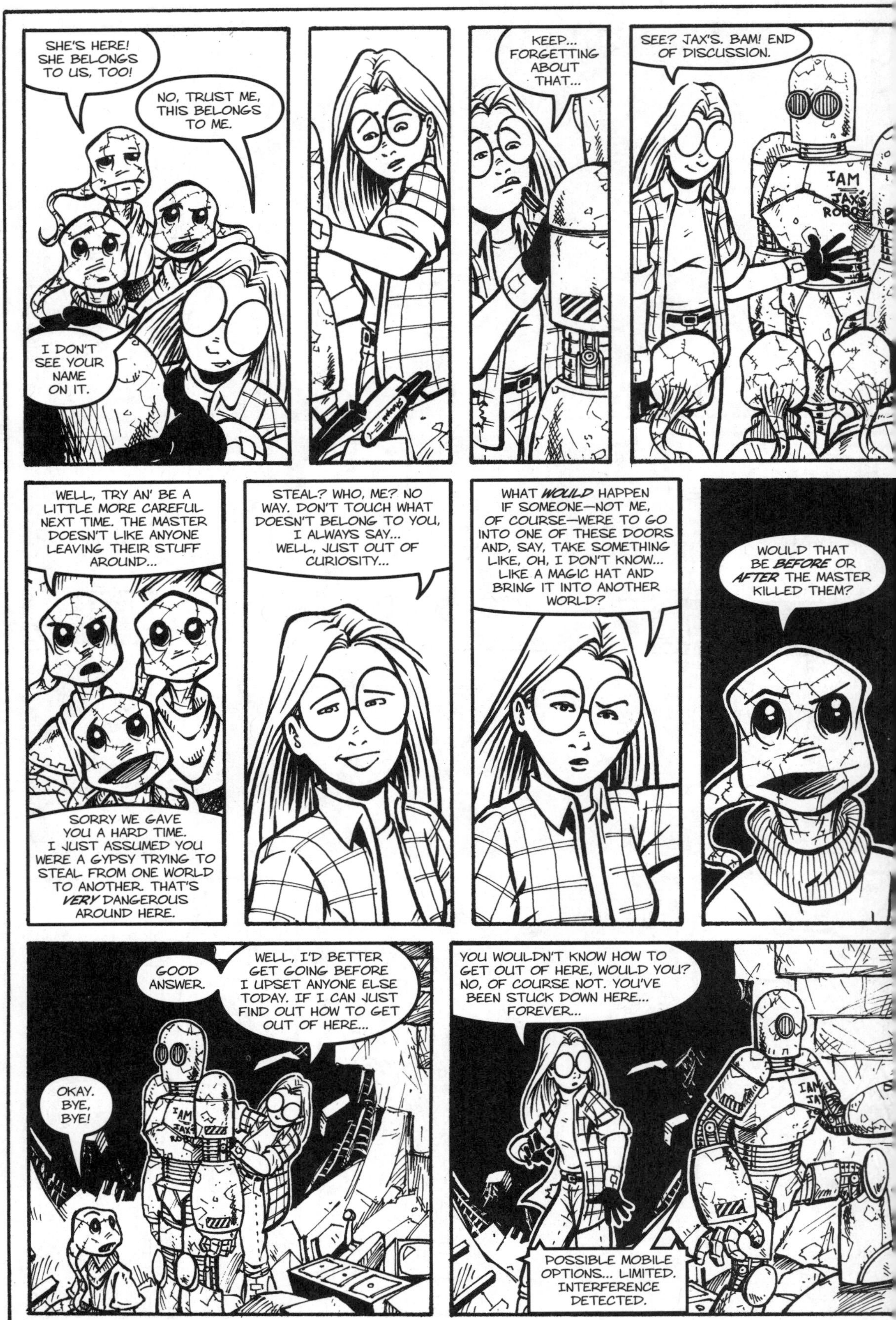
SHE'S HERE! SHE BELONGS TO US, TOO!
NO, TRUST ME, THIS BELONGS TO ME.
I DON'T SEE YOUR NAME ON IT.
KEEP... FORGETTING ABOUT THAT...
SEE? JAX'S. BAM! END OF DISCUSSION.
I AM JAX'S ROBO
WELL, TRY AN' BE A LITTLE MORE CAREFUL NEXT TIME. THE MASTER DOESN'T LIKE ANYONE LEAVING THEIR STUFF AROUND...
SORRY WE GAVE YOU A HARD TIME. I JUST ASSUMED YOU WERE A GYPSY TRYING TO STEAL FROM ONE WORLD TO ANOTHER. THAT'S *VERY* DANGEROUS AROUND HERE.
STEAL? WHO, ME? NO WAY. DON'T TOUCH WHAT DOESN'T BELONG TO YOU, I ALWAYS SAY... WELL, JUST OUT OF CURIOSITY...
WHAT *WOULD* HAPPEN IF SOMEONE—NOT ME, OF COURSE—WERE TO GO INTO ONE OF THESE DOORS AND, SAY, TAKE SOMETHING LIKE, OH, I DON'T KNOW... LIKE A MAGIC HAT AND BRING IT INTO ANOTHER WORLD?
WOULD THAT BE *BEFORE* OR *AFTER* THE MASTER KILLED THEM?
GOOD ANSWER.
WELL, I'D BETTER GET GOING BEFORE I UPSET ANYONE ELSE TODAY. IF I CAN JUST FIND OUT HOW TO GET OUT OF HERE...
OKAY. BYE, BYE!
YOU WOULDN'T KNOW HOW TO GET OUT OF HERE, WOULD YOU? NO, OF COURSE NOT. YOU'VE BEEN STUCK DOWN HERE... FOREVER...
POSSIBLE MOBILE OPTIONS... LIMITED. INTERFERENCE DETECTED.

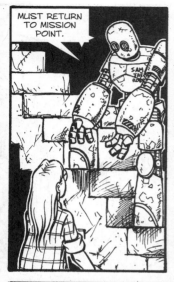

MUST RETURN TO MISSION POINT.

YEAH, WELL... I SORT OF LOST MY SENSE OF DIRECTION.

BUT IF YOU KNOW THE WAY...

IF THIS PLACE KEEPS CHANGING, HOW WILL YOU FIND THE WAY BACK?

FOLLOW SIGNAL... HOMING BEACON... PORTAL NOT FAR...

THAT SOUNDS A BIT FAR-FETCHED TO ME. HOW CAN IT PENETRA--

WAIT A SECOND-- NOW WHAT'S *THIS* PLACE?

A *LIBRARY!* COME ON, LET'S TAKE A LOOK!

NEGATIVE. MUST RETURN TO MISSION POINT. NOT FAR FROM HOME.

SETTLE DOWN, BUCKET-HEAD, SURELY EVEN ROBOTS APPRECIATE THE DISCOVERY OF VAST AMOUNTS OF KNOWLEDGE.

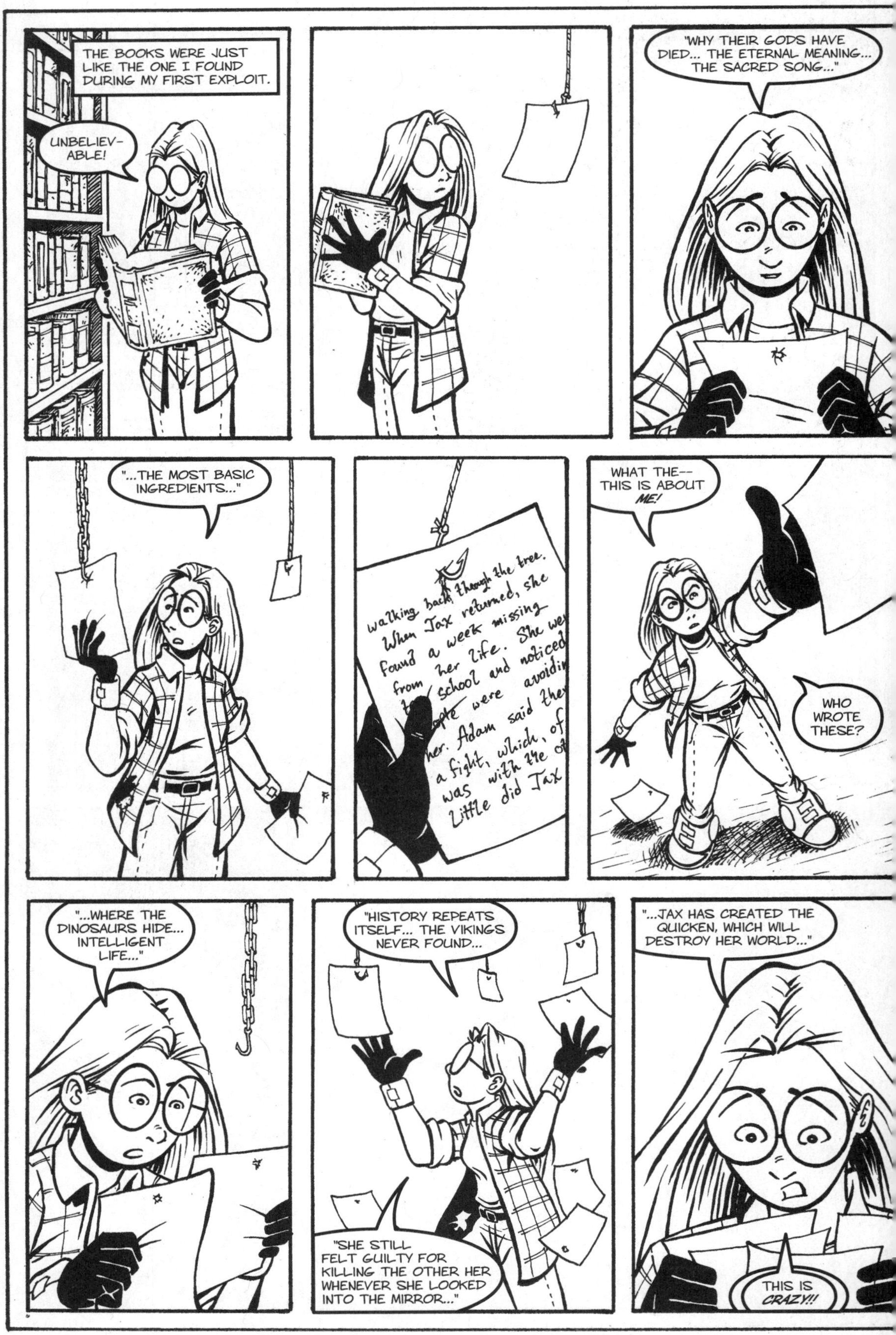
THE BOOKS WERE JUST LIKE THE ONE I FOUND DURING MY FIRST EXPLOIT.
UNBELIEVABLE!
"WHY THEIR GODS HAVE DIED... THE ETERNAL MEANING... THE SACRED SONG..."
"...THE MOST BASIC INGREDIENTS..."
walking back through the tree.
When Jax returned, she
found a week missing
from her life. She we
school and noticed
were avoidi
her. Adam said the
a fight, which, of
was with the o
Little did Jax
WHAT THE-- THIS IS ABOUT ME!
WHO WROTE THESE?
"...WHERE THE DINOSAURS HIDE... INTELLIGENT LIFE..."
"HISTORY REPEATS ITSELF... THE VIKINGS NEVER FOUND...
"SHE STILL FELT GUILTY FOR KILLING THE OTHER HER WHENEVER SHE LOOKED INTO THE MIRROR..."
"...JAX HAS CREATED THE QUICKEN, WHICH WILL DESTROY HER WORLD..."
THIS IS CRAZY!!

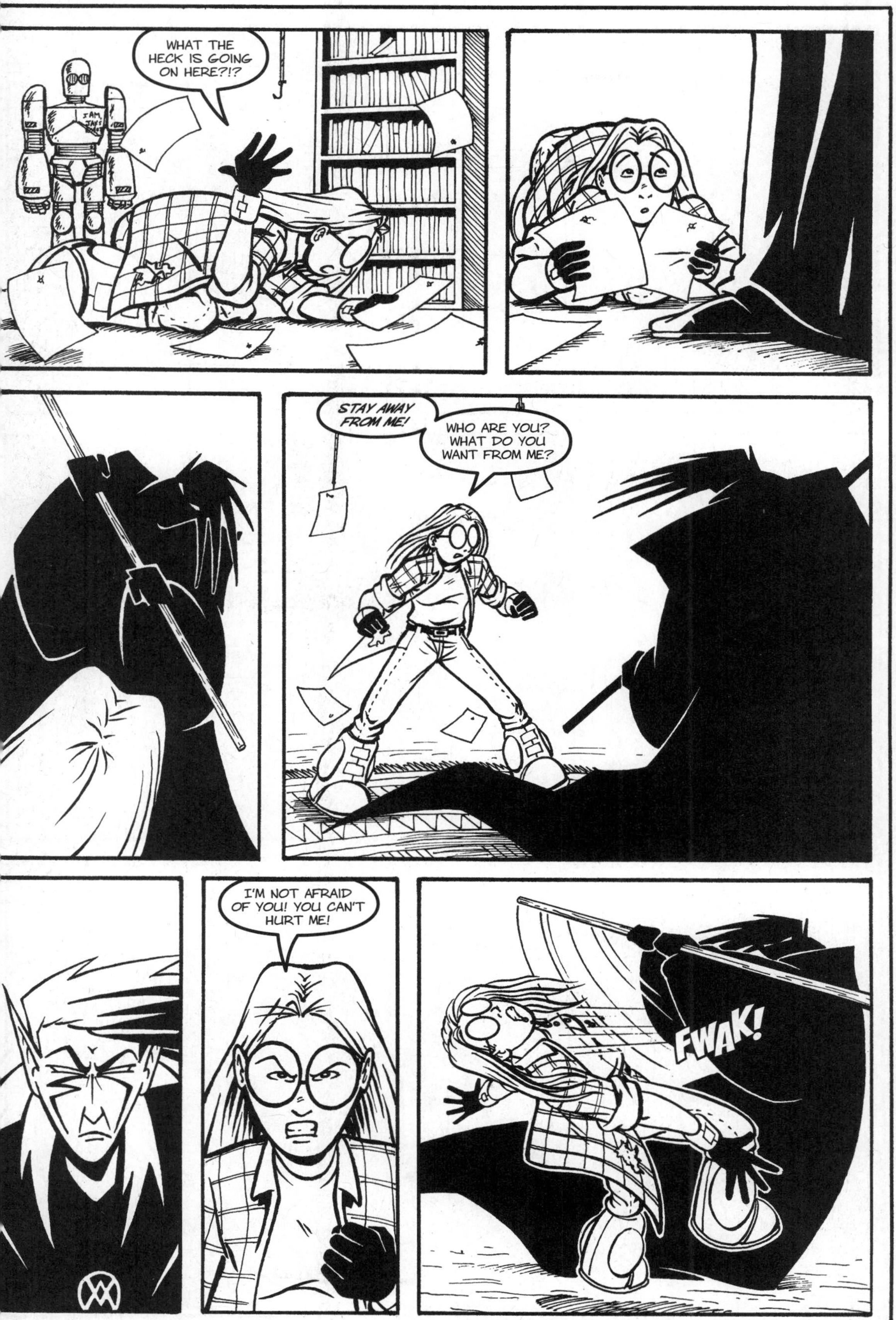
WHAT THE HECK IS GOING ON HERE?!?
STAY AWAY FROM ME!
WHO ARE YOU? WHAT DO YOU WANT FROM ME?
I'M NOT AFRAID OF YOU! YOU CAN'T HURT ME!
FWAK!

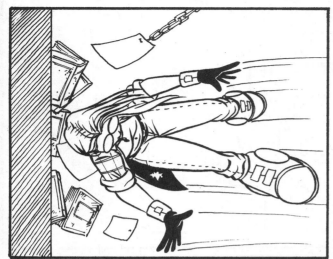

OW!! THAT... DIDN'T... FEEL GOOD.

FWOOSH

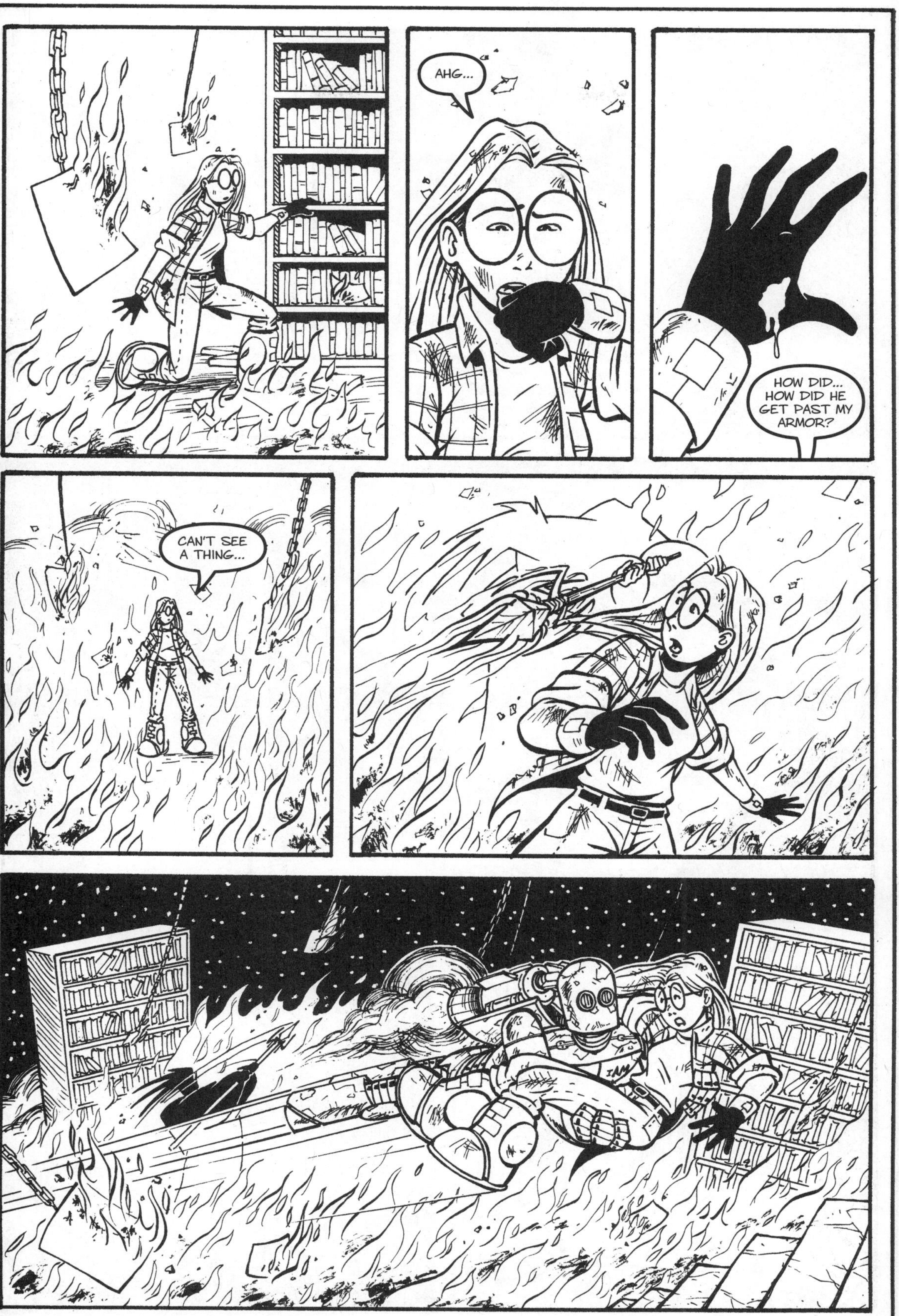
AHG...
HOW DID... HOW DID HE GET PAST MY ARMOR?
CAN'T SEE A THING...

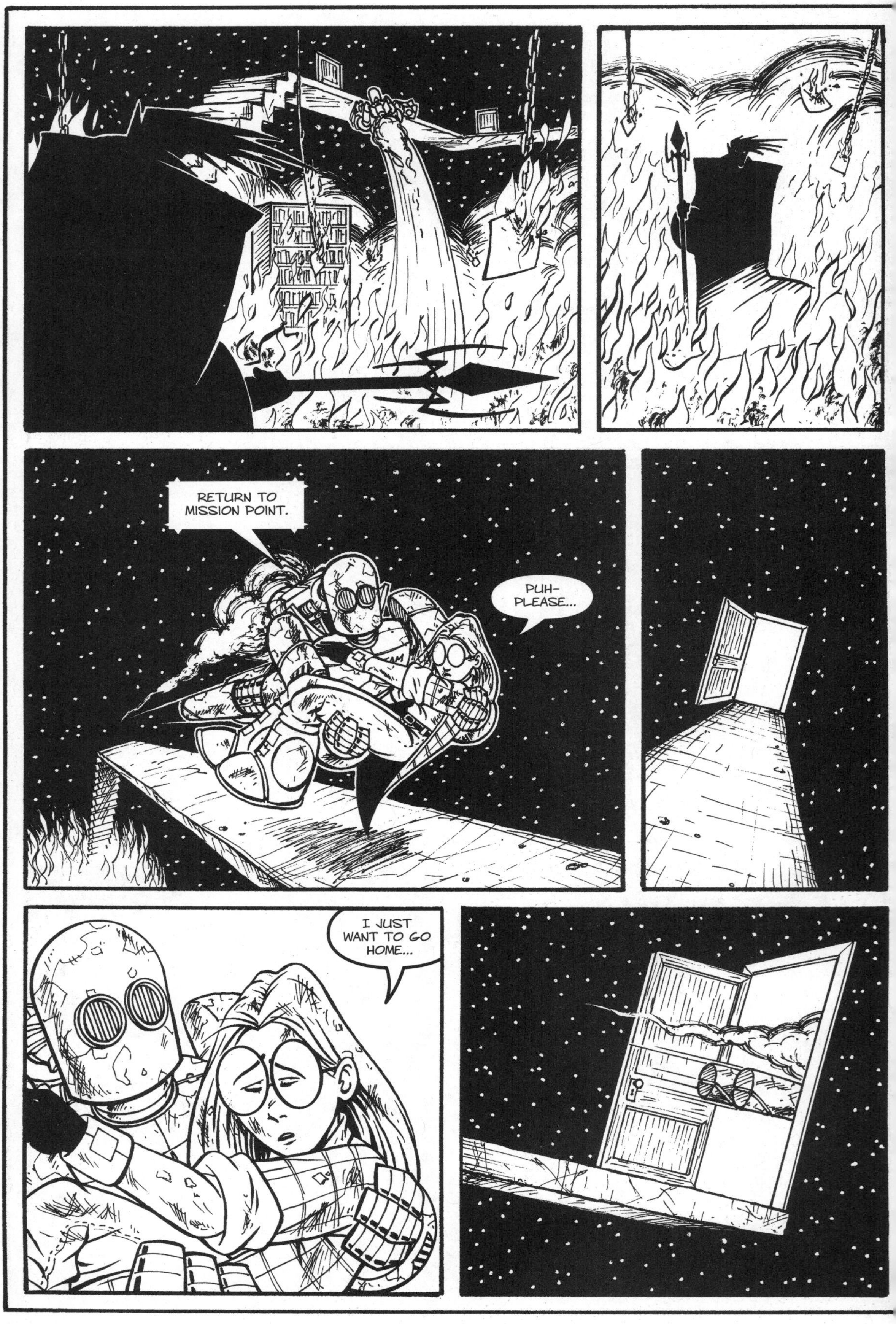
RETURN TO MISSION POINT.
PUH-PLEASE...
I JUST WANT TO GO HOME...

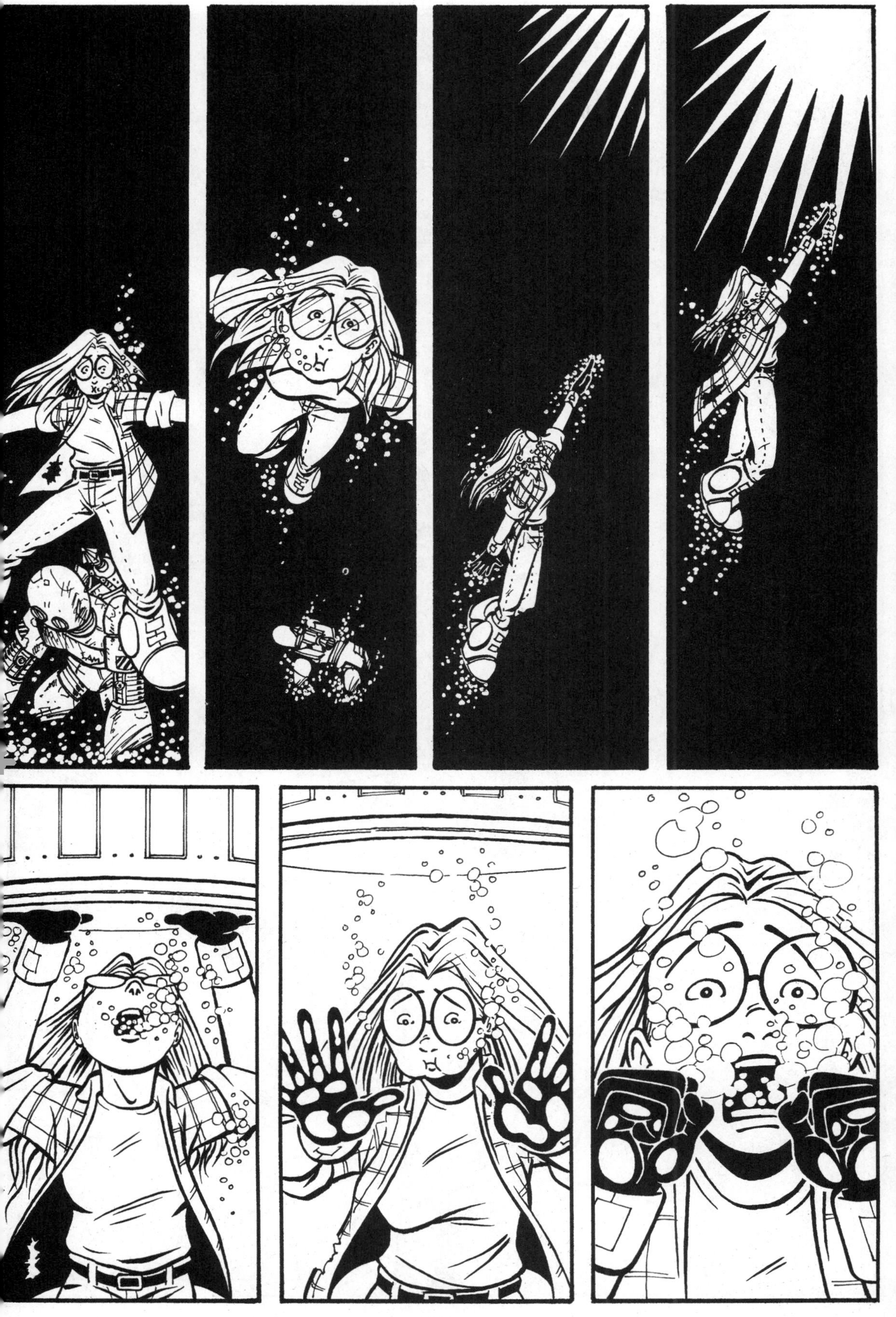

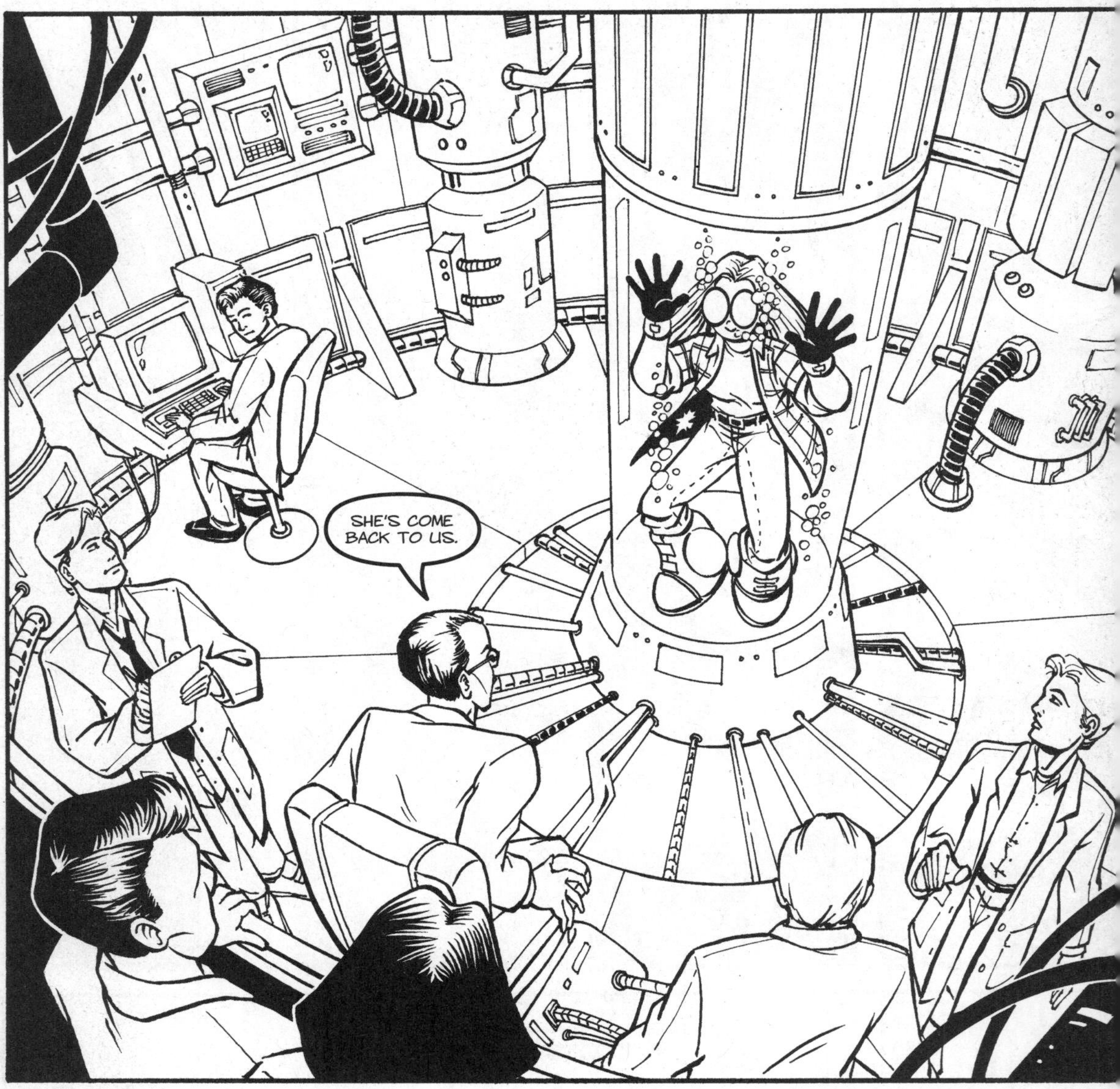
SHE'S COME BACK TO US.

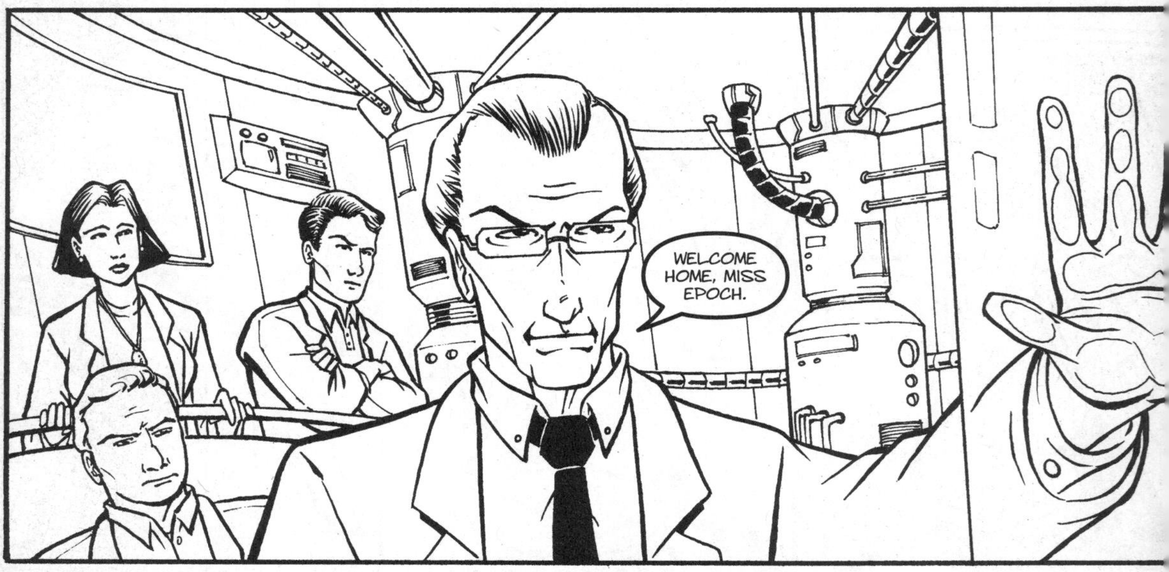
WELCOME HOME, MISS EPOCH.

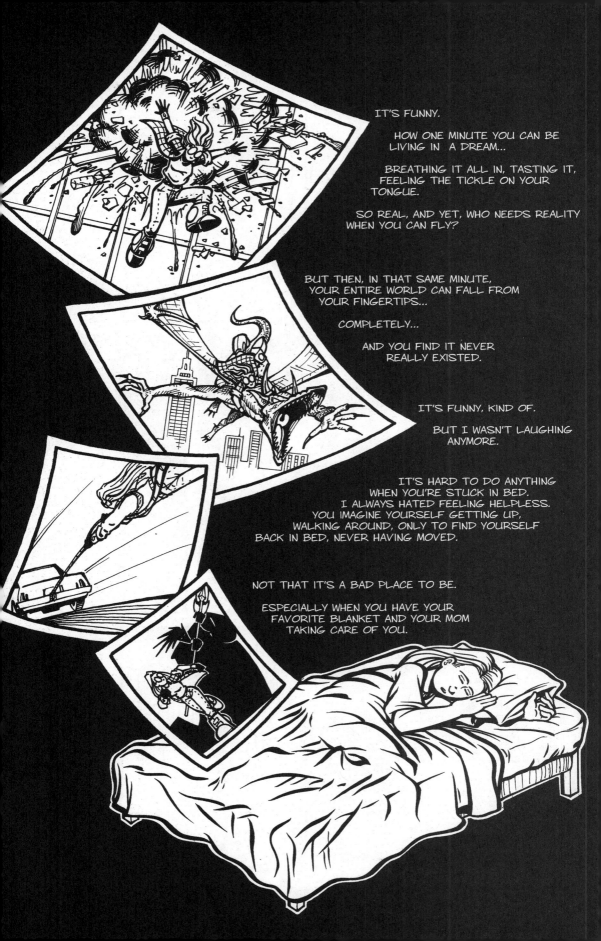

IT'S FUNNY.

HOW ONE MINUTE YOU CAN BE LIVING IN A DREAM...

BREATHING IT ALL IN, TASTING IT, FEELING THE TICKLE ON YOUR TONGUE.

SO REAL, AND YET, WHO NEEDS REALITY WHEN YOU CAN FLY?

BUT THEN, IN THAT SAME MINUTE, YOUR ENTIRE WORLD CAN FALL FROM YOUR FINGERTIPS...

COMPLETELY...

AND YOU FIND IT NEVER REALLY EXISTED.

IT'S FUNNY, KIND OF.

BUT I WASN'T LAUGHING ANYMORE.

IT'S HARD TO DO ANYTHING WHEN YOU'RE STUCK IN BED. I ALWAYS HATED FEELING HELPLESS. YOU IMAGINE YOURSELF GETTING UP, WALKING AROUND, ONLY TO FIND YOURSELF BACK IN BED, NEVER HAVING MOVED.

NOT THAT IT'S A BAD PLACE TO BE.

ESPECIALLY WHEN YOU HAVE YOUR FAVORITE BLANKET AND YOUR MOM TAKING CARE OF YOU.

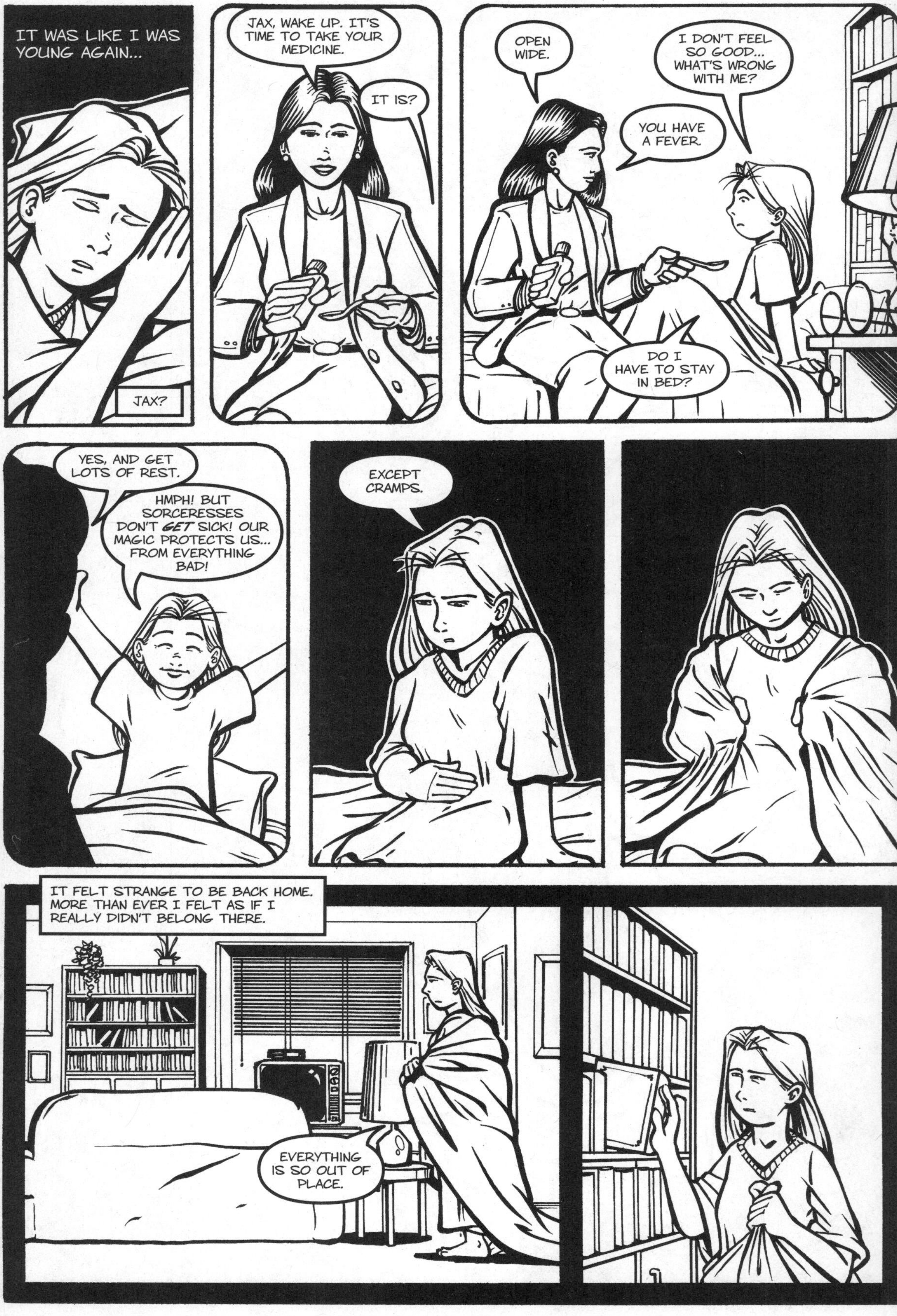

IT WAS LIKE I WAS YOUNG AGAIN...
JAX?
JAX, WAKE UP. IT'S TIME TO TAKE YOUR MEDICINE.
IT IS?
OPEN WIDE.
I DON'T FEEL SO GOOD... WHAT'S WRONG WITH ME?
YOU HAVE A FEVER.
DO I HAVE TO STAY IN BED?
YES, AND GET LOTS OF REST.
HMPH! BUT SORCERESSES DON'T GET SICK! OUR MAGIC PROTECTS US... FROM EVERYTHING BAD!
EXCEPT CRAMPS.
IT FELT STRANGE TO BE BACK HOME. MORE THAN EVER I FELT AS IF I REALLY DIDN'T BELONG THERE.
EVERYTHING IS SO OUT OF PLACE.

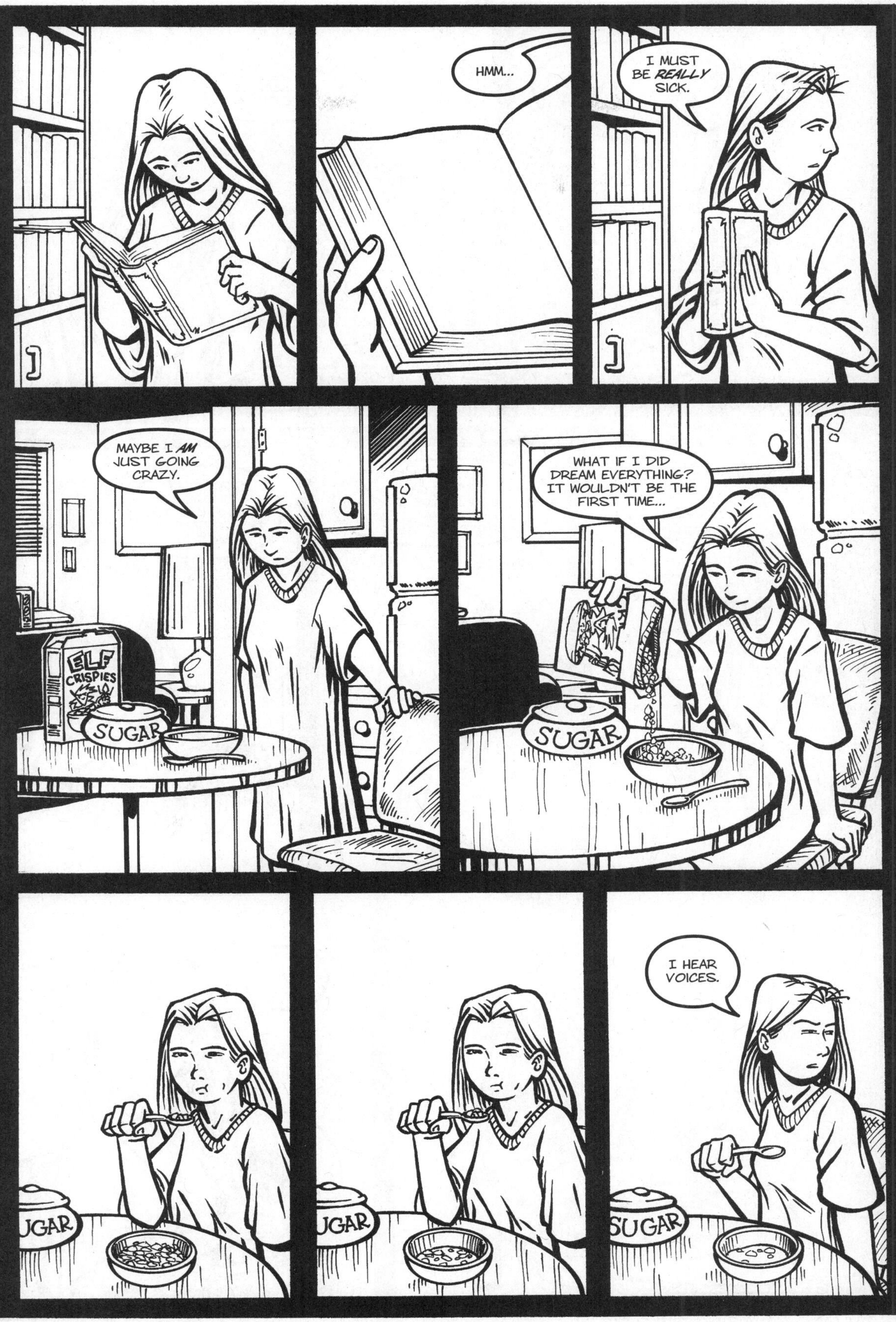
HMM...
I MUST BE *REALLY* SICK.
MAYBE I *AM* JUST GOING CRAZY.
ELF CRISPIES
SUGAR
WHAT IF I DID DREAM EVERYTHING? IT WOULDN'T BE THE FIRST TIME...
SUGAR
UGAR
UGAR
I HEAR VOICES.
SUGAR

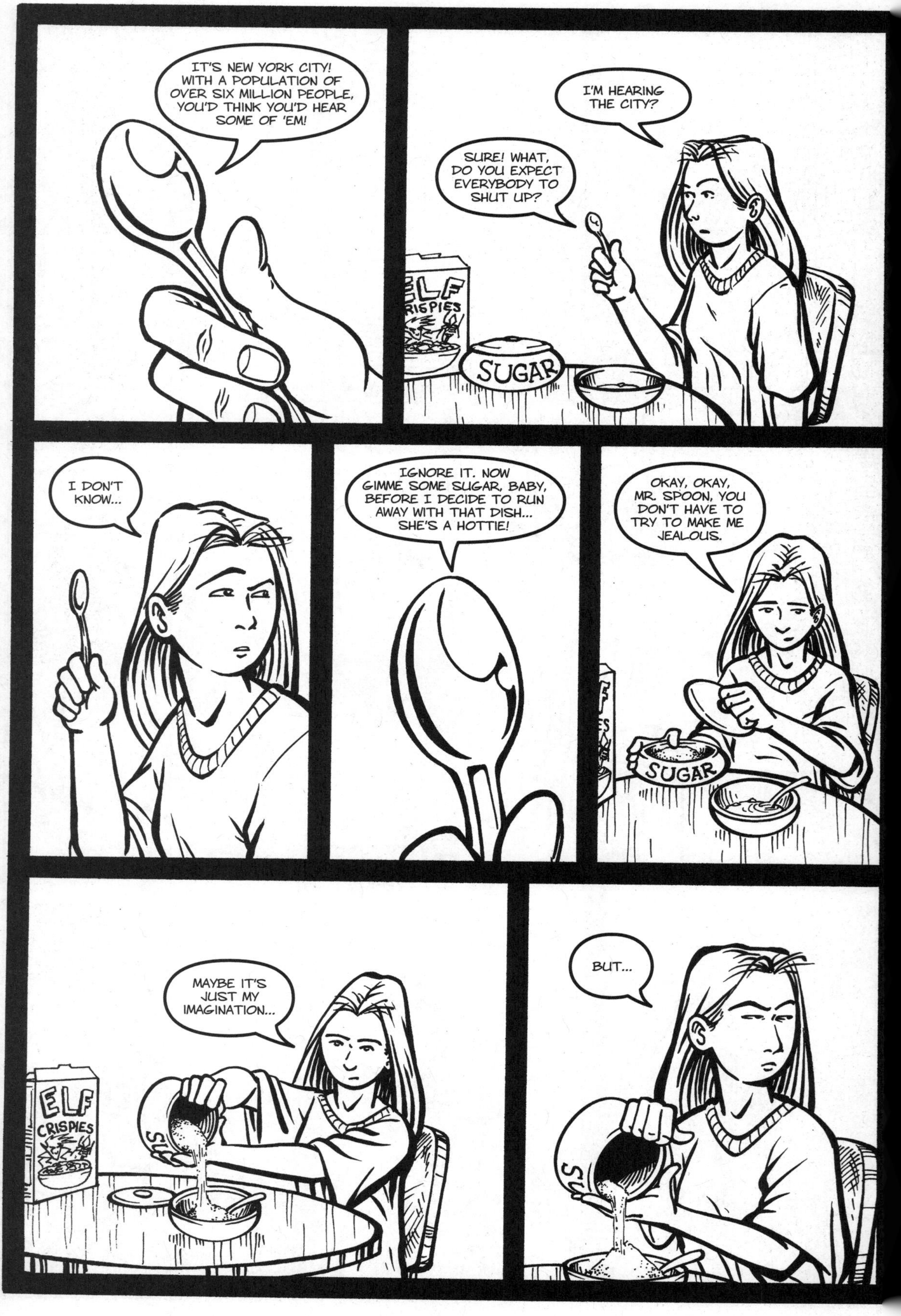
IT'S NEW YORK CITY! WITH A POPULATION OF OVER SIX MILLION PEOPLE, YOU'D THINK YOU'D HEAR SOME OF 'EM!
I'M HEARING THE CITY?
SURE! WHAT, DO YOU EXPECT EVERYBODY TO SHUT UP?
ELF CRISPIES
SUGAR
I DON'T KNOW...
IGNORE IT. NOW GIMME SOME SUGAR, BABY, BEFORE I DECIDE TO RUN AWAY WITH THAT DISH... SHE'S A HOTTIE!
OKAY, OKAY, MR. SPOON, YOU DON'T HAVE TO TRY TO MAKE ME JEALOUS.
SUGAR
MAYBE IT'S JUST MY IMAGINATION...
ELF CRISPIES
BUT...

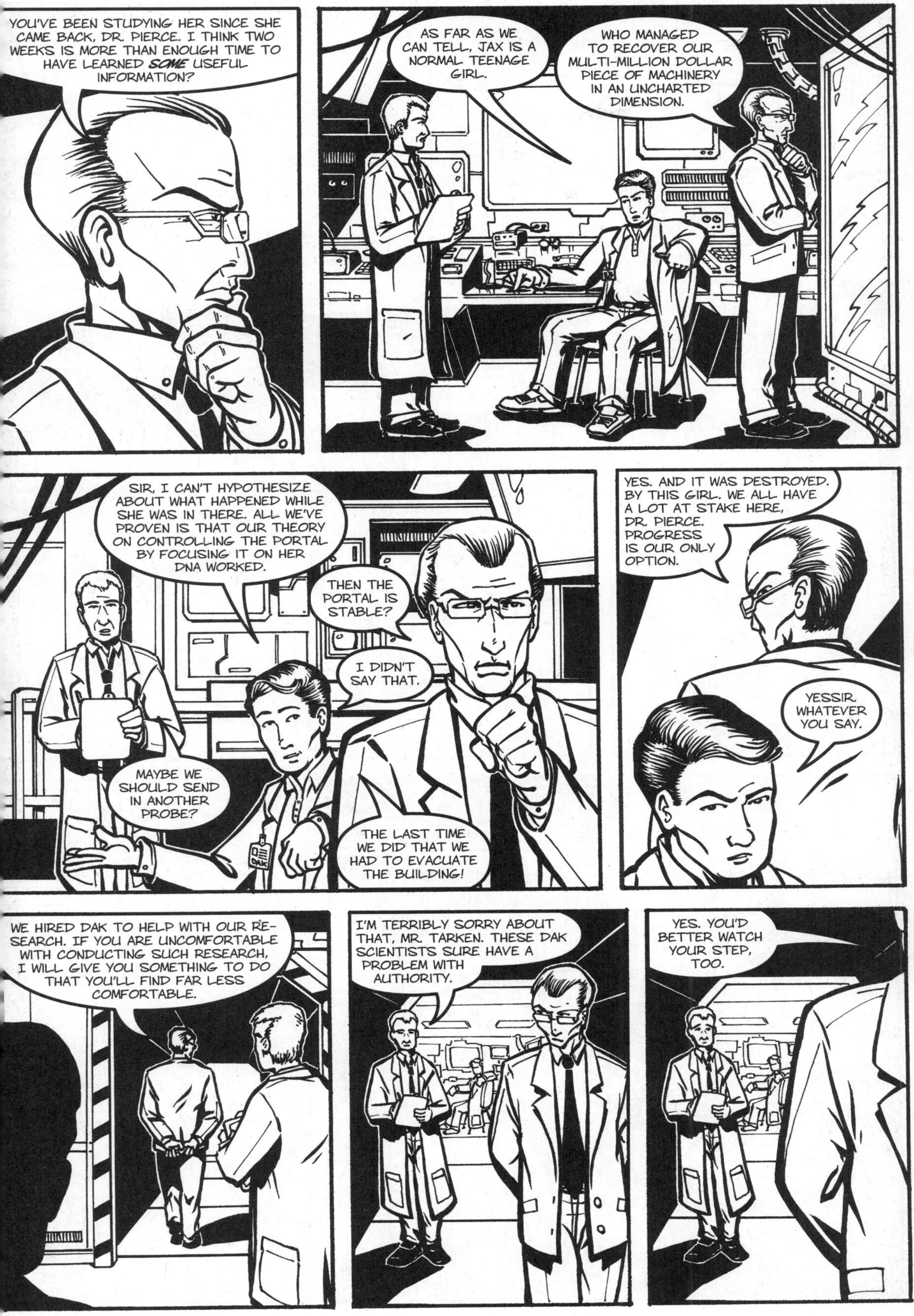
YOU'VE BEEN STUDYING HER SINCE SHE CAME BACK, DR. PIERCE. I THINK TWO WEEKS IS MORE THAN ENOUGH TIME TO HAVE LEARNED SOME USEFUL INFORMATION?
AS FAR AS WE CAN TELL, JAX IS A NORMAL TEENAGE GIRL.
WHO MANAGED TO RECOVER OUR MULTI-MILLION DOLLAR PIECE OF MACHINERY IN AN UNCHARTED DIMENSION.
SIR, I CAN'T HYPOTHESIZE ABOUT WHAT HAPPENED WHILE SHE WAS IN THERE. ALL WE'VE PROVEN IS THAT OUR THEORY ON CONTROLLING THE PORTAL BY FOCUSING IT ON HER DNA WORKED.
THEN THE PORTAL IS STABLE?
I DIDN'T SAY THAT.
MAYBE WE SHOULD SEND IN ANOTHER PROBE?
THE LAST TIME WE DID THAT WE HAD TO EVACUATE THE BUILDING!
DAK
YES. AND IT WAS DESTROYED. BY THIS GIRL. WE ALL HAVE A LOT AT STAKE HERE, DR. PIERCE. PROGRESS IS OUR ONLY OPTION.
YESSIR. WHATEVER YOU SAY.
WE HIRED DAK TO HELP WITH OUR RESEARCH. IF YOU ARE UNCOMFORTABLE WITH CONDUCTING SUCH RESEARCH, I WILL GIVE YOU SOMETHING TO DO THAT YOU'LL FIND FAR LESS COMFORTABLE.
I'M TERRIBLY SORRY ABOUT THAT, MR. TARKEN. THESE DAK SCIENTISTS SURE HAVE A PROBLEM WITH AUTHORITY.
YES. YOU'D BETTER WATCH YOUR STEP, TOO.

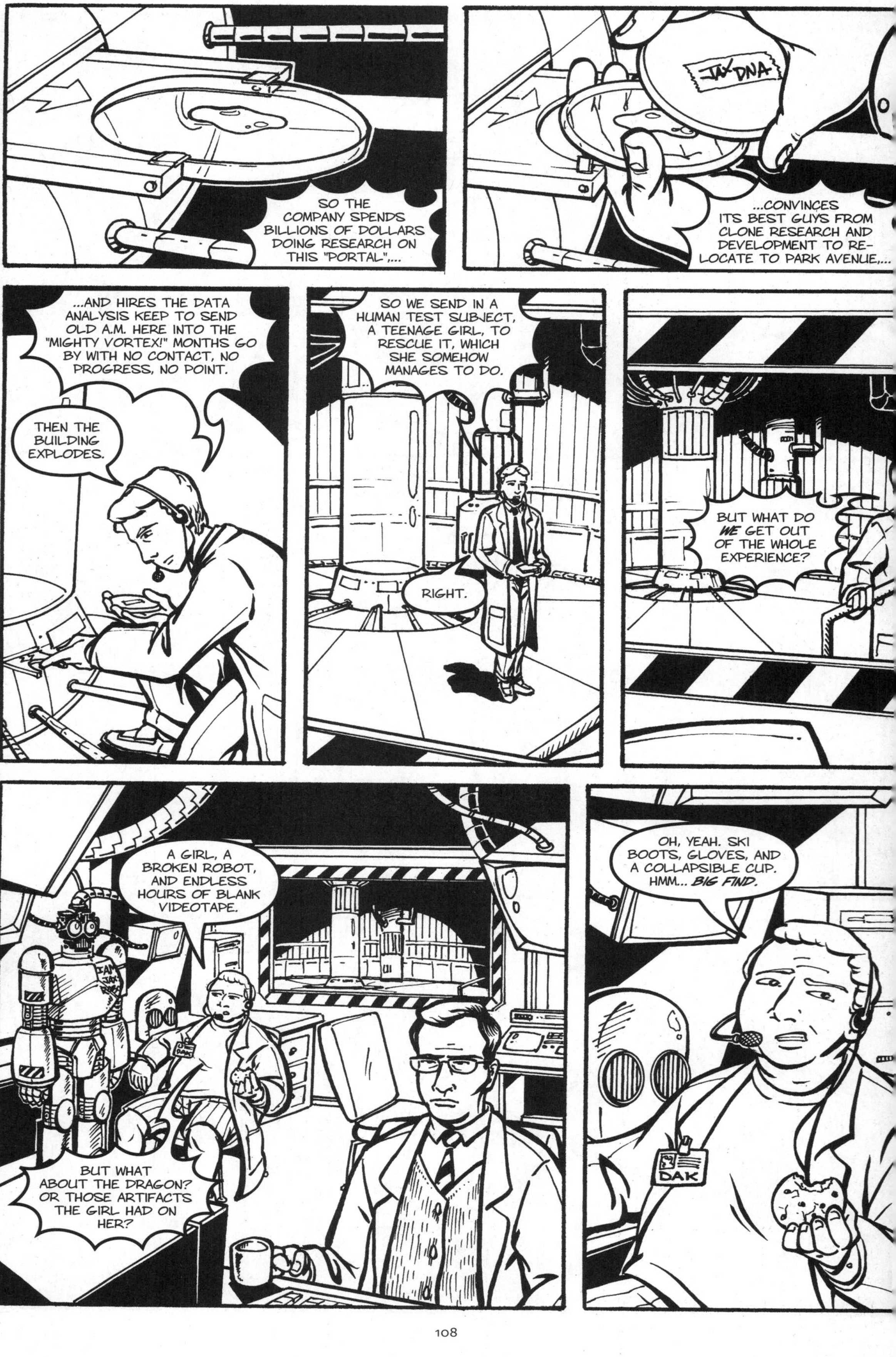
SO THE COMPANY SPENDS BILLIONS OF DOLLARS DOING RESEARCH ON THIS "PORTAL",...
JAX DNA
...CONVINCES ITS BEST GUYS FROM CLONE RESEARCH AND DEVELOPMENT TO RE-LOCATE TO PARK AVENUE,...
...AND HIRES THE DATA ANALYSIS KEEP TO SEND OLD A.M. HERE INTO THE "MIGHTY VORTEX!" MONTHS GO BY WITH NO CONTACT, NO PROGRESS, NO POINT.
THEN THE BUILDING EXPLODES.
SO WE SEND IN A HUMAN TEST SUBJECT, A TEENAGE GIRL, TO RESCUE IT, WHICH SHE SOMEHOW MANAGES TO DO.
RIGHT.
BUT WHAT DO *WE* GET OUT OF THE WHOLE EXPERIENCE?
A GIRL, A BROKEN ROBOT, AND ENDLESS HOURS OF BLANK VIDEOTAPE.
BUT WHAT ABOUT THE DRAGON? OR THOSE ARTIFACTS THE GIRL HAD ON HER?
OH, YEAH. SKI BOOTS, GLOVES, AND A COLLAPSIBLE CUP. HMM... ***BIG FIND.***
DAK

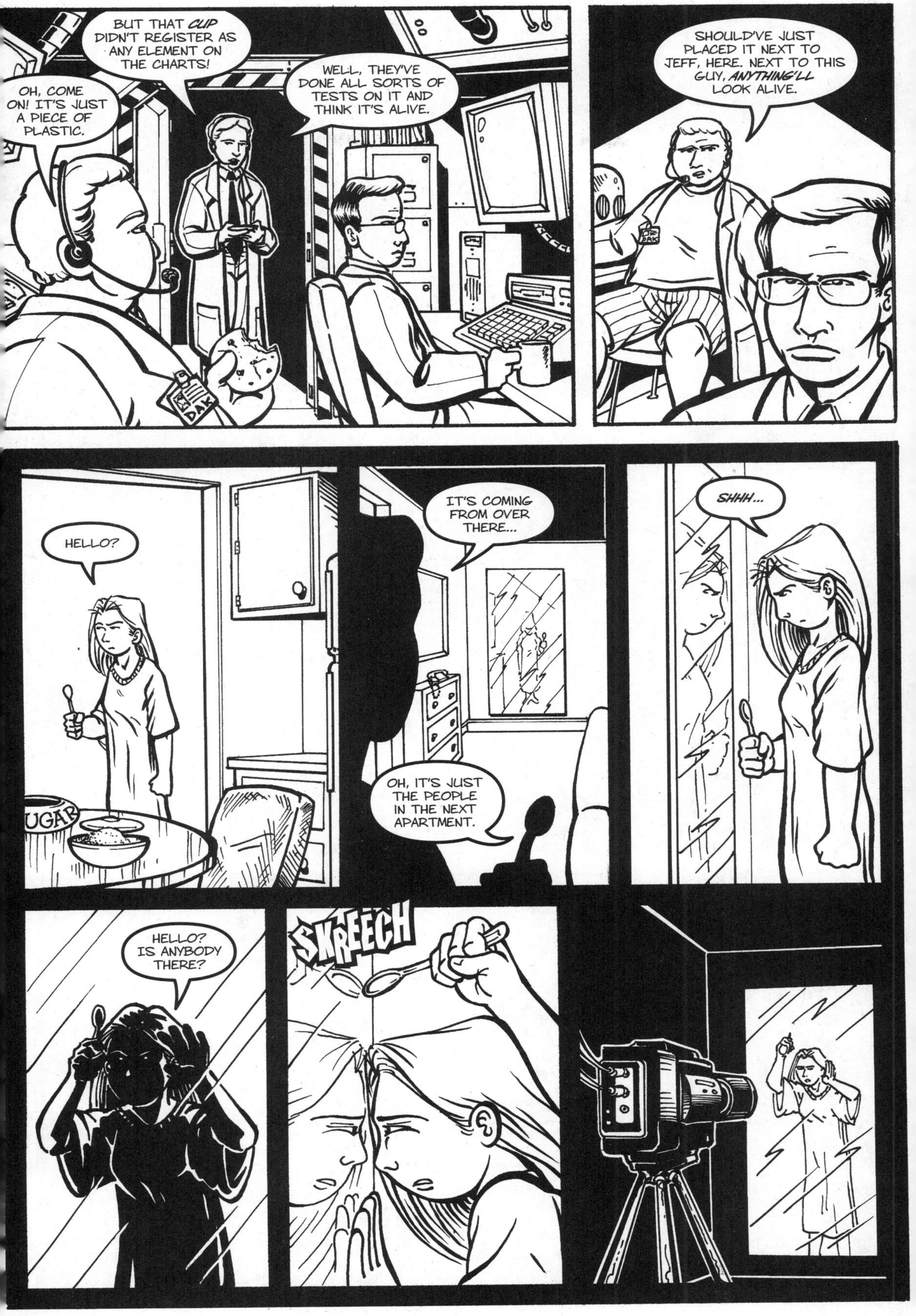
BUT THAT CUP DIDN'T REGISTER AS ANY ELEMENT ON THE CHARTS!
OH, COME ON! IT'S JUST A PIECE OF PLASTIC.
WELL, THEY'VE DONE ALL SORTS OF TESTS ON IT AND THINK IT'S ALIVE.
DAK
SHOULD'VE JUST PLACED IT NEXT TO JEFF, HERE. NEXT TO THIS GUY, ANYTHING'LL LOOK ALIVE.
HELLO?
UGAR
IT'S COMING FROM OVER THERE...
OH, IT'S JUST THE PEOPLE IN THE NEXT APARTMENT.
SHHH...
HELLO? IS ANYBODY THERE?
SKREECH

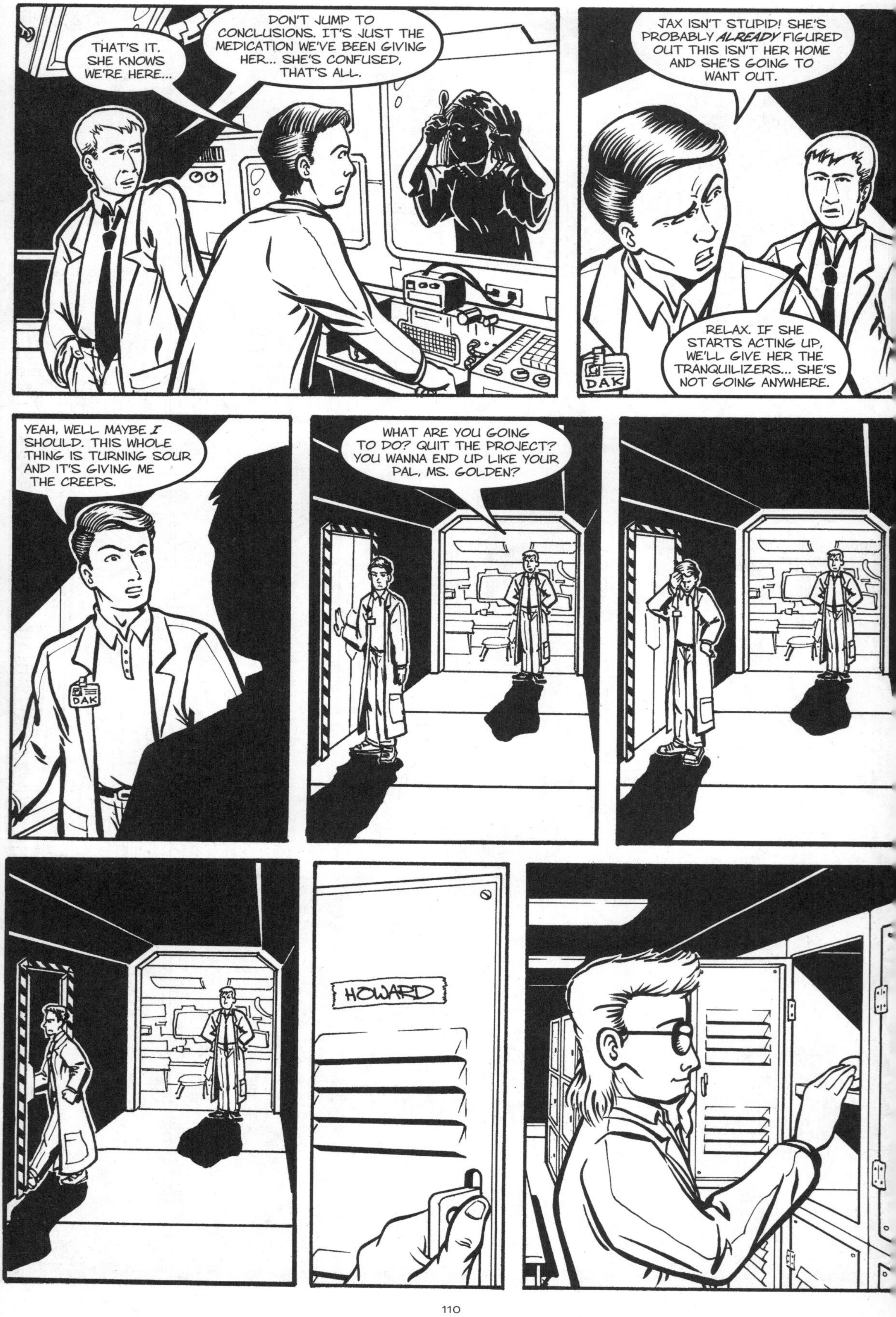
THAT'S IT. SHE KNOWS WE'RE HERE...
DON'T JUMP TO CONCLUSIONS. IT'S JUST THE MEDICATION WE'VE BEEN GIVING HER... SHE'S CONFUSED, THAT'S ALL.
JAX ISN'T STUPID! SHE'S PROBABLY ALREADY FIGURED OUT THIS ISN'T HER HOME AND SHE'S GOING TO WANT OUT.
DAK
RELAX. IF SHE STARTS ACTING UP, WE'LL GIVE HER THE TRANQUILIZERS... SHE'S NOT GOING ANYWHERE.
YEAH, WELL MAYBE I SHOULD. THIS WHOLE THING IS TURNING SOUR AND IT'S GIVING ME THE CREEPS.
DAK
WHAT ARE YOU GOING TO DO? QUIT THE PROJECT? YOU WANNA END UP LIKE YOUR PAL, MS. GOLDEN?
HOWARD

OH, HEY, TEDD!

MMPH.

SOMEBODY WOKE UP ON THE WRONG SIDE OF THE BED THIS MORNING.

YEAH, *JAX.* THIS THING SUCKS... WHY DO I PUT UP WITH THEM?

HEY, WELL, AT LEAST *YOU* DON'T HAVE TO PRETEND TO BE HER MOTHER.

I'M WORRIED, CAL. I THINK THE MEDICATION THEY'RE MAKING YOU GIVE TO JAX IS MAKING HER GO CRAZY.

DON'T JUMP TO ANY CONCLUSIONS.

WHY DOES EVERYONE *SAY* THAT?!

THIS ISN'T A JOKE! JAX IS HALLUCINATING, TALKING TO HERSELF... THE MEDICATION IS TOO STRONG...

OF COURSE IT IS! THAT'S WHY I'VE ONLY BEEN GIVING HER A *PLACEBO!* YOU DON'T THINK I ACTUALLY LISTEN TO THOSE PEOPLE, DO YOU?

CRASH

THAT WASN'T A FISHTANK.

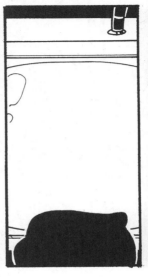

WOO HOO! LOOK AT ME!

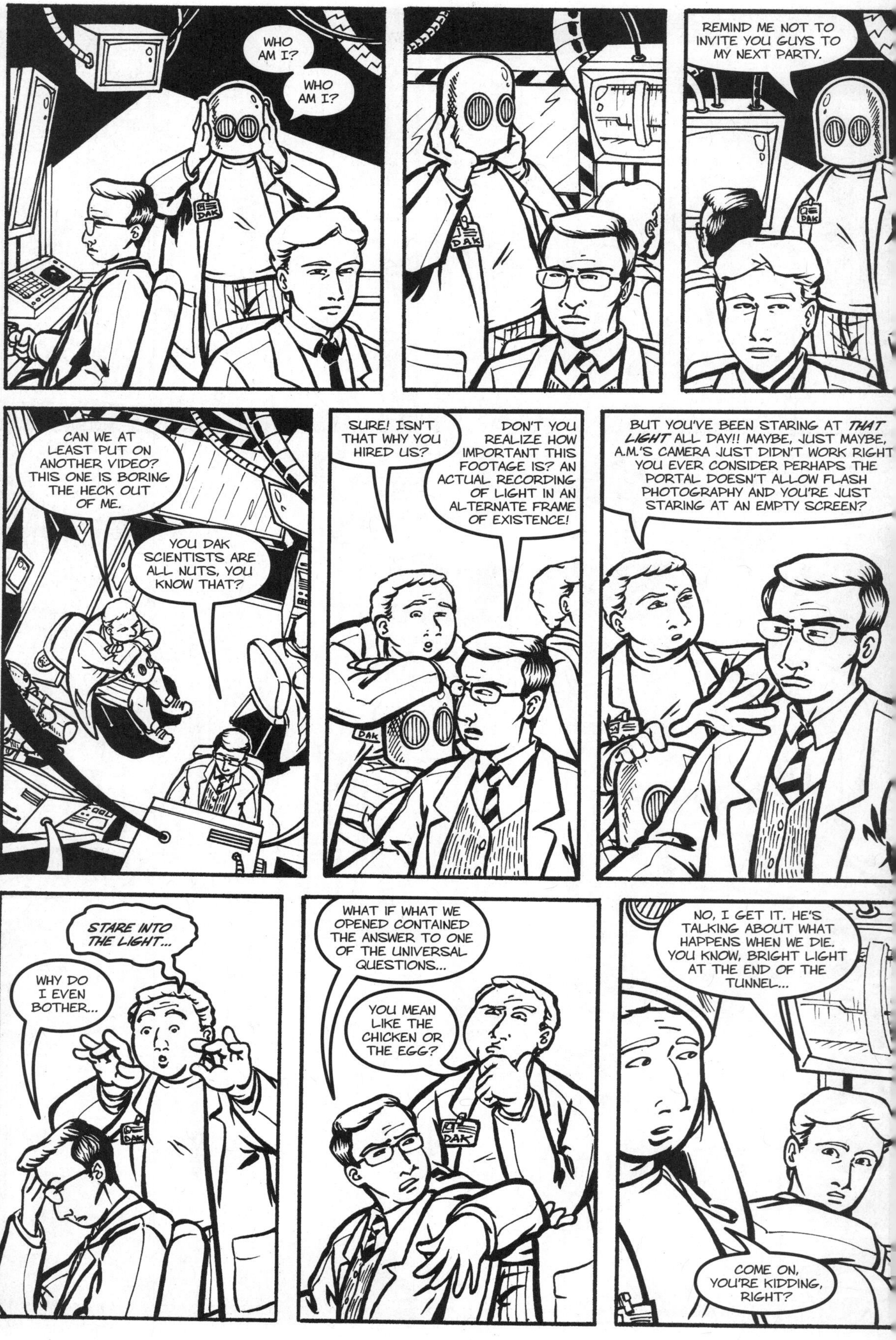
WHO AM I?
WHO AM I?
REMIND ME NOT TO INVITE YOU GUYS TO MY NEXT PARTY.
CAN WE AT LEAST PUT ON ANOTHER VIDEO? THIS ONE IS BORING THE HECK OUT OF ME.
YOU DAK SCIENTISTS ARE ALL NUTS, YOU KNOW THAT?
SURE! ISN'T THAT WHY YOU HIRED US?
DON'T YOU REALIZE HOW IMPORTANT THIS FOOTAGE IS? AN ACTUAL RECORDING OF LIGHT IN AN ALTERNATE FRAME OF EXISTENCE!
BUT YOU'VE BEEN STARING AT *THAT LIGHT* ALL DAY!! MAYBE, JUST MAYBE, A.M.'S CAMERA JUST DIDN'T WORK RIGHT. YOU EVER CONSIDER PERHAPS THE PORTAL DOESN'T ALLOW FLASH PHOTOGRAPHY AND YOU'RE JUST STARING AT AN EMPTY SCREEN?
STARE INTO THE LIGHT...
WHY DO I EVEN BOTHER...
WHAT IF WHAT WE OPENED CONTAINED THE ANSWER TO ONE OF THE UNIVERSAL QUESTIONS...
YOU MEAN LIKE THE CHICKEN OR THE EGG?
NO, I GET IT. HE'S TALKING ABOUT WHAT HAPPENS WHEN WE DIE. YOU KNOW, BRIGHT LIGHT AT THE END OF THE TUNNEL...
COME ON, YOU'RE KIDDING, RIGHT?

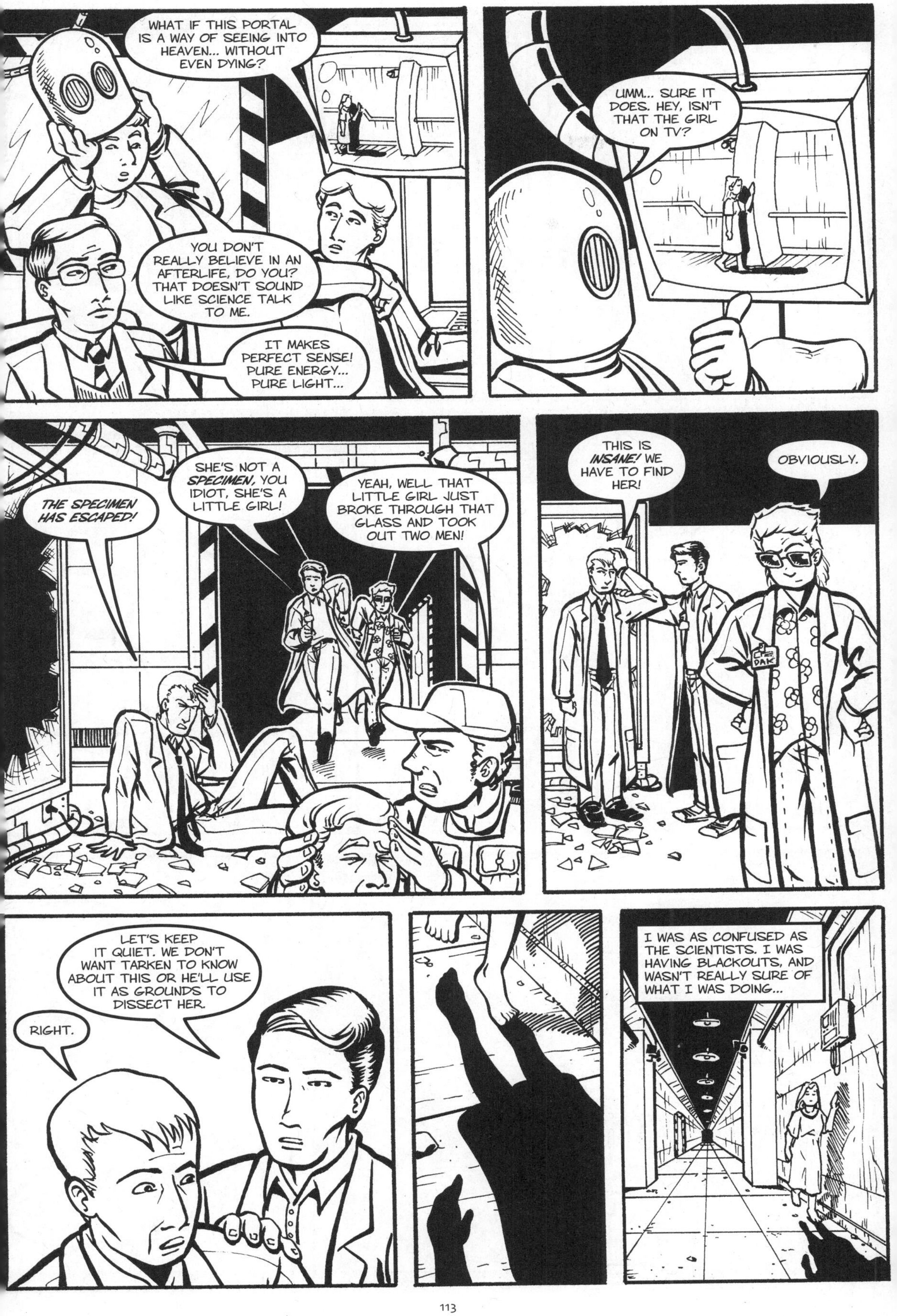
WHAT IF THIS PORTAL IS A WAY OF SEEING INTO HEAVEN... WITHOUT EVEN DYING?
YOU DON'T REALLY BELIEVE IN AN AFTERLIFE, DO YOU? THAT DOESN'T SOUND LIKE SCIENCE TALK TO ME.
IT MAKES PERFECT SENSE! PURE ENERGY... PURE LIGHT...
UMM... SURE IT DOES. HEY, ISN'T THAT THE GIRL ON TV?
THE SPECIMEN HAS ESCAPED!
SHE'S NOT A SPECIMEN, YOU IDIOT, SHE'S A LITTLE GIRL!
YEAH, WELL THAT LITTLE GIRL JUST BROKE THROUGH THAT GLASS AND TOOK OUT TWO MEN!
THIS IS INSANE! WE HAVE TO FIND HER!
OBVIOUSLY.
DAK
LET'S KEEP IT QUIET. WE DON'T WANT TARKEN TO KNOW ABOUT THIS OR HE'LL USE IT AS GROUNDS TO DISSECT HER.
RIGHT.
I WAS AS CONFUSED AS THE SCIENTISTS. I WAS HAVING BLACKOUTS, AND WASN'T REALLY SURE OF WHAT I WAS DOING...

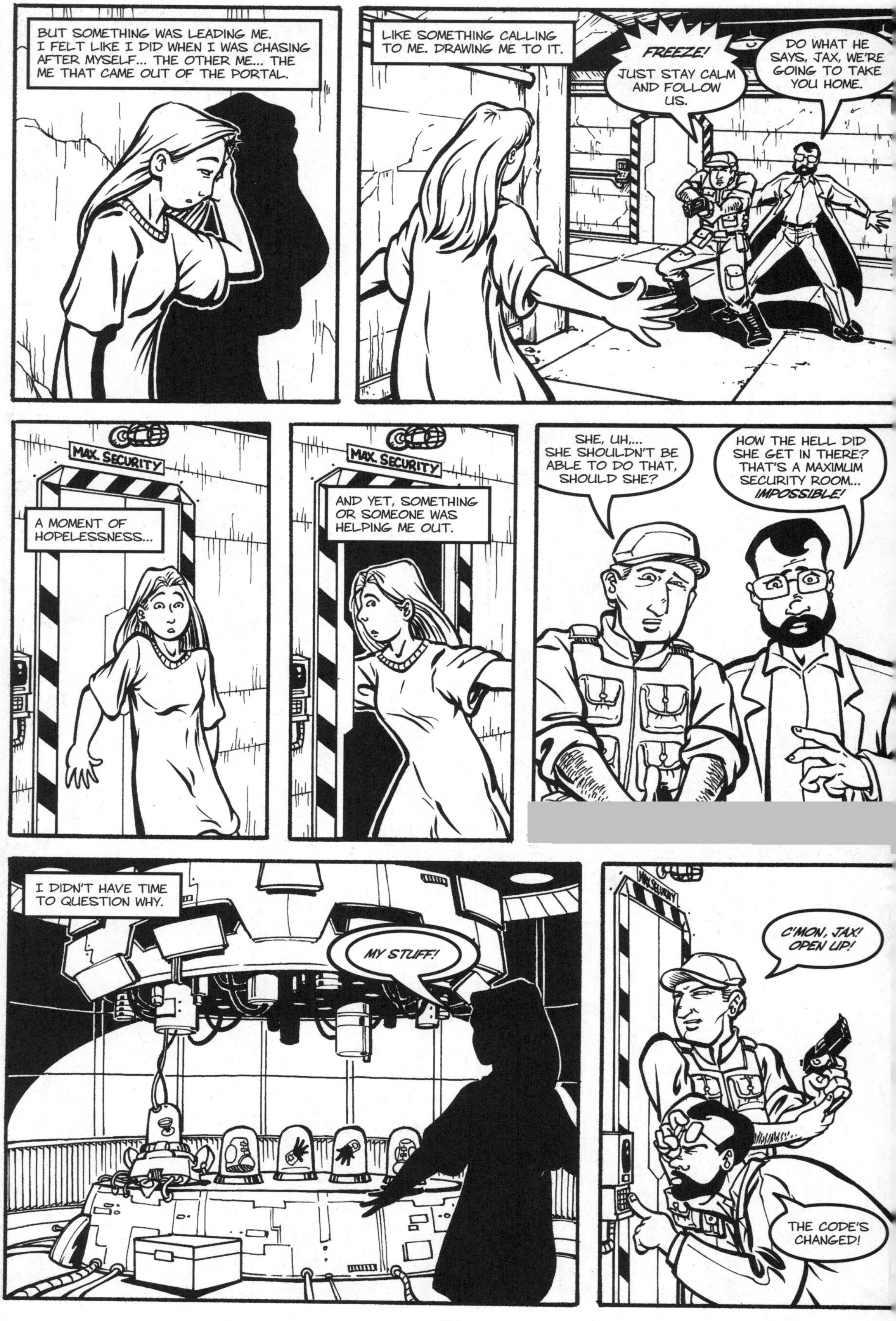
BUT SOMETHING WAS LEADING ME. I FELT LIKE I DID WHEN I WAS CHASING AFTER MYSELF... THE OTHER ME... THE ME THAT CAME OUT OF THE PORTAL.
LIKE SOMETHING CALLING TO ME. DRAWING ME TO IT.
FREEZE! JUST STAY CALM AND FOLLOW US.
DO WHAT HE SAYS, JAX, WE'RE GOING TO TAKE YOU HOME.
MAX. SECURITY
A MOMENT OF HOPELESSNESS...
MAX. SECURITY
AND YET, SOMETHING OR SOMEONE WAS HELPING ME OUT.
SHE, UH,... SHE SHOULDN'T BE ABLE TO DO THAT, SHOULD SHE?
HOW THE HELL DID SHE GET IN THERE? THAT'S A MAXIMUM SECURITY ROOM... IMPOSSIBLE!
I DIDN'T HAVE TIME TO QUESTION WHY.
MY STUFF!
C'MON, JAX! OPEN UP!
THE CODE'S CHANGED!

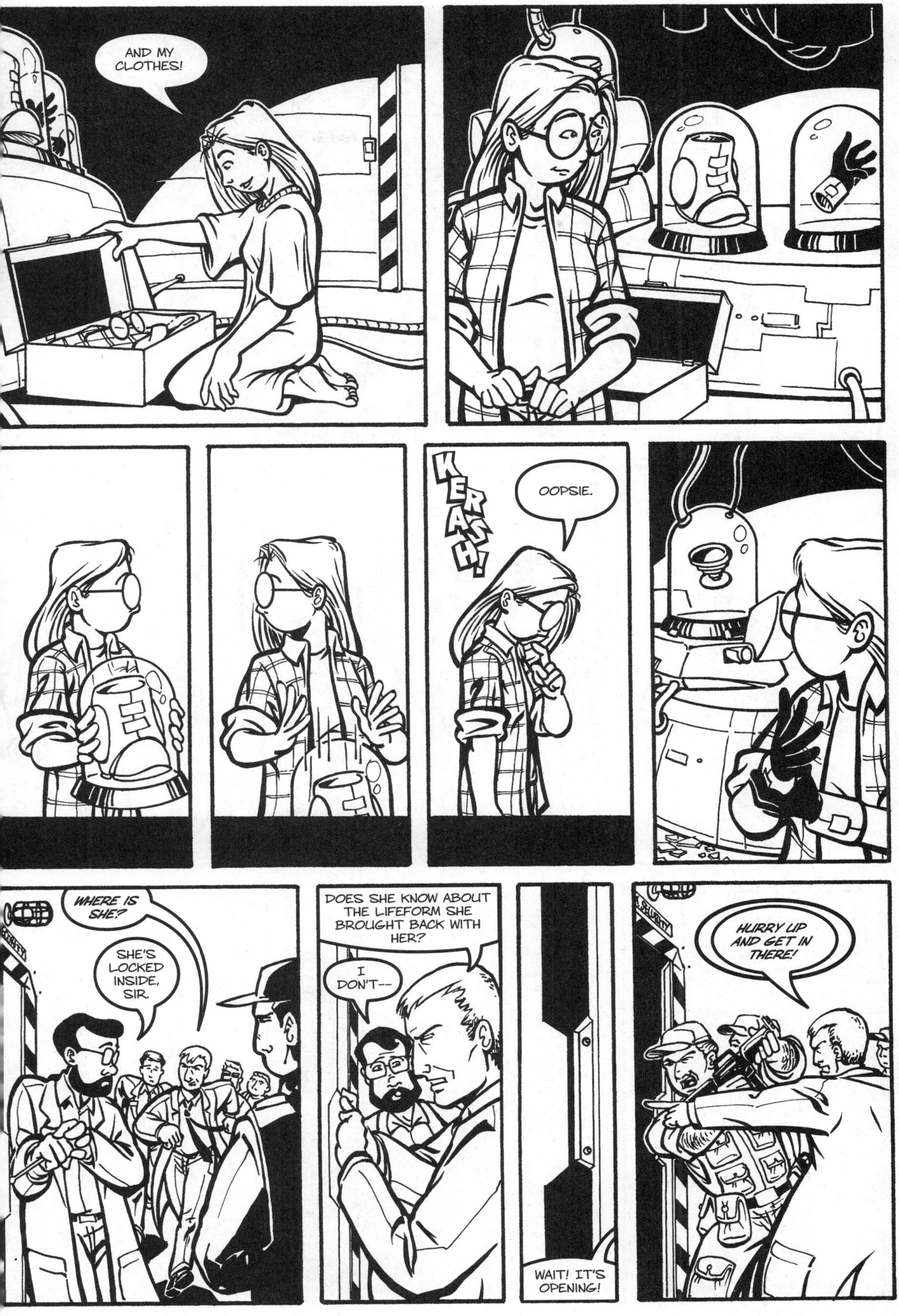
AND MY CLOTHES!
KERASH!
OOPSIE.
WHERE IS SHE?
SHE'S LOCKED INSIDE, SIR.
DOES SHE KNOW ABOUT THE LIFEFORM SHE BROUGHT BACK WITH HER?
I DON'T--
WAIT! IT'S OPENING!
HURRY UP AND GET IN THERE!

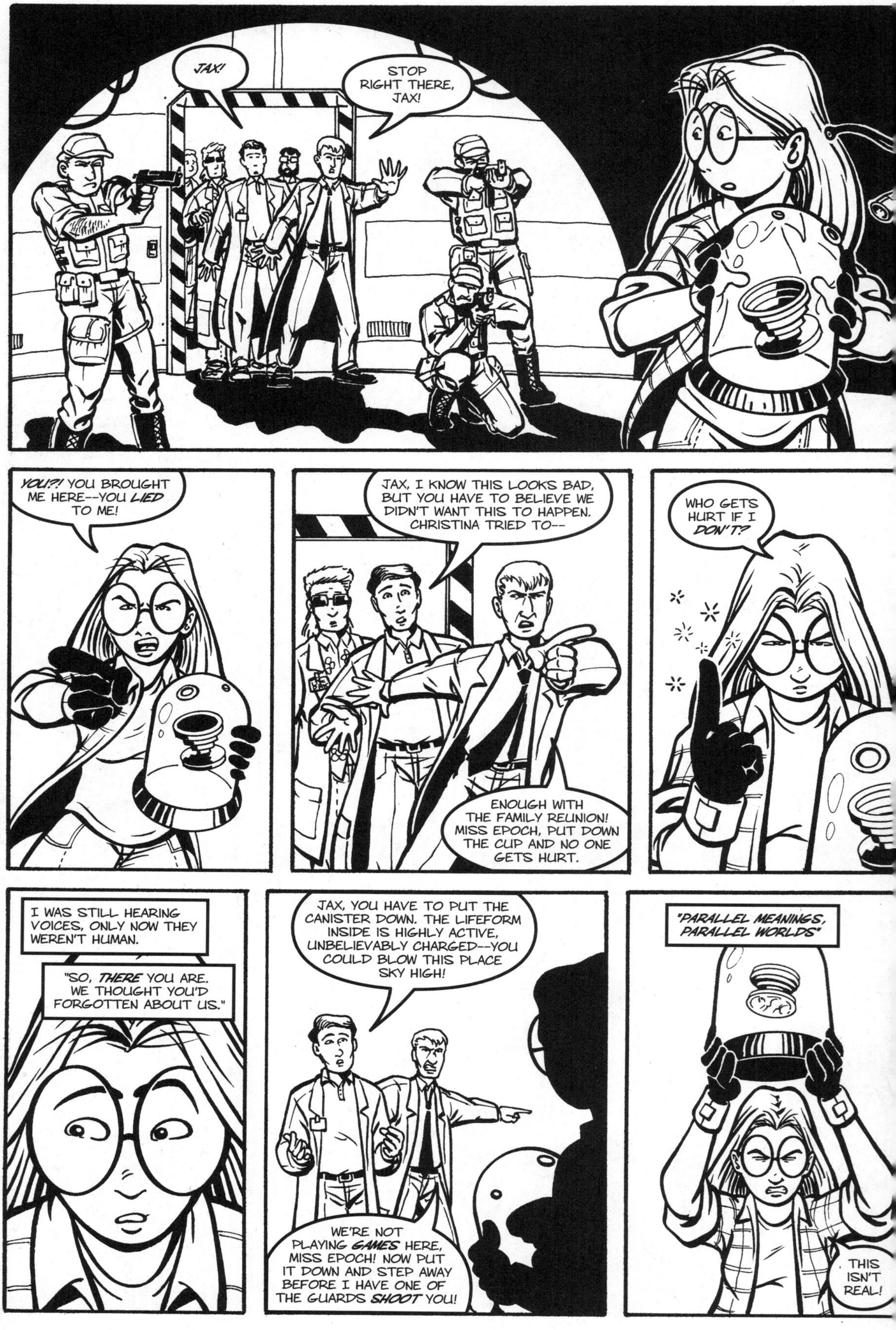
JAX!
STOP RIGHT THERE, JAX!
YOU!?! YOU BROUGHT ME HERE--YOU LIED TO ME!
JAX, I KNOW THIS LOOKS BAD, BUT YOU HAVE TO BELIEVE WE DIDN'T WANT THIS TO HAPPEN. CHRISTINA TRIED TO--
ENOUGH WITH THE FAMILY REUNION! MISS EPOCH, PUT DOWN THE CUP AND NO ONE GETS HURT.
WHO GETS HURT IF I DON'T?
I WAS STILL HEARING VOICES, ONLY NOW THEY WEREN'T HUMAN.
"SO, THERE YOU ARE. WE THOUGHT YOU'D FORGOTTEN ABOUT US."
JAX, YOU HAVE TO PUT THE CANISTER DOWN. THE LIFEFORM INSIDE IS HIGHLY ACTIVE, UNBELIEVABLY CHARGED--YOU COULD BLOW THIS PLACE SKY HIGH!
WE'RE NOT PLAYING GAMES HERE, MISS EPOCH! NOW PUT IT DOWN AND STEP AWAY BEFORE I HAVE ONE OF THE GUARDS SHOOT YOU!
"PARALLEL MEANINGS, PARALLEL WORLDS"
THIS ISN'T REAL!

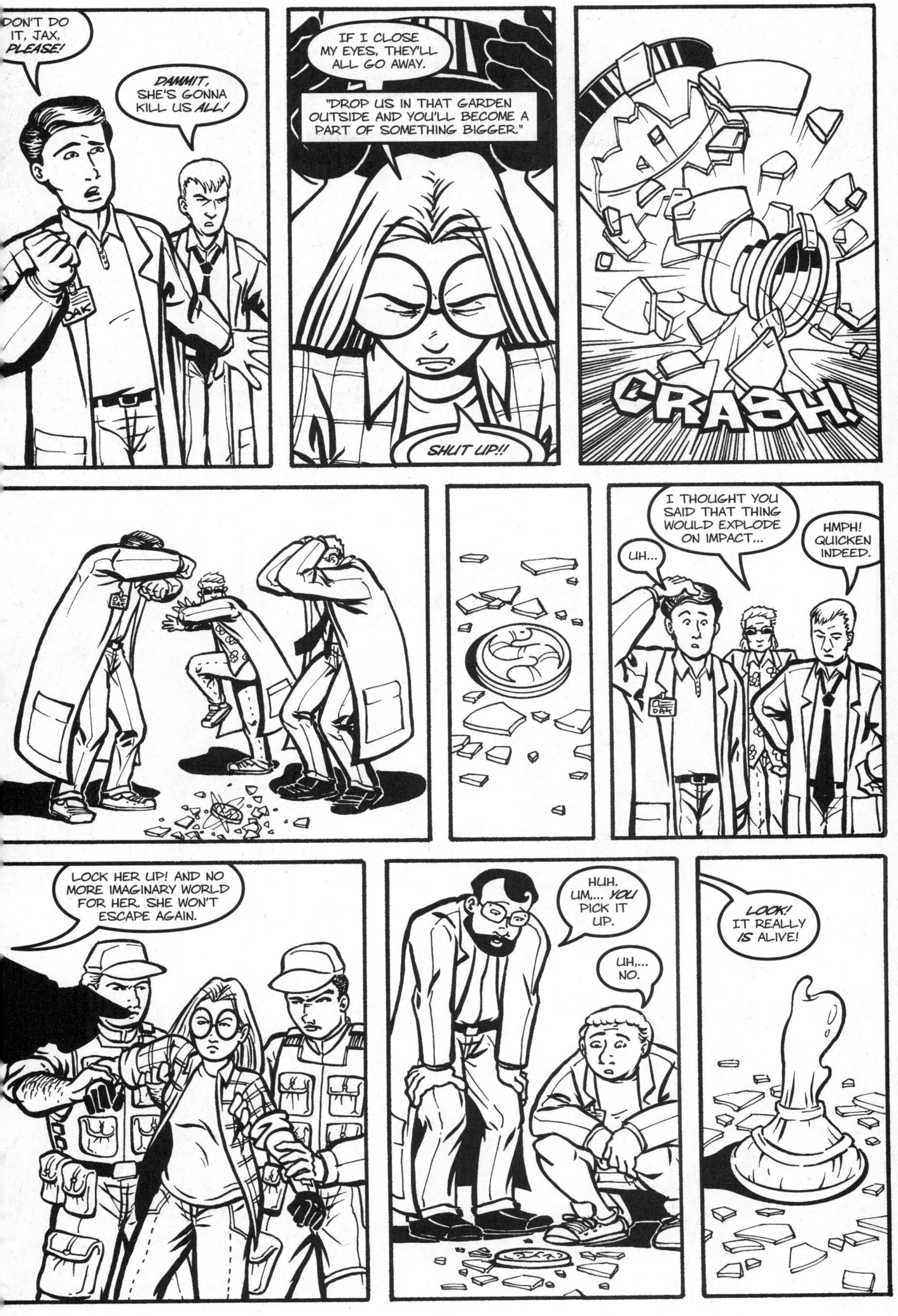
DON'T DO IT, JAX, *PLEASE!*
DAMMIT, SHE'S GONNA KILL US *ALL!*
DAK
IF I CLOSE MY EYES, THEY'LL ALL GO AWAY.
"DROP US IN THAT GARDEN OUTSIDE AND YOU'LL BECOME A PART OF SOMETHING BIGGER."
SHUT UP!!
CRASH!
I THOUGHT YOU SAID THAT THING WOULD EXPLODE ON IMPACT...
UH...
HMPH! QUICKEN INDEED.
LOCK HER UP! AND NO MORE IMAGINARY WORLD FOR HER. SHE WON'T ESCAPE AGAIN.
HUH. UM,... *YOU* PICK IT UP.
UH,... NO.
LOOK! IT REALLY *IS* ALIVE!

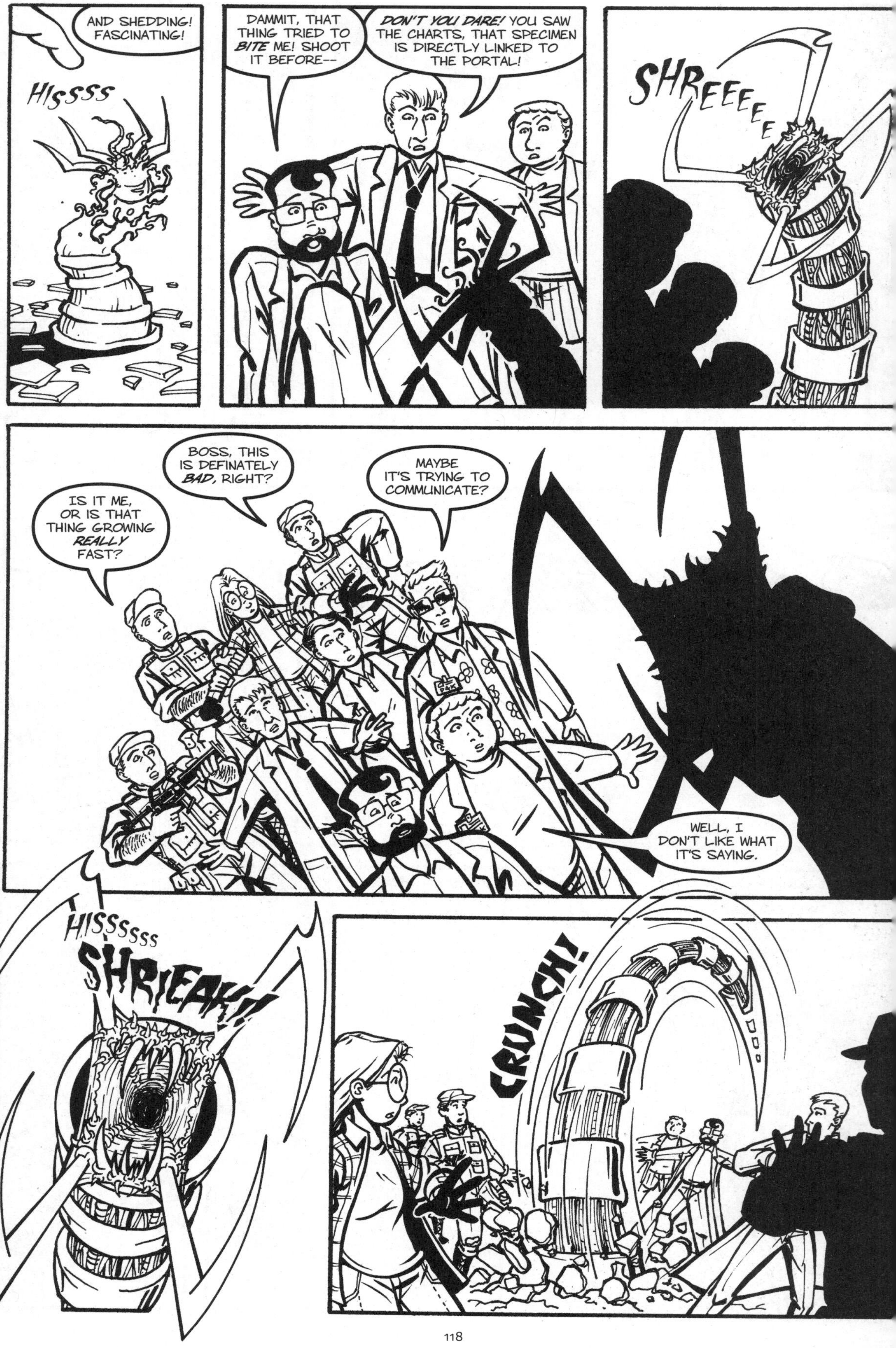
AND SHEDDING! FASCINATING!
HISSSS
DAMMIT, THAT THING TRIED TO *BITE* ME! SHOOT IT BEFORE--
DON'T YOU DARE! YOU SAW THE CHARTS, THAT SPECIMEN IS DIRECTLY LINKED TO THE PORTAL!
SHREEEEEE
IS IT ME, OR IS THAT THING GROWING *REALLY* FAST?
BOSS, THIS IS DEFINATELY *BAD*, RIGHT?
MAYBE IT'S TRYING TO COMMUNICATE?
WELL, I DON'T LIKE WHAT IT'S SAYING.
HISSSSSS
SHRIEAK!!
CRUNCH!

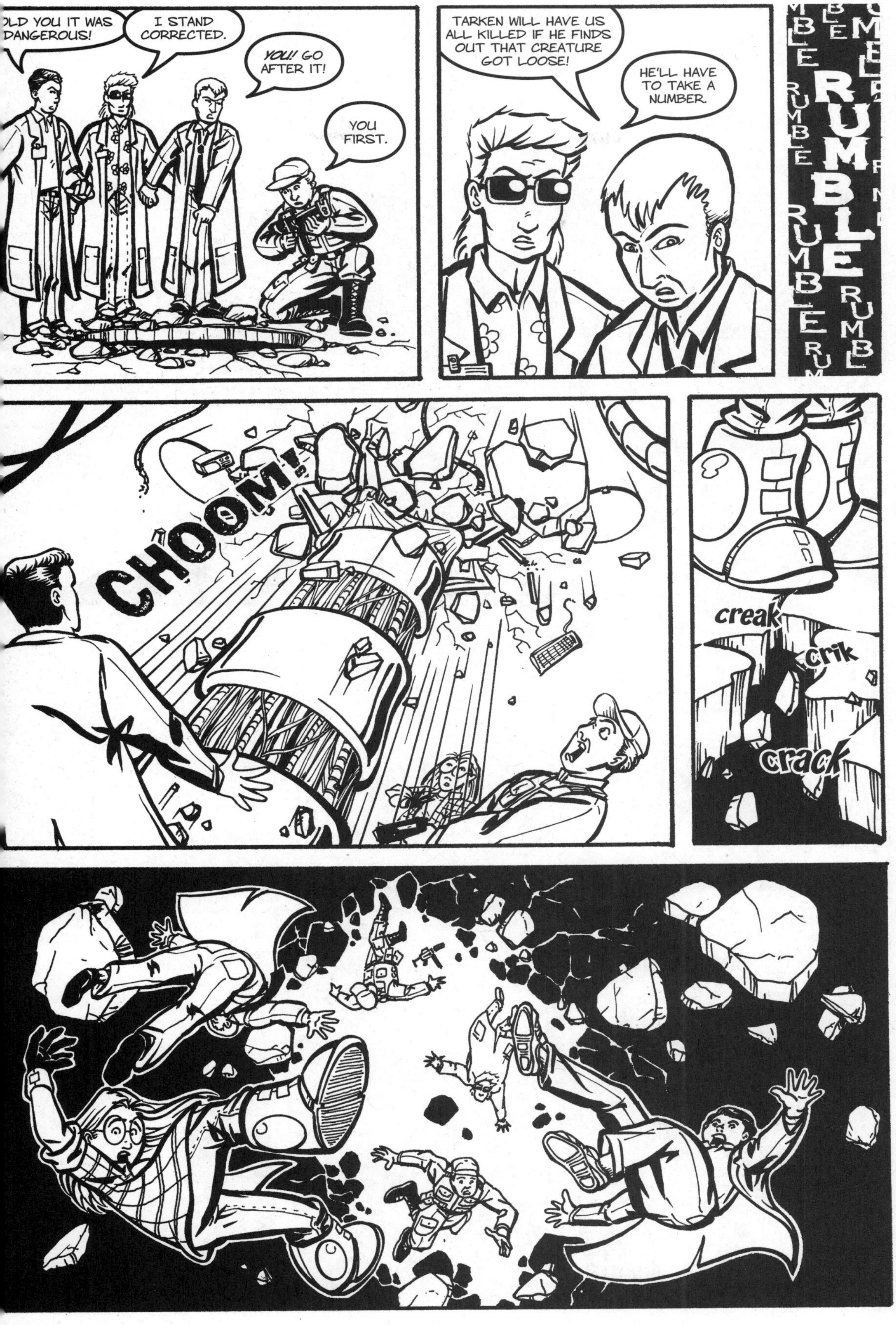
OLD YOU IT WAS DANGEROUS!
I STAND CORRECTED.
YOU!! GO AFTER IT!
YOU FIRST.
TARKEN WILL HAVE US ALL KILLED IF HE FINDS OUT THAT CREATURE GOT LOOSE!
HE'LL HAVE TO TAKE A NUMBER.
RUMBLE
CHOOM!
creak
crik
crack

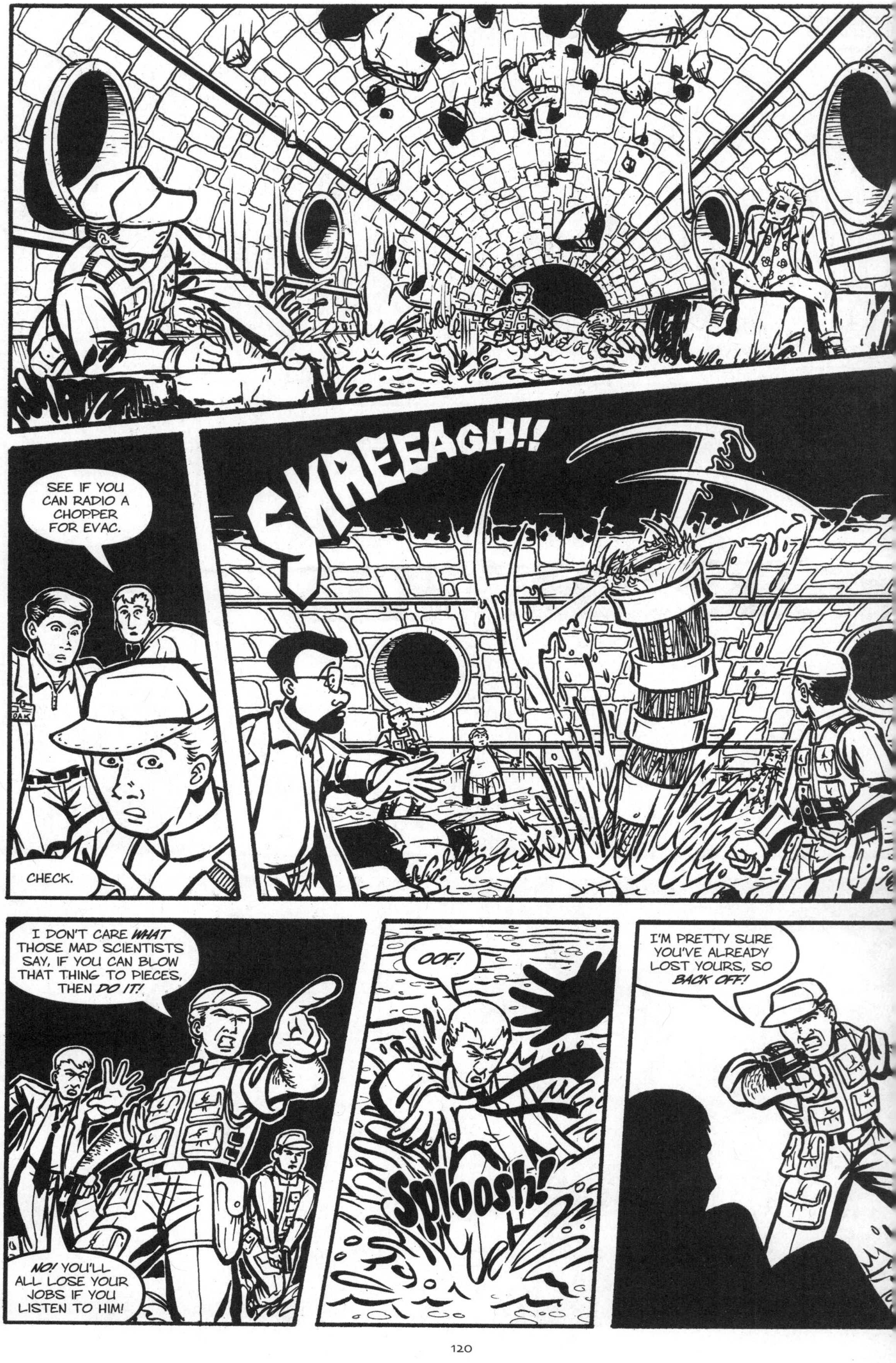
SEE IF YOU CAN RADIO A CHOPPER FOR EVAC.
CHECK.
SKREEAGH!!
I DON'T CARE WHAT THOSE MAD SCIENTISTS SAY, IF YOU CAN BLOW THAT THING TO PIECES, THEN DO IT!
NO! YOU'LL ALL LOSE YOUR JOBS IF YOU LISTEN TO HIM!
OOF!
Sploosh!
I'M PRETTY SURE YOU'VE ALREADY LOST YOURS, SO BACK OFF!

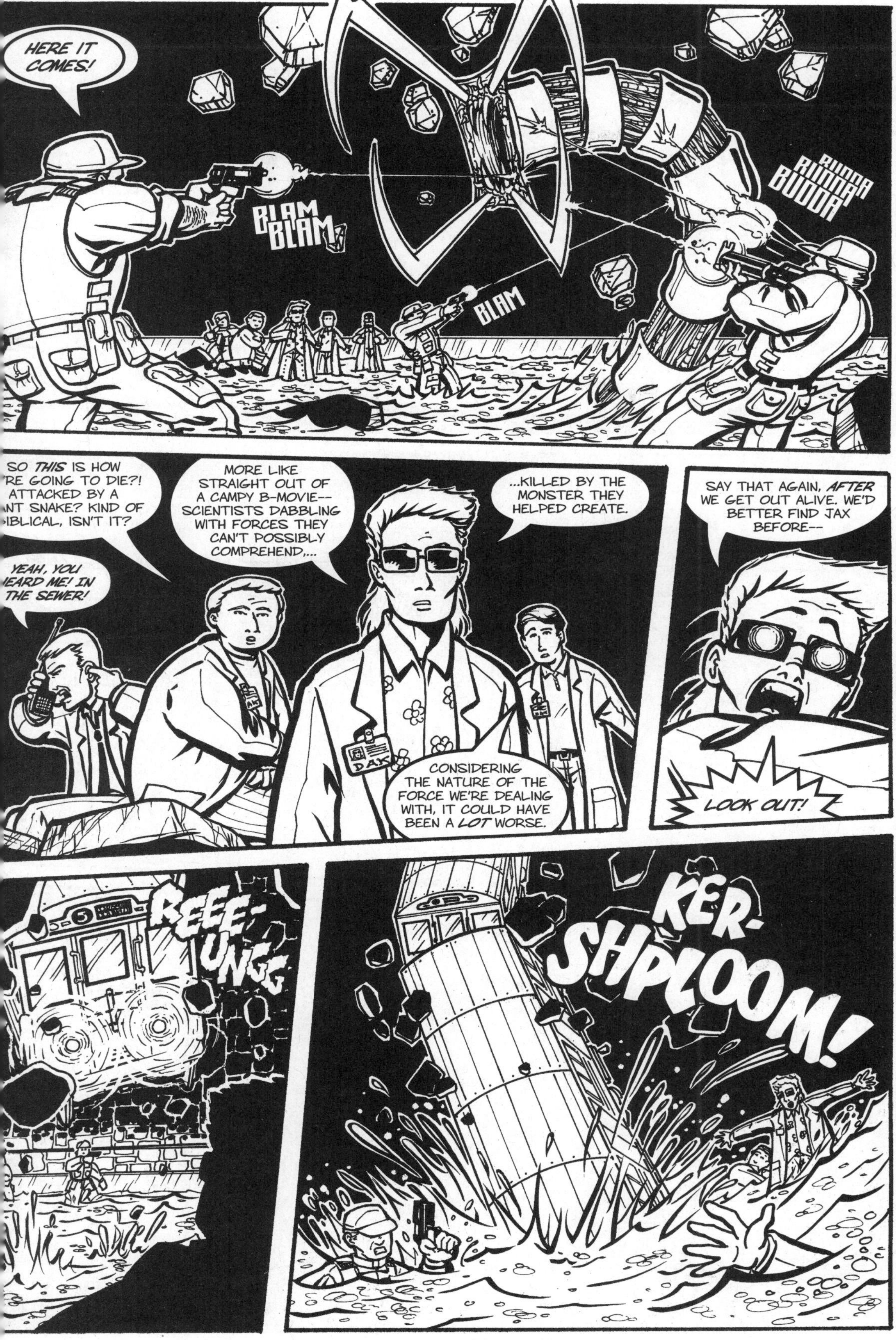
HERE IT COMES!
BLAM BLAM
BLAM
BUDDA BUDDA BUDDA
SO THIS IS HOW 'RE GOING TO DIE?! ATTACKED BY A ANT SNAKE? KIND OF BIBLICAL, ISN'T IT?
YEAH, YOU HEARD ME! IN THE SEWER!
MORE LIKE STRAIGHT OUT OF A CAMPY B-MOVIE-- SCIENTISTS DABBLING WITH FORCES THEY CAN'T POSSIBLY COMPREHEND,...
...KILLED BY THE MONSTER THEY HELPED CREATE.
CONSIDERING THE NATURE OF THE FORCE WE'RE DEALING WITH, IT COULD HAVE BEEN A LOT WORSE.
DAK
SAY THAT AGAIN, AFTER WE GET OUT ALIVE. WE'D BETTER FIND JAX BEFORE--
LOOK OUT!
REEE-UNGG
KER-SHPLOOM!

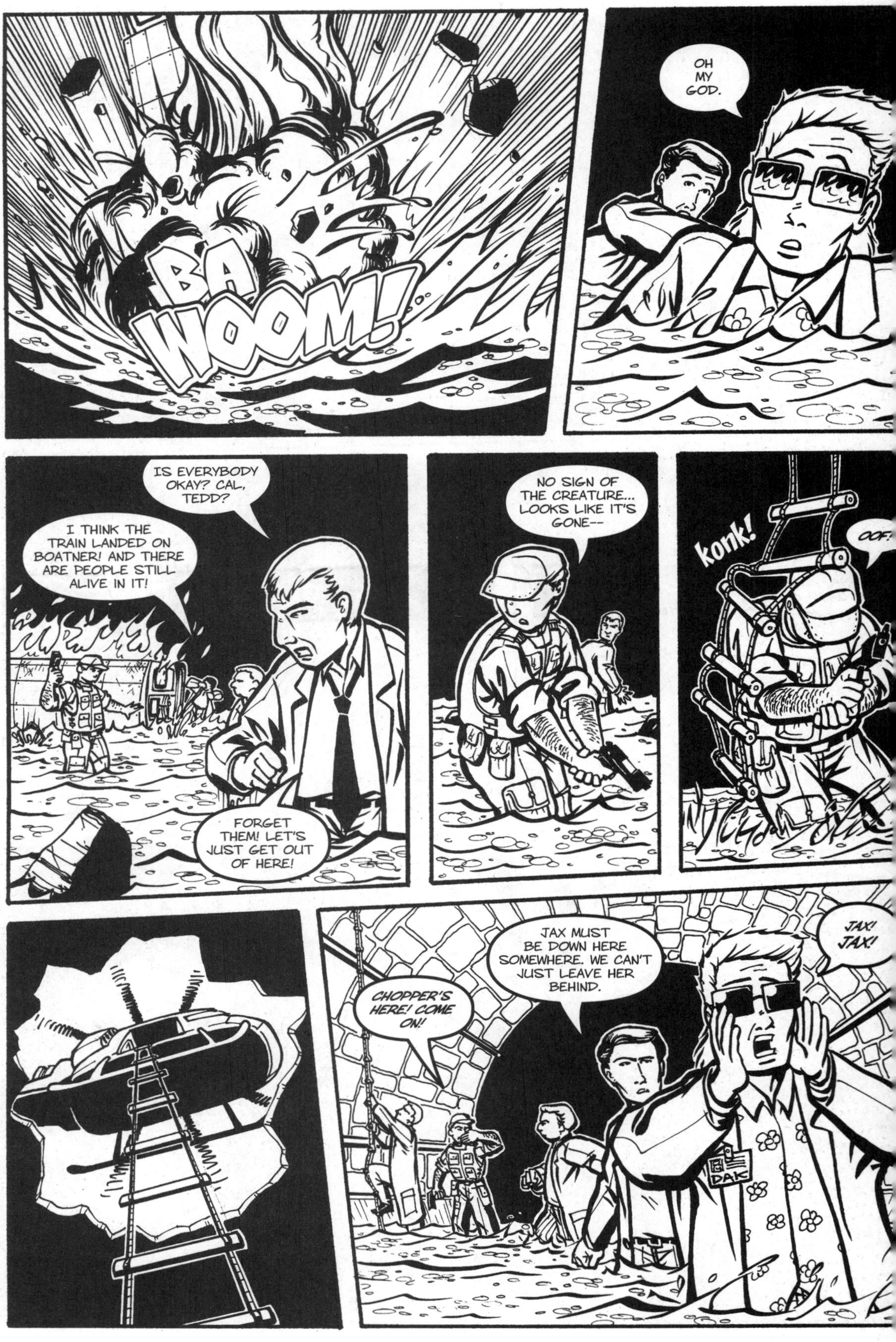
BA WOOM!
OH MY GOD.
IS EVERYBODY OKAY? CAL, TEDD?
I THINK THE TRAIN LANDED ON BOATNER! AND THERE ARE PEOPLE STILL ALIVE IN IT!
FORGET THEM! LET'S JUST GET OUT OF HERE!
NO SIGN OF THE CREATURE... LOOKS LIKE IT'S GONE--
konk!
OOF!
JAX MUST BE DOWN HERE SOMEWHERE. WE CAN'T JUST LEAVE HER BEHIND.
JAX! JAX!
CHOPPER'S HERE! COME ON!
DAK

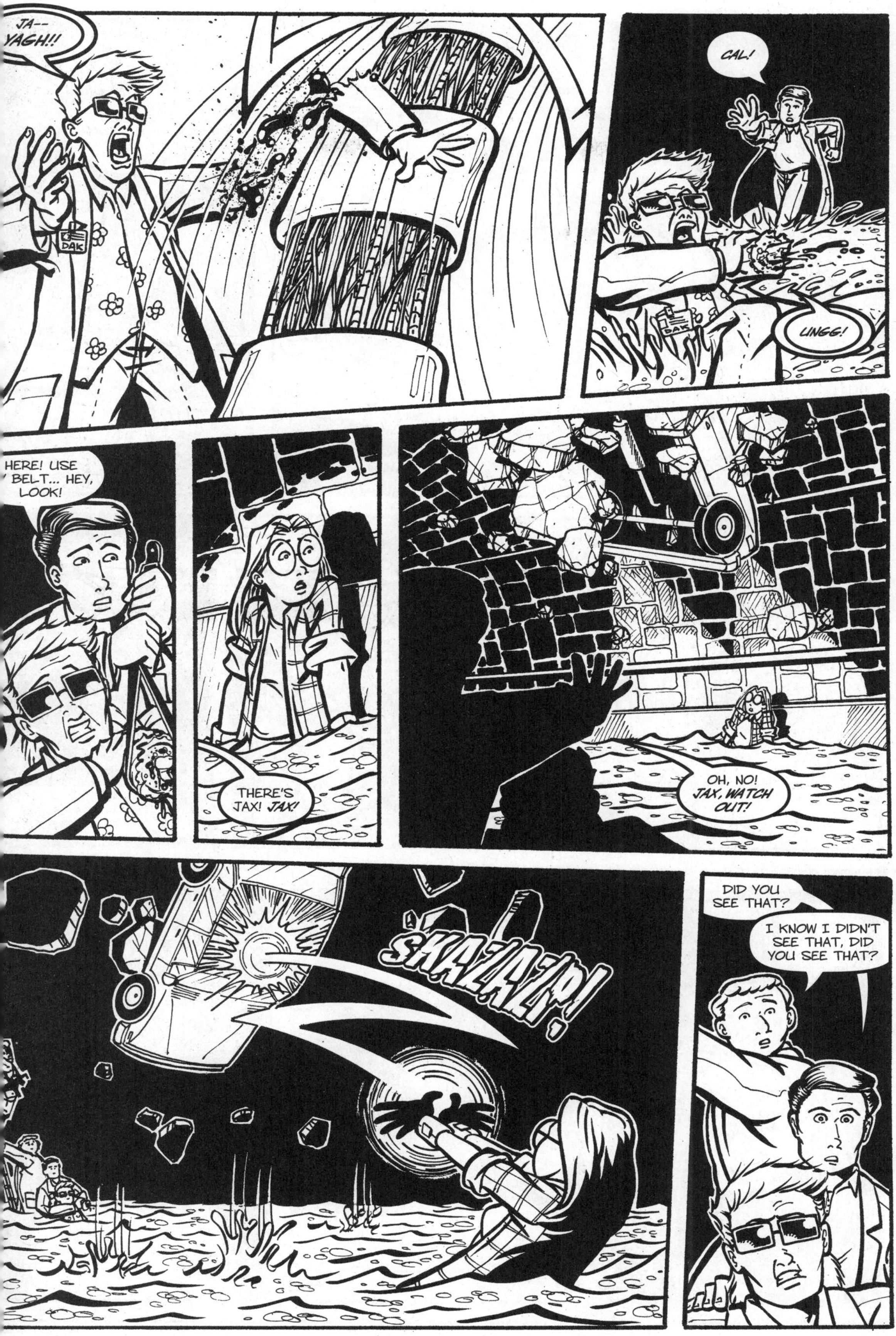
JA-- YAGH!!
CAL!
UNGG!
HERE! USE MY BELT... HEY, LOOK!
THERE'S JAX! JAX!
OH, NO! JAX, WATCH OUT!
SKAZAZAZP!
DID YOU SEE THAT?
I KNOW I DIDN'T SEE THAT, DID YOU SEE THAT?

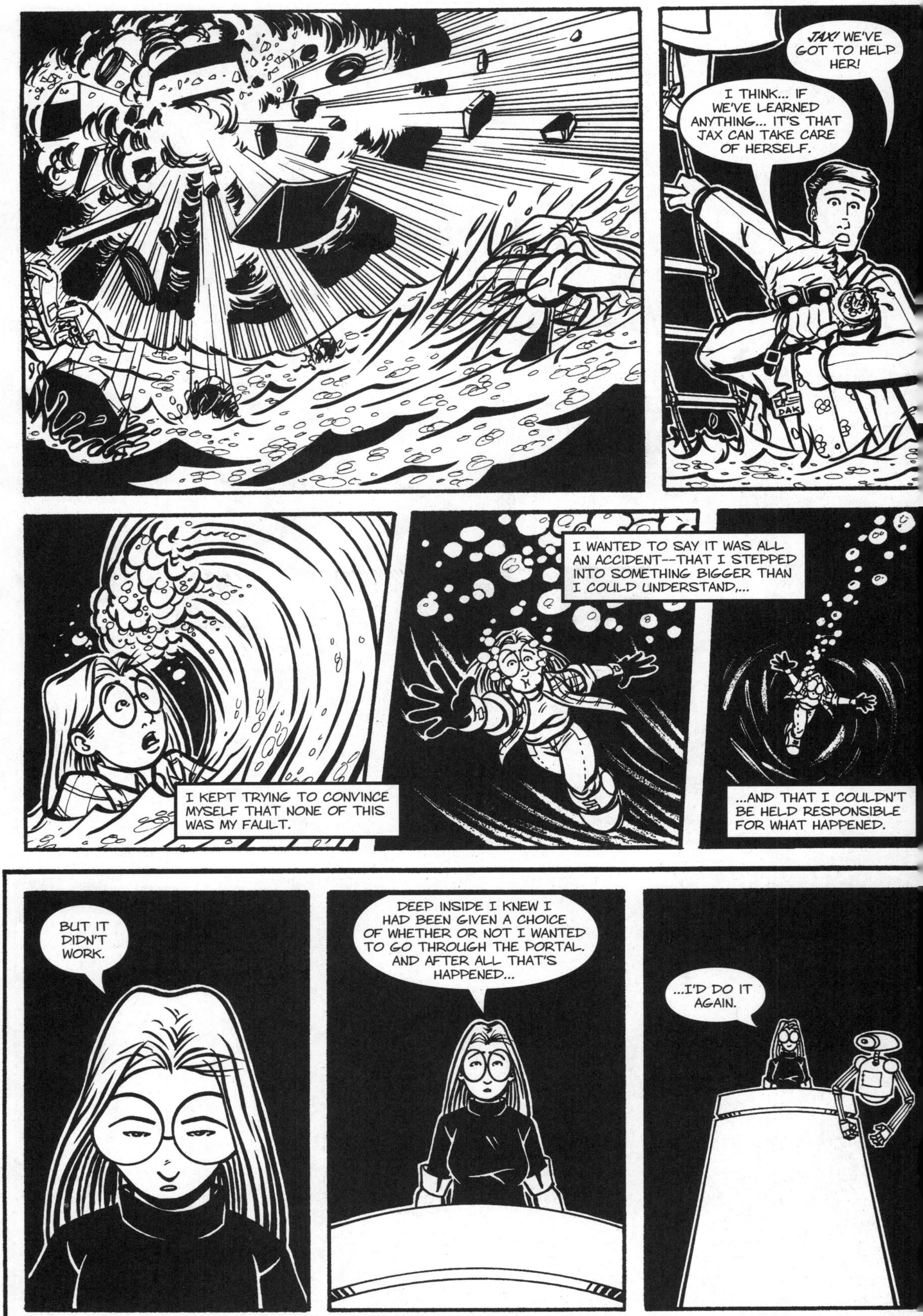
JAX! WE'VE GOT TO HELP HER!
I THINK... IF WE'VE LEARNED ANYTHING... IT'S THAT JAX CAN TAKE CARE OF HERSELF.
DAK
I KEPT TRYING TO CONVINCE MYSELF THAT NONE OF THIS WAS MY FAULT.
I WANTED TO SAY IT WAS ALL AN ACCIDENT--THAT I STEPPED INTO SOMETHING BIGGER THAN I COULD UNDERSTAND,...
...AND THAT I COULDN'T BE HELD RESPONSIBLE FOR WHAT HAPPENED.
BUT IT DIDN'T WORK.
DEEP INSIDE I KNEW I HAD BEEN GIVEN A CHOICE OF WHETHER OR NOT I WANTED TO GO THROUGH THE PORTAL. AND AFTER ALL THAT'S HAPPENED...
...I'D DO IT AGAIN.

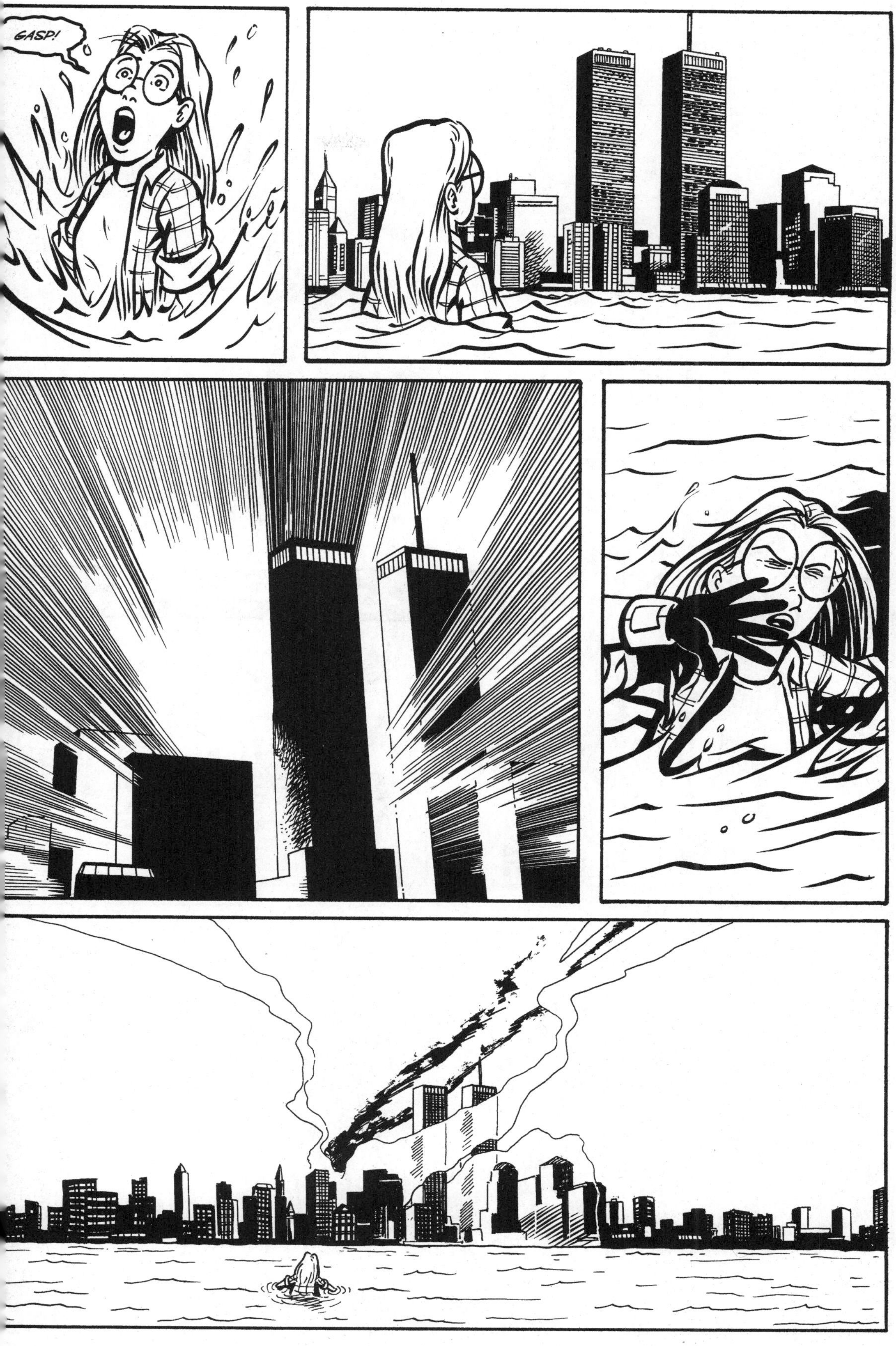
GASP!

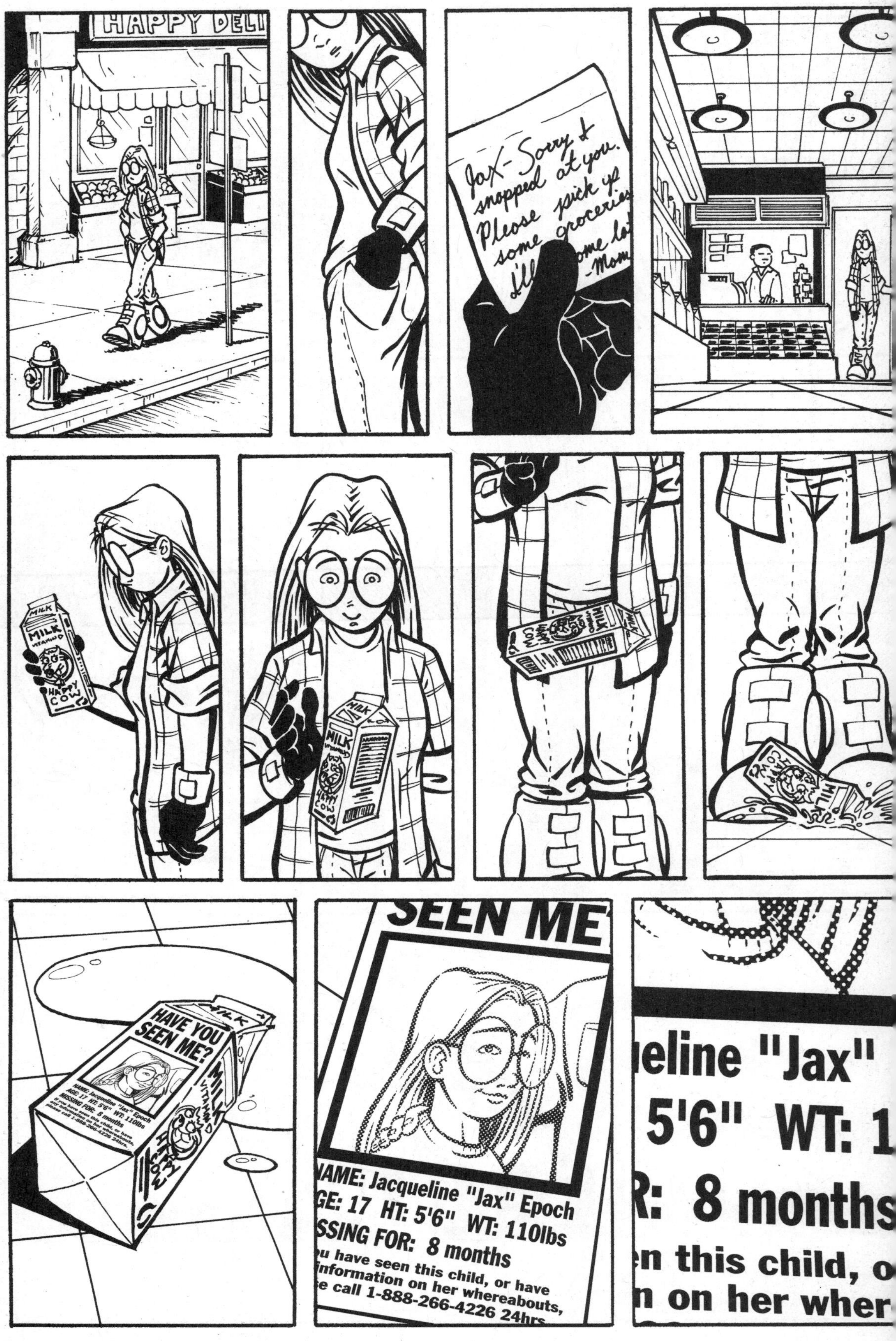
HAPPY DELI
Jax- Sorry I snapped at you. Please pick up some groceries I'll ... home lat... -Mom
MILK
MILK VITAMIN D
HAPPY COW
HAVE YOU SEEN ME?
SEEN ME
NAME: Jacqueline "Jax" Epoch
GE: 17 HT: 5'6" WT: 110lbs
SSING FOR: 8 months
u have seen this child, or have
information on her whereabouts,
e call 1-888-266-4226 24hrs
ueline "Jax"
5'6" WT: 1
R: 8 months
en this child, o
n on her wher

"Reality is an illusion, albeit a persistent one."
-Albert Einstein

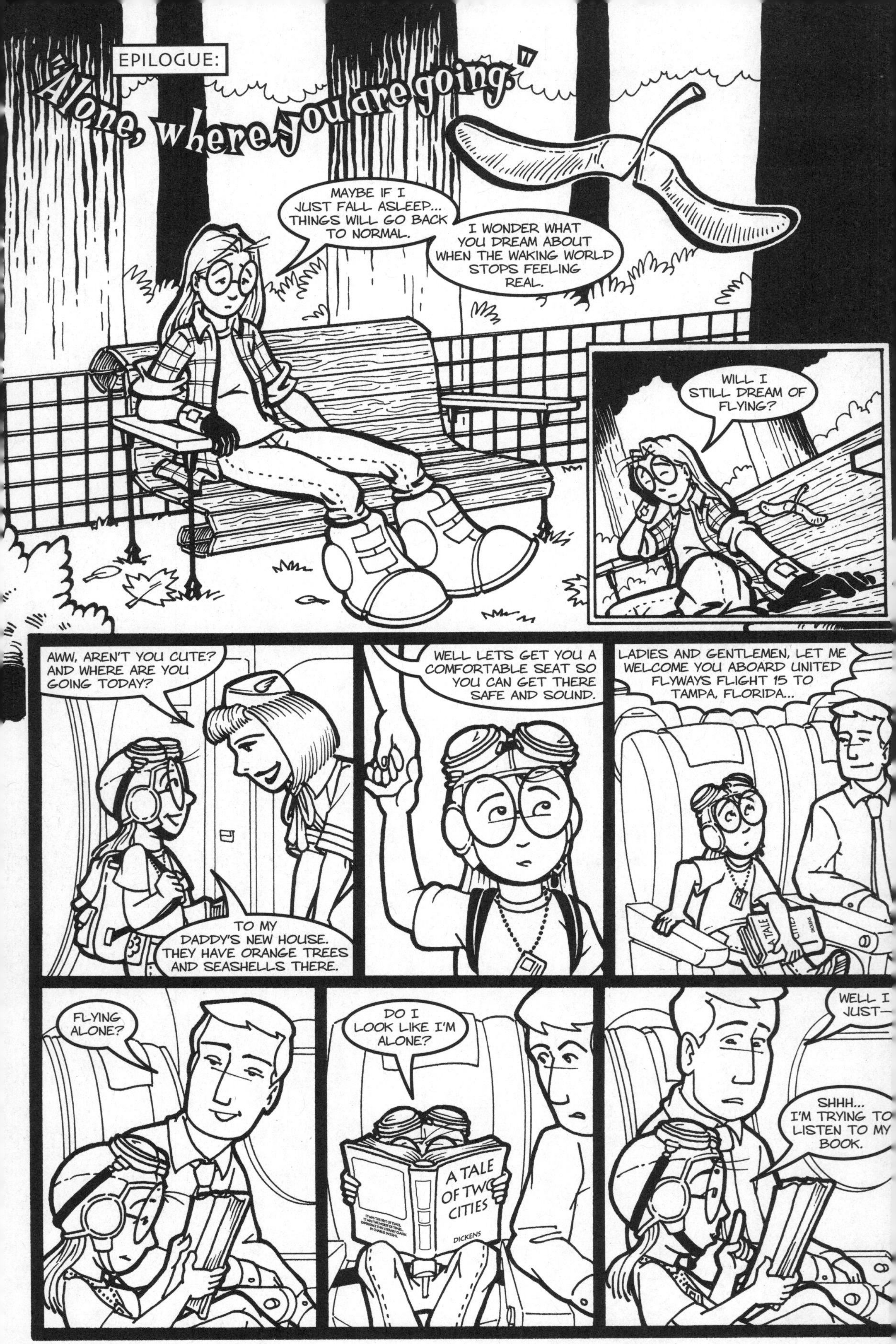

EPILOGUE:
"Alone, where you are going."
MAYBE IF I JUST FALL ASLEEP... THINGS WILL GO BACK TO NORMAL.
I WONDER WHAT YOU DREAM ABOUT WHEN THE WAKING WORLD STOPS FEELING REAL.
WILL I STILL DREAM OF FLYING?
AWW, AREN'T YOU CUTE? AND WHERE ARE YOU GOING TODAY?
TO MY DADDY'S NEW HOUSE. THEY HAVE ORANGE TREES AND SEASHELLS THERE.
WELL LETS GET YOU A COMFORTABLE SEAT SO YOU CAN GET THERE SAFE AND SOUND.
LADIES AND GENTLEMEN, LET ME WELCOME YOU ABOARD UNITED FLYWAYS FLIGHT 15 TO TAMPA, FLORIDA...
FLYING ALONE?
DO I LOOK LIKE I'M ALONE?
A TALE OF TWO CITIES
DICKENS
WELL I JUST—
SHHH... I'M TRYING TO LISTEN TO MY BOOK.

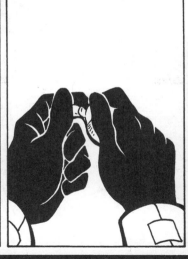

MOM, WHAT IS THIS STUFF? IT FEELS LIKE *GUTS* WITH LITTLE THINGS INSIDE...

THOSE ARE PUMPKINS SEEDS.

REALLY? IF I PLANT THEM WILL IT GROW INTO A PUMPKIN TREE?

PUMPKINS DON'T GROW ON TREES.

TOO BAD, CUZ I'D LIKE TO HAVE A PUMPKIN TREE TO CLIMB. AND ALL THE PUMPKINS ON IT CAN HAVE SCARY *JACK-O-LANTERN* FACES.

HOW COME THERE AREN'T TREES TO CLIMB HERE IN NEW YORK, MOM?

THERE ARE, IF YOU KNOW WHERE TO LOOK. BUT MOSTLY WE HAVE SKYSCRAPERS INSTEAD. YOU JUST USE *ELEVATORS* TO CLIMB THEM.

YEAH, BUT YOU CAN'T SWING ON 'EM OR JUMP OFF OF 'EM, RIGHT?

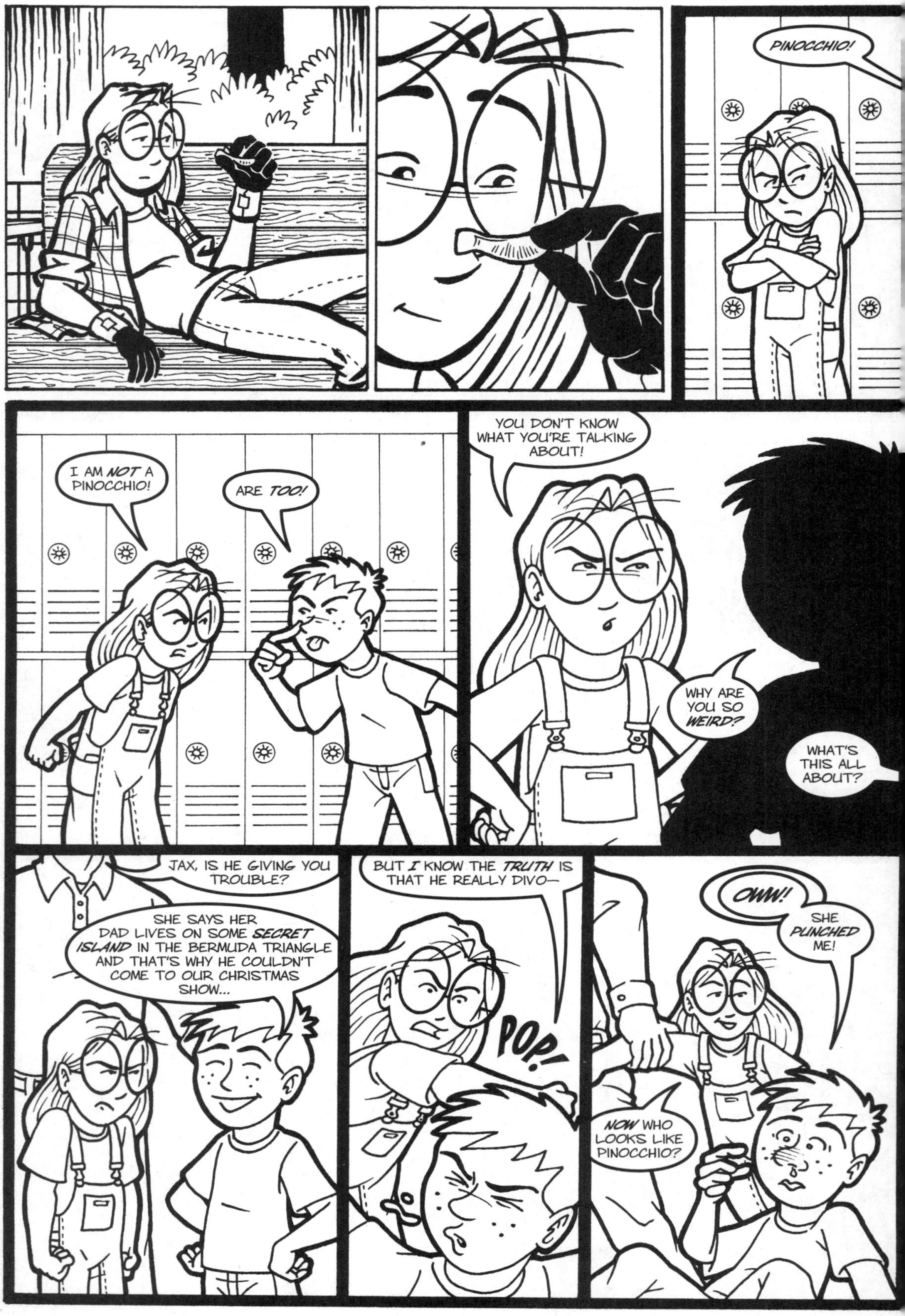
PINOCCHIO!
I AM *NOT* A PINOCCHIO!
ARE *TOO!*
YOU DON'T KNOW WHAT YOU'RE TALKING ABOUT!
WHY ARE YOU SO *WEIRD?*
WHAT'S THIS ALL ABOUT?
JAX, IS HE GIVING YOU TROUBLE?
SHE SAYS HER DAD LIVES ON SOME *SECRET ISLAND* IN THE BERMUDA TRIANGLE AND THAT'S WHY HE COULDN'T COME TO OUR CHRISTMAS SHOW...
BUT *I* KNOW THE *TRUTH* IS THAT HE REALLY DIVO—
POP!
OWW!
SHE *PUNCHED* ME!
NOW WHO LOOKS LIKE PINOCCHIO?

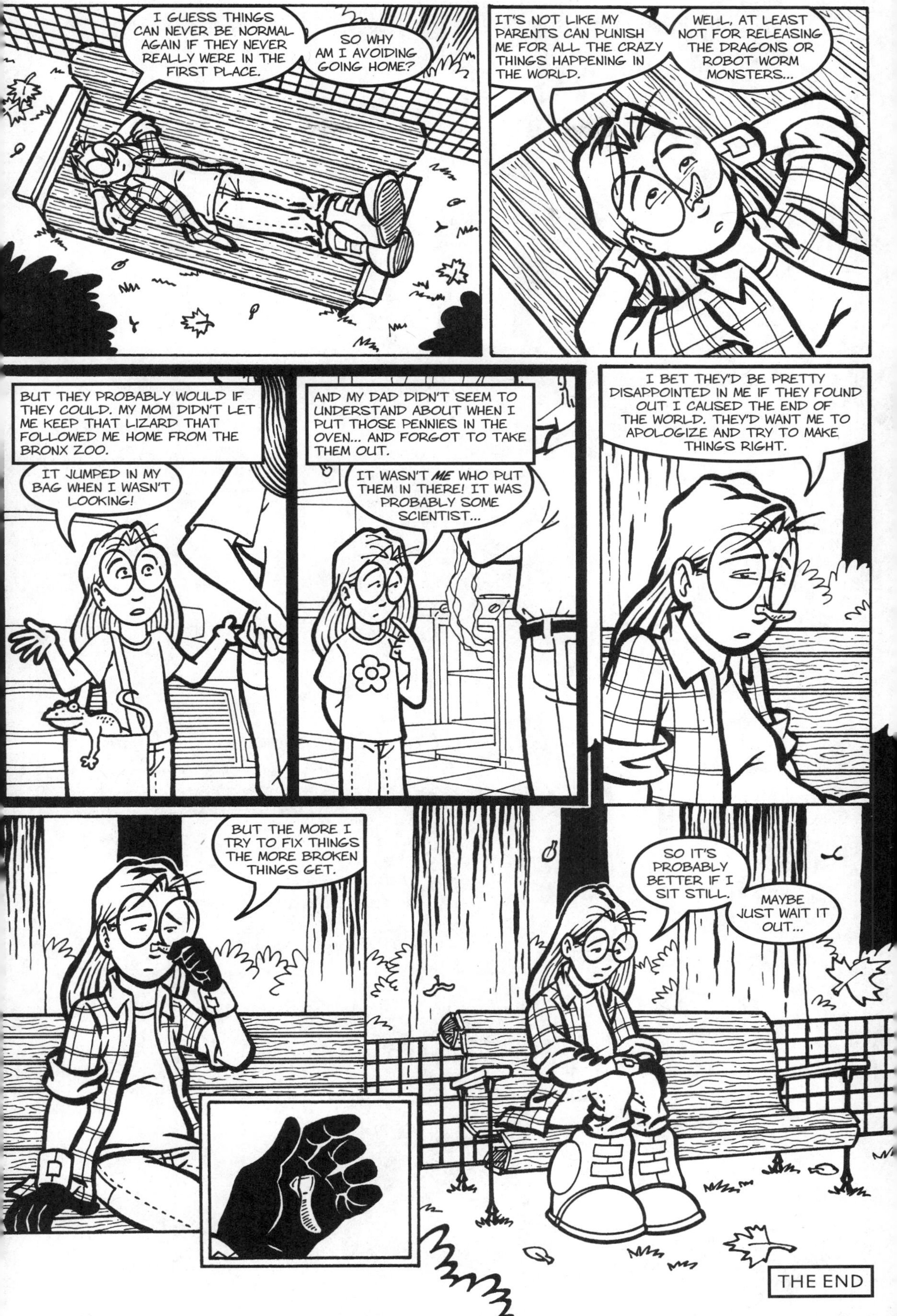

I GUESS THINGS CAN NEVER BE NORMAL AGAIN IF THEY NEVER REALLY WERE IN THE FIRST PLACE.
SO WHY AM I AVOIDING GOING HOME?
IT'S NOT LIKE MY PARENTS CAN PUNISH ME FOR ALL THE CRAZY THINGS HAPPENING IN THE WORLD.
WELL, AT LEAST NOT FOR RELEASING THE DRAGONS OR ROBOT WORM MONSTERS...
BUT THEY PROBABLY WOULD IF THEY COULD. MY MOM DIDN'T LET ME KEEP THAT LIZARD THAT FOLLOWED ME HOME FROM THE BRONX ZOO.
IT JUMPED IN MY BAG WHEN I WASN'T LOOKING!
AND MY DAD DIDN'T SEEM TO UNDERSTAND ABOUT WHEN I PUT THOSE PENNIES IN THE OVEN... AND FORGOT TO TAKE THEM OUT.
IT WASN'T *ME* WHO PUT THEM IN THERE! IT WAS PROBABLY SOME SCIENTIST...
I BET THEY'D BE PRETTY DISAPPOINTED IN ME IF THEY FOUND OUT I CAUSED THE END OF THE WORLD. THEY'D WANT ME TO APOLOGIZE AND TRY TO MAKE THINGS RIGHT.
BUT THE MORE I TRY TO FIX THINGS THE MORE BROKEN THINGS GET.
SO IT'S PROBABLY BETTER IF I SIT STILL.
MAYBE JUST WAIT IT OUT...
THE END

forbidden TREATS

DAVE ROMAN

DAVE by dave

Although Dave Roman has always existed throughout time, this particular manifestation of him was created in May 1977 (to coincide with the release of the original *STAR WARS*). Dave decided he wanted to make his own comic books very early in life after realizing he couldn't afford the expensive equipment needed for animation or film. With comics, all he needed was a Bic pen, access to a photo copier and a big stapler. Best of all, getting into comics was a great way to meet girls.

Dave studied the Art of Happiness (also known as Cartooning) at the School of Invisible Arts. He's worked freelance for 181 Productions, a stop motion/puppet animation studio owned by award winning animator Becky Wible, and for DC Comics where he got paid to answer Scooby-Doo's fan mail. Currently Dave works for *Nickelodeon Magazine* and is the comics editor for their Nick Mag Specials. He has also written stories for DC Comics' *Dexter's Laboratory* including "Chicken Scratch" which inspired the short film that debuted in front of *The Powerpuff Girls Movie*.

Dave's own illustrated work appears on the website www.realmsend.com and recently in *Alternative Comics 9-11: Emergency Relief* as well as several mini-comics including *Keep Warm* , *Go Tortoise Boy Go!* and *Astronaut Elementary*.

Dave's turn ons are: long walks in the park, cold mornings under the blanket covers and late night cereal binges. His pet peeves are: smoking, people who don't watch cartoons and having to be awake.

Bust: 32 Waist: 22 Hips: 32

JOHN GREEN

John Patrick Green was born on Long Island, NY on March 20th, 1975. Like many children of the late seventies his biggest influence growing up was *Star Wars*. John also fell in love with comic books early on in life, but stopped reading them in the late eighties when he reached his mutant crossover limit. With little access to independent and alternative comic books, John's love for comics went dormant.

John majored in Graphic Design at Manhattan's School of Visual Arts. During those years he met Dave Roman and Rich Zimmer, who were soon-to-be-students at SVA. Their love of the comics medium ignited a flame in the big, black, sucking void that John's love for comics had previously become. The three formed Cryptic Press and began publishing their own comic books.

After working on books such as *Melon Head, Tyrant: KM-67*, and his own creation *Hellbent,* John wanted to work on a project that would break new ground, expand his horizons... all that creative-type mumbo-jumbo. That opportunity came along when he had to illustrate a full length comic for Klaus Janson's visual storytelling class. So, joining up with Dave, the two created *Quicken Forbidden*. Years later, the duo would make history with *Teen Boat*.

JOHN by john

John currently resides in New York City. There he does freelance illustration, design and comic book production, writes and colors numerous comics for *Disney Adventures,* and letters the occassional story for *Nickelodeon Magazine*. He watches way too many movies and has way too many Legos.

Quicken FORBIDDEN ™

"A GUIDE TO JAX EPOCH"

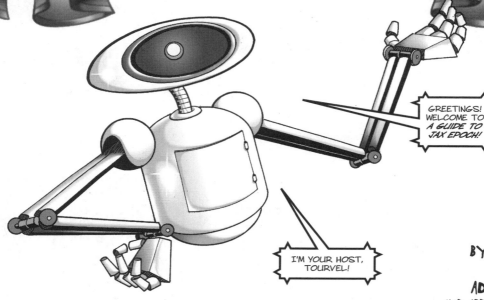

GREETINGS! WELCOME TO A GUIDE TO JAX EPOCH!

I'M YOUR HOST, TOURVEL!

BY JOHN GREE
DAVE ROMA
ADAM DEKRAKER
AND STU CHAIFET

TODAY WE'LL WITNESS JAX IN ACTION DURING AN EARLY EXPLOIT, EXAMINE WHAT MAKES JAX WHO SHE IS, AND WATCH HER HER MAKE USE OF HER ABILITIES IN A SKILLED AND RESPONSIBLE MANNER.

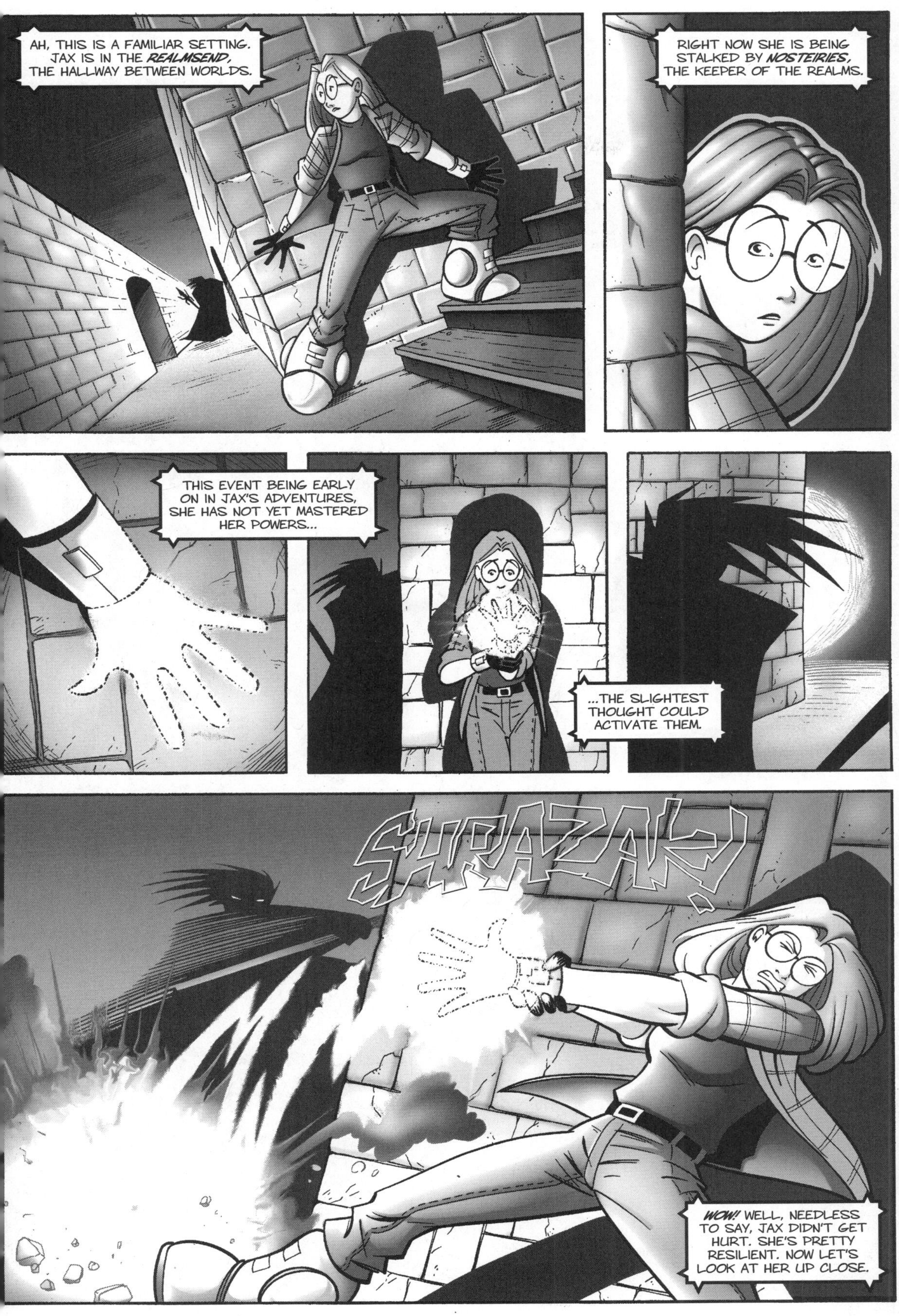
AH, THIS IS A FAMILIAR SETTING. JAX IS IN THE REALMSEND, THE HALLWAY BETWEEN WORLDS.
RIGHT NOW SHE IS BEING STALKED BY NOSTEIRIES, THE KEEPER OF THE REALMS.
THIS EVENT BEING EARLY ON IN JAX'S ADVENTURES, SHE HAS NOT YET MASTERED HER POWERS...
...THE SLIGHTEST THOUGHT COULD ACTIVATE THEM.
SHRAZAK!
WOW! WELL, NEEDLESS TO SAY, JAX DIDN'T GET HURT. SHE'S PRETTY RESILIENT. NOW LET'S LOOK AT HER UP CLOSE.

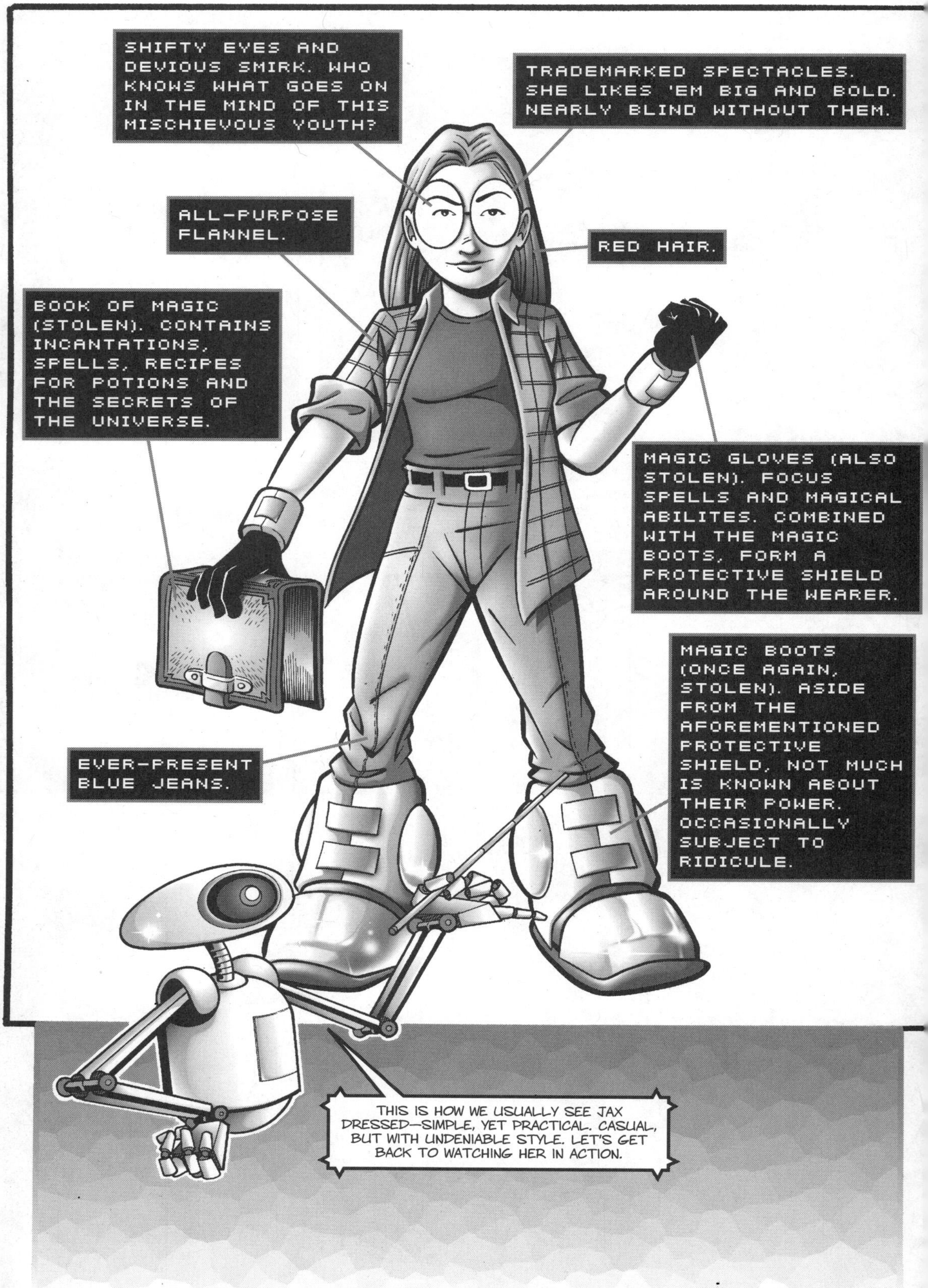

SHIFTY EYES AND DEVIOUS SMIRK. WHO KNOWS WHAT GOES ON IN THE MIND OF THIS MISCHIEVOUS YOUTH?
TRADEMARKED SPECTACLES. SHE LIKES 'EM BIG AND BOLD. NEARLY BLIND WITHOUT THEM.
ALL-PURPOSE FLANNEL.
RED HAIR.
BOOK OF MAGIC (STOLEN). CONTAINS INCANTATIONS, SPELLS, RECIPES FOR POTIONS AND THE SECRETS OF THE UNIVERSE.
MAGIC GLOVES (ALSO STOLEN). FOCUS SPELLS AND MAGICAL ABILITES. COMBINED WITH THE MAGIC BOOTS, FORM A PROTECTIVE SHIELD AROUND THE WEARER.
MAGIC BOOTS (ONCE AGAIN, STOLEN). ASIDE FROM THE AFOREMENTIONED PROTECTIVE SHIELD, NOT MUCH IS KNOWN ABOUT THEIR POWER. OCCASIONALLY SUBJECT TO RIDICULE.
EVER-PRESENT BLUE JEANS.
THIS IS HOW WE USUALLY SEE JAX DRESSED—SIMPLE, YET PRACTICAL. CASUAL, BUT WITH UNDENIABLE STYLE. LET'S GET BACK TO WATCHING HER IN ACTION.

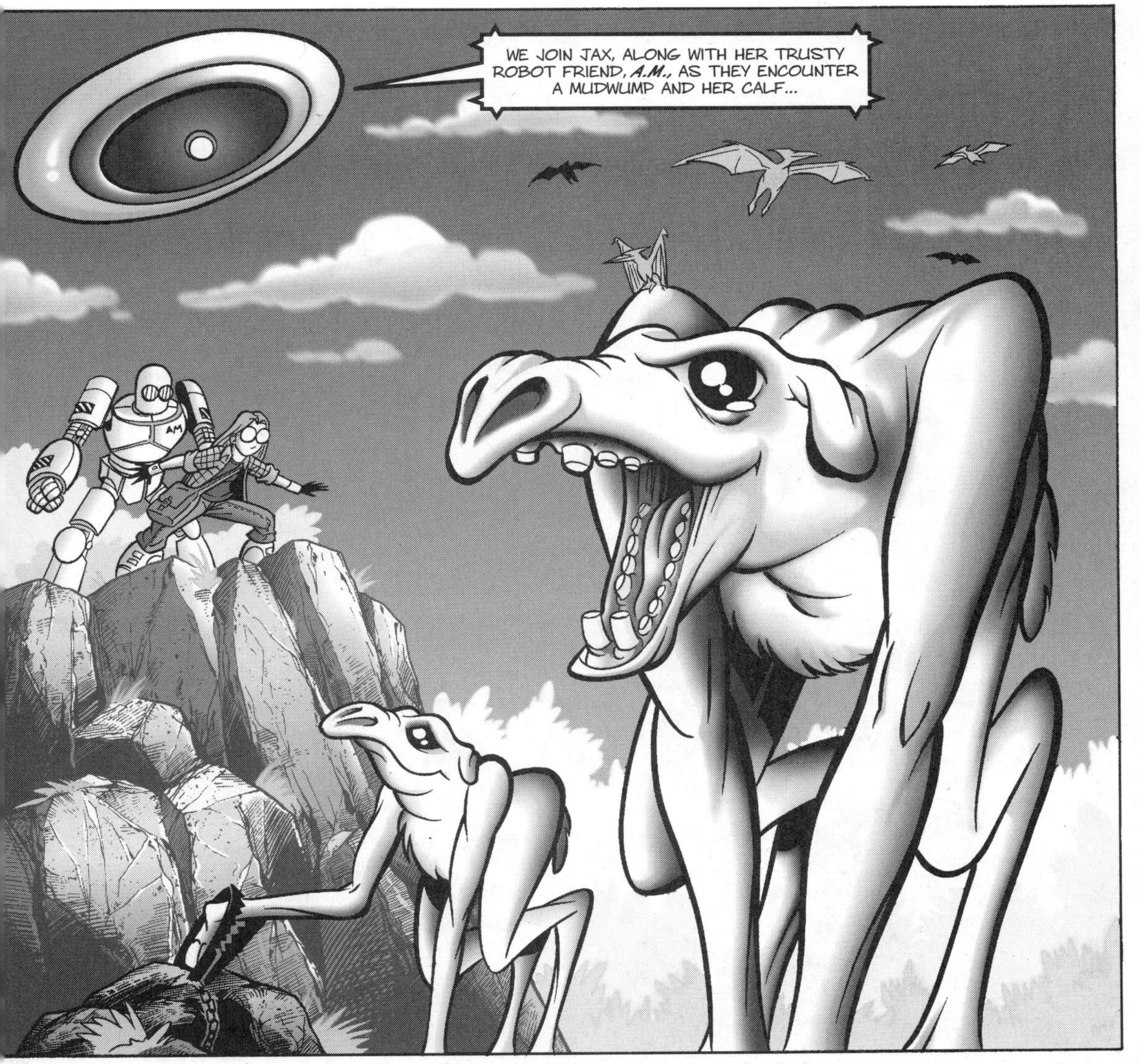
WE JOIN JAX, ALONG WITH HER TRUSTY ROBOT FRIEND, ***A.M.,*** AS THEY ENCOUNTER A MUDWUMP AND HER CALF...
AM

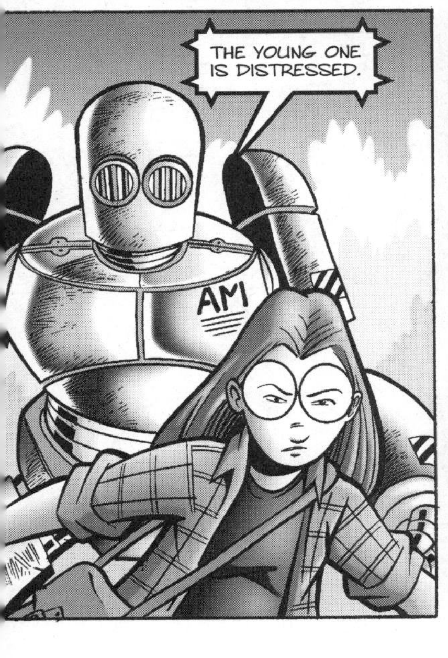
THE YOUNG ONE IS DISTRESSED.
AM

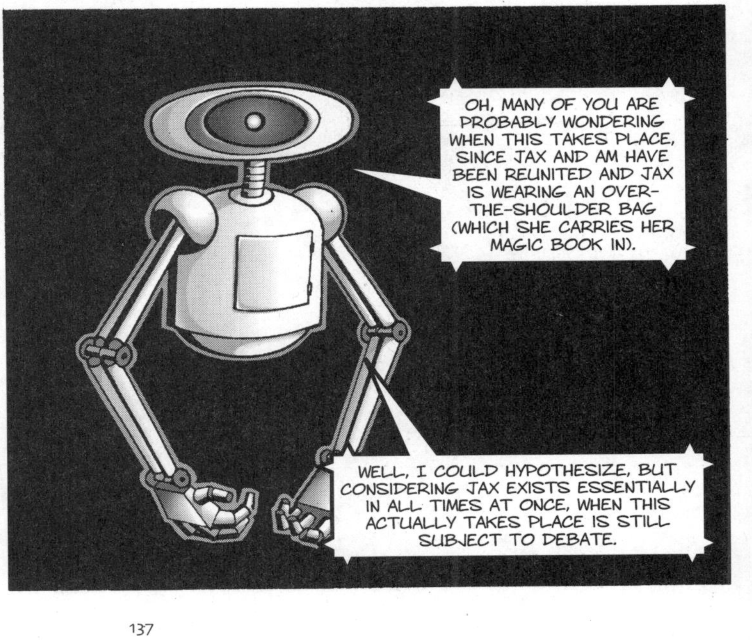
OH, MANY OF YOU ARE PROBABLY WONDERING WHEN THIS TAKES PLACE, SINCE JAX AND AM HAVE BEEN REUNITED AND JAX IS WEARING AN OVER-THE-SHOULDER BAG (WHICH SHE CARRIES HER MAGIC BOOK IN).
WELL, I COULD HYPOTHESIZE, BUT CONSIDERING JAX EXISTS ESSENTIALLY IN ALL TIMES AT ONCE, WHEN THIS ACTUALLY TAKES PLACE IS STILL SUBJECT TO DEBATE.

SHOULD WE ASSIST?

YEAH, YOU JUST WAIT HERE AND I'LL SET HIM FREE.

EASY, EASY— THERE!

DARN POACHERS. I CAN'T BELIEVE THEY'D DO THIS TO SUCH A PEACEFUL ANIMAL.

OF COURSE, NONE OF THIS WOULD HAVE HAPPENED IF IT WEREN'T FOR ME.

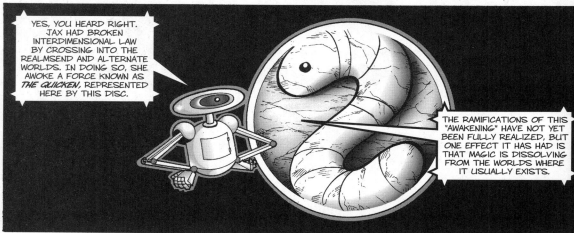

YES, YOU HEARD RIGHT. JAX HAD BROKEN INTERDIMENSIONAL LAW BY CROSSING INTO THE REALMSEND AND ALTERNATE WORLDS. IN DOING SO, SHE AWOKE A FORCE KNOWN AS *THE QUICKEN*, REPRESENTED HERE BY THIS DISC.

THE RAMIFICATIONS OF THIS "AWAKENING" HAVE NOT YET BEEN FULLY REALIZED, BUT ONE EFFECT IT HAS HAD IS THAT MAGIC IS DISSOLVING FROM THE WORLDS WHERE IT USUALLY EXISTS.

IT'S MY FAULT THESE CREATURES AREN'T THOUGHT OF AS MYSTICAL ANYMORE. NO LONGER FEARED... NO LONGER SACRED.

AND BECAUSE OF THAT, POACHERS TRAP THEM FOR THEIR TUSKS.

USUALLY THEY'RE KILLED. I GUESS THIS ONE WAS LUCKY.

THERE WE GO! GOOD THING I FINALLY GOT A HANG OF THAT REGENERATION SPELL.

AW... BEAUTIFUL THING, AIN'T IT, A.M.?

YUP! AND WITH ORDER RESTORED, I, JAX EPOCH, BECOME SAVIOR OF THE WOR—

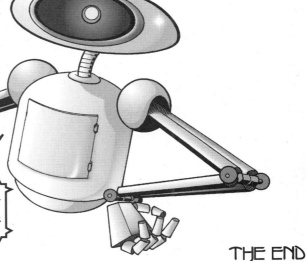

AND OFF THEY GO TO ANOTHER DIMENSION! WHERE WILL THEY END UP? WHERE WILL JAX'S NEXT ADVENTURE TAKE US? WHO KNOWS!

WHAT IS FOR SURE IS THAT WE'VE RUN OUT OF TIME. PLEASE JOIN US AGAIN SOMETIME. THIS IS TOURVEL, SIGNING OFF.

THE END

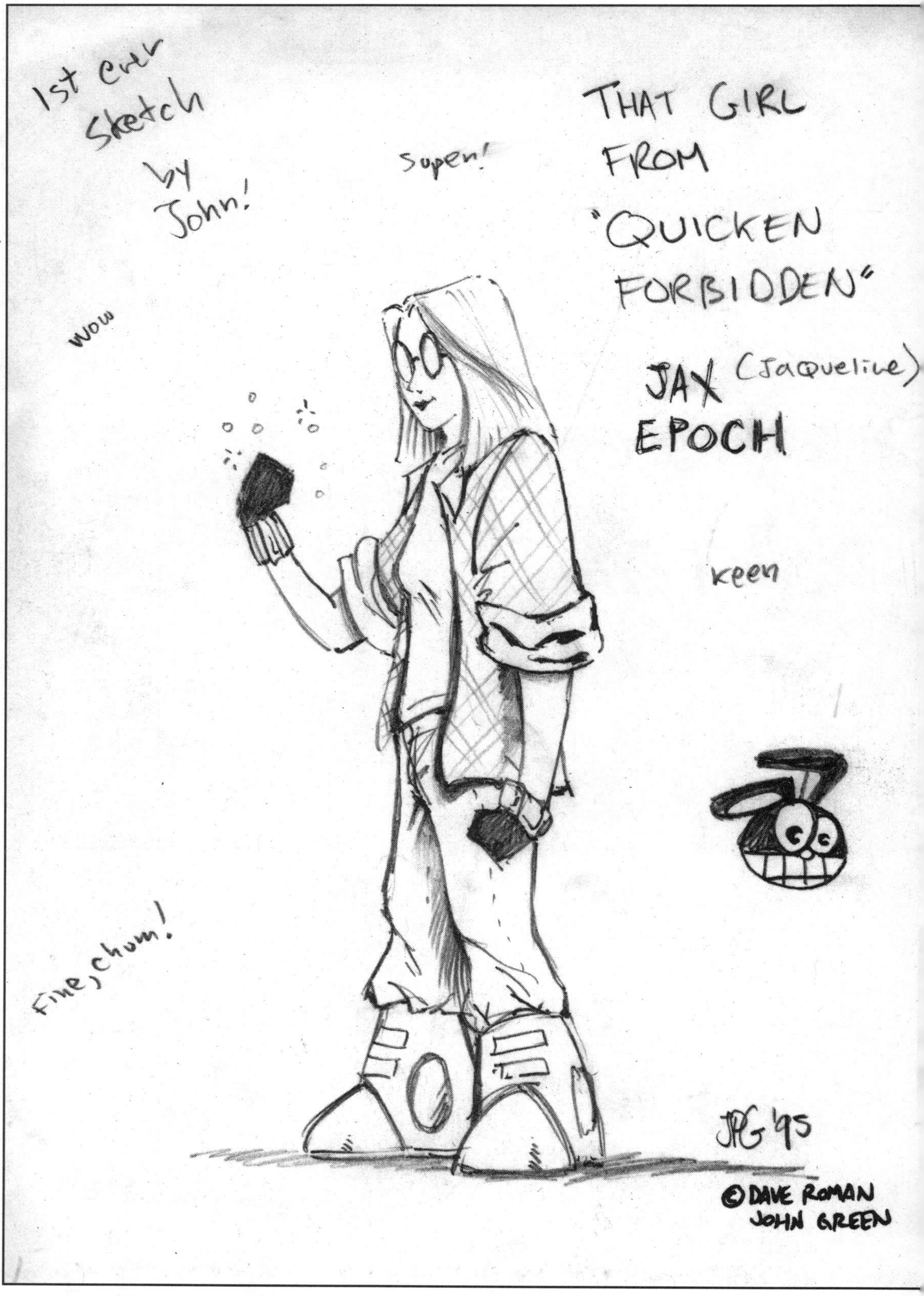

1st ever Sketch by John!
Super!
THAT GIRL FROM "QUICKEN FORBIDDEN"
JAX (Jaqueline) EPOCH
wow
keen
Fine, chum!
JPG '95
© DAVE ROMAN JOHN GREEN

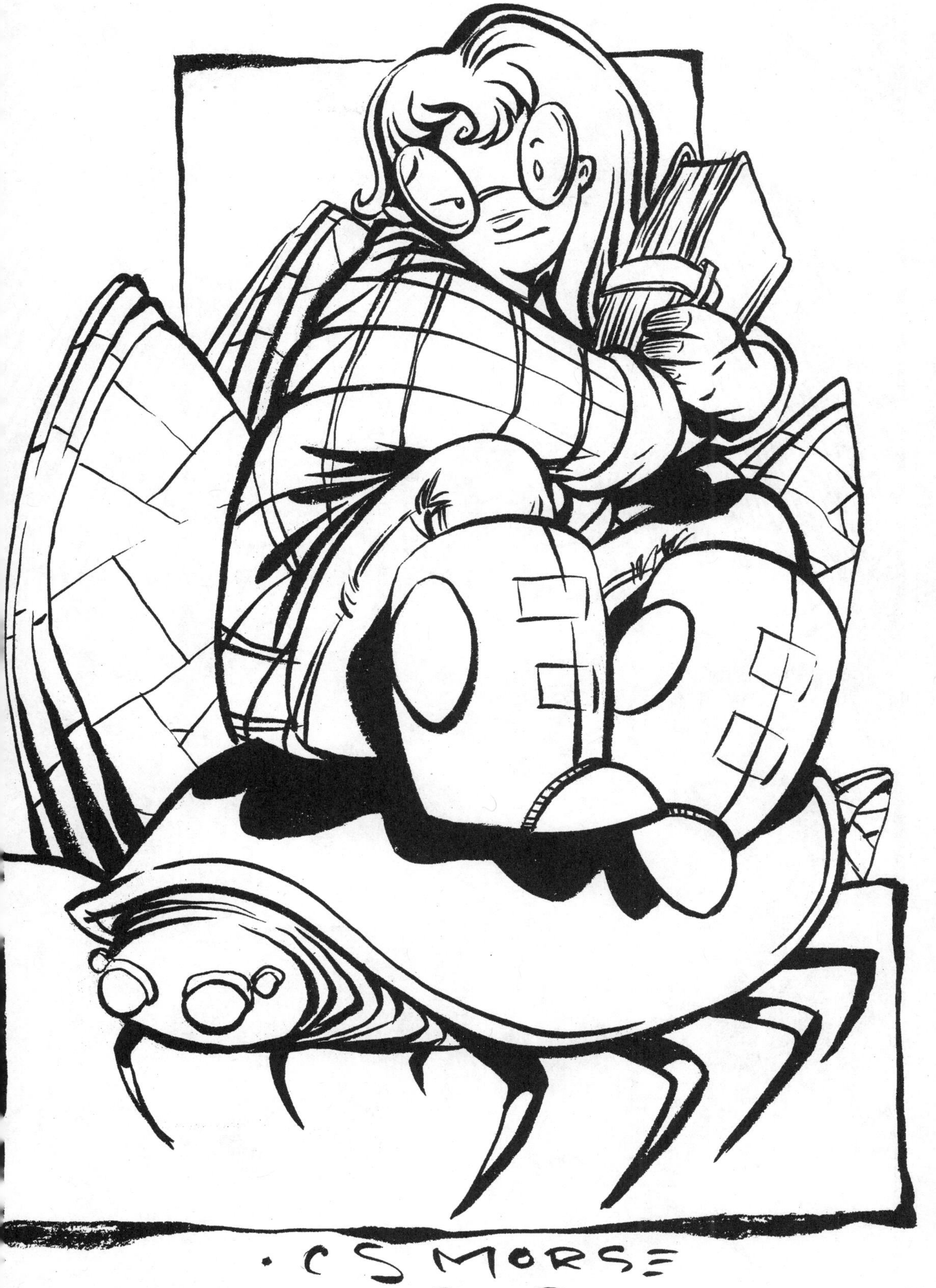
C S MORSE
1997

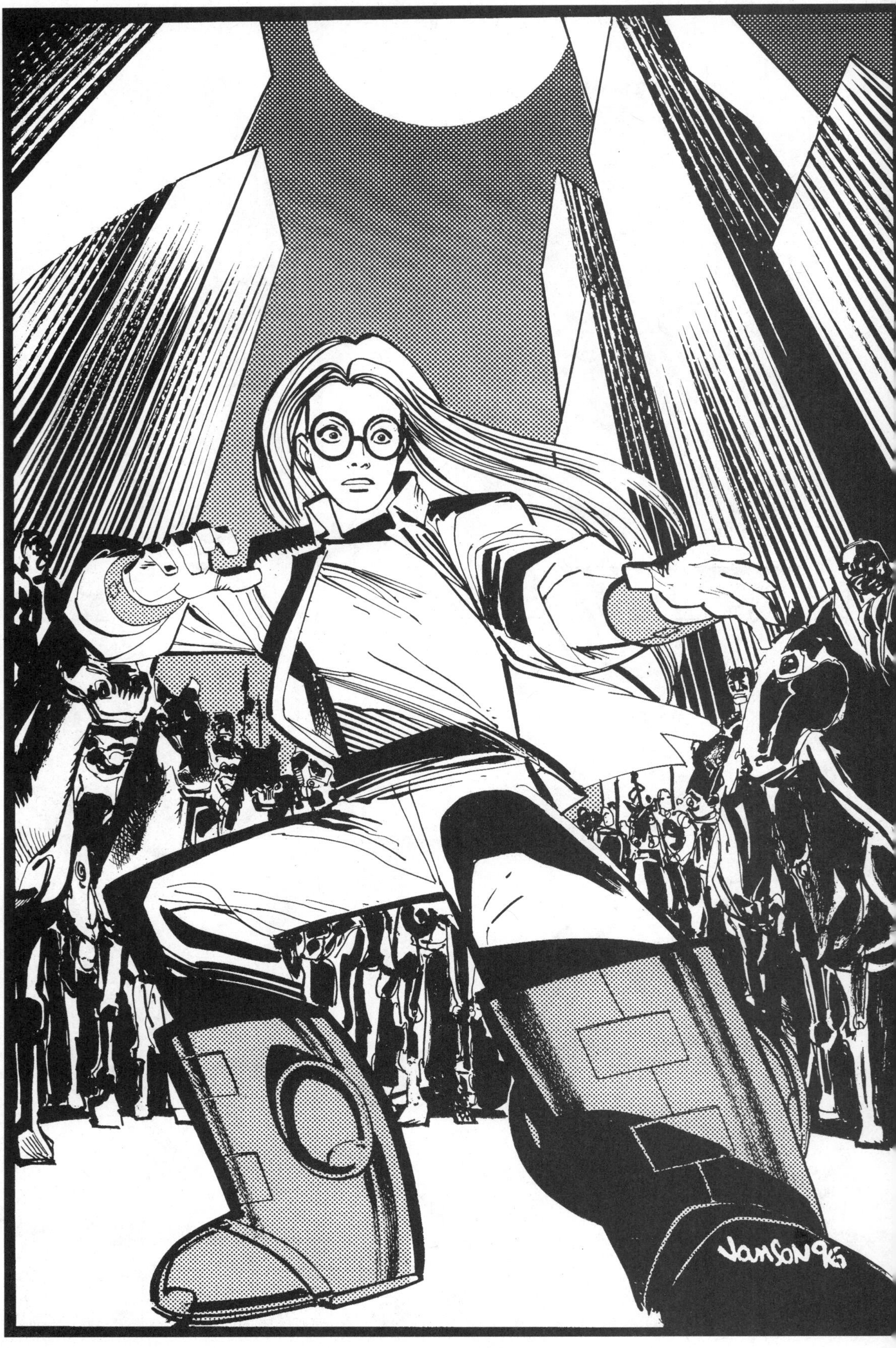
JANSON 95

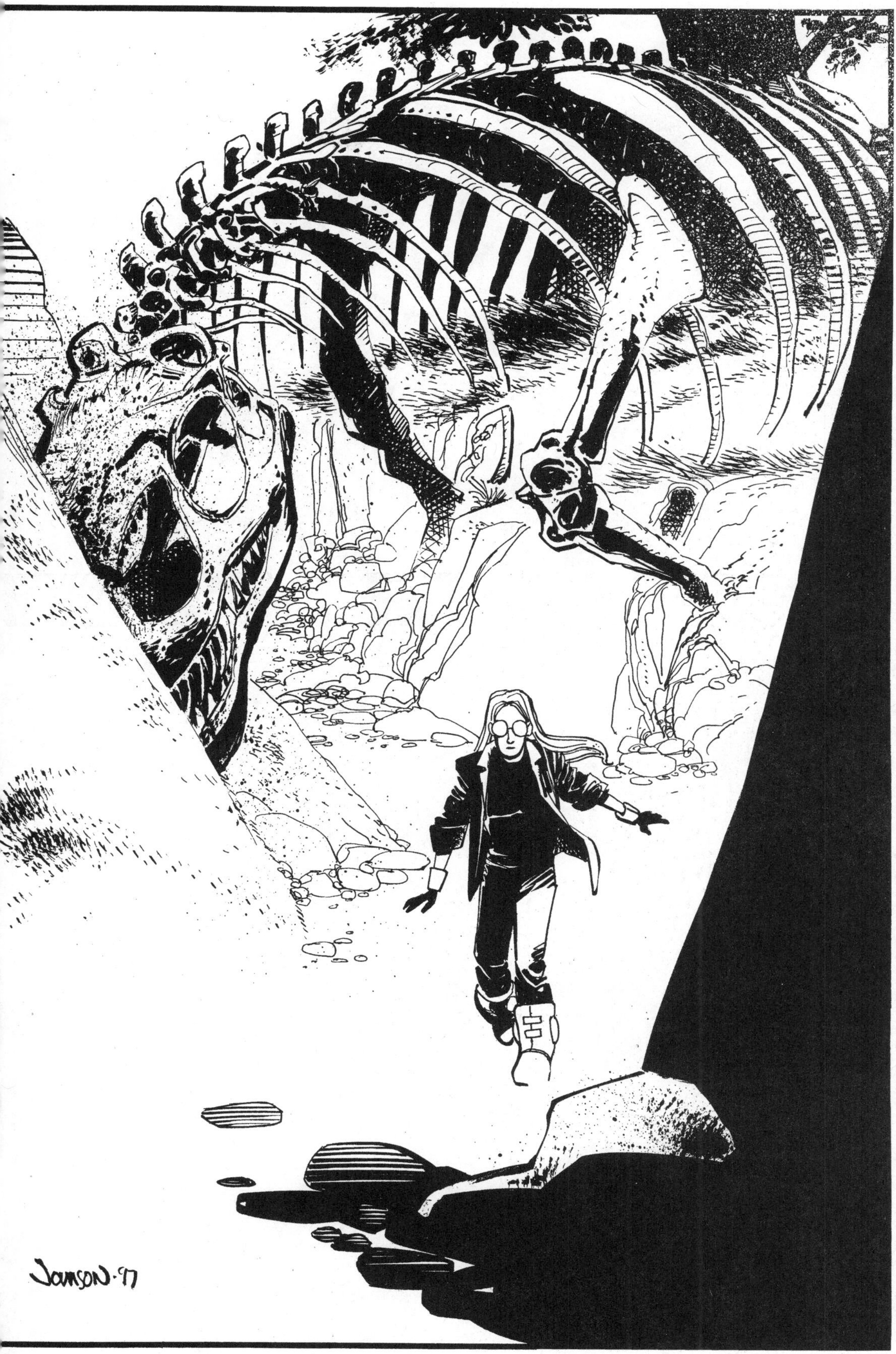
Jonson·97

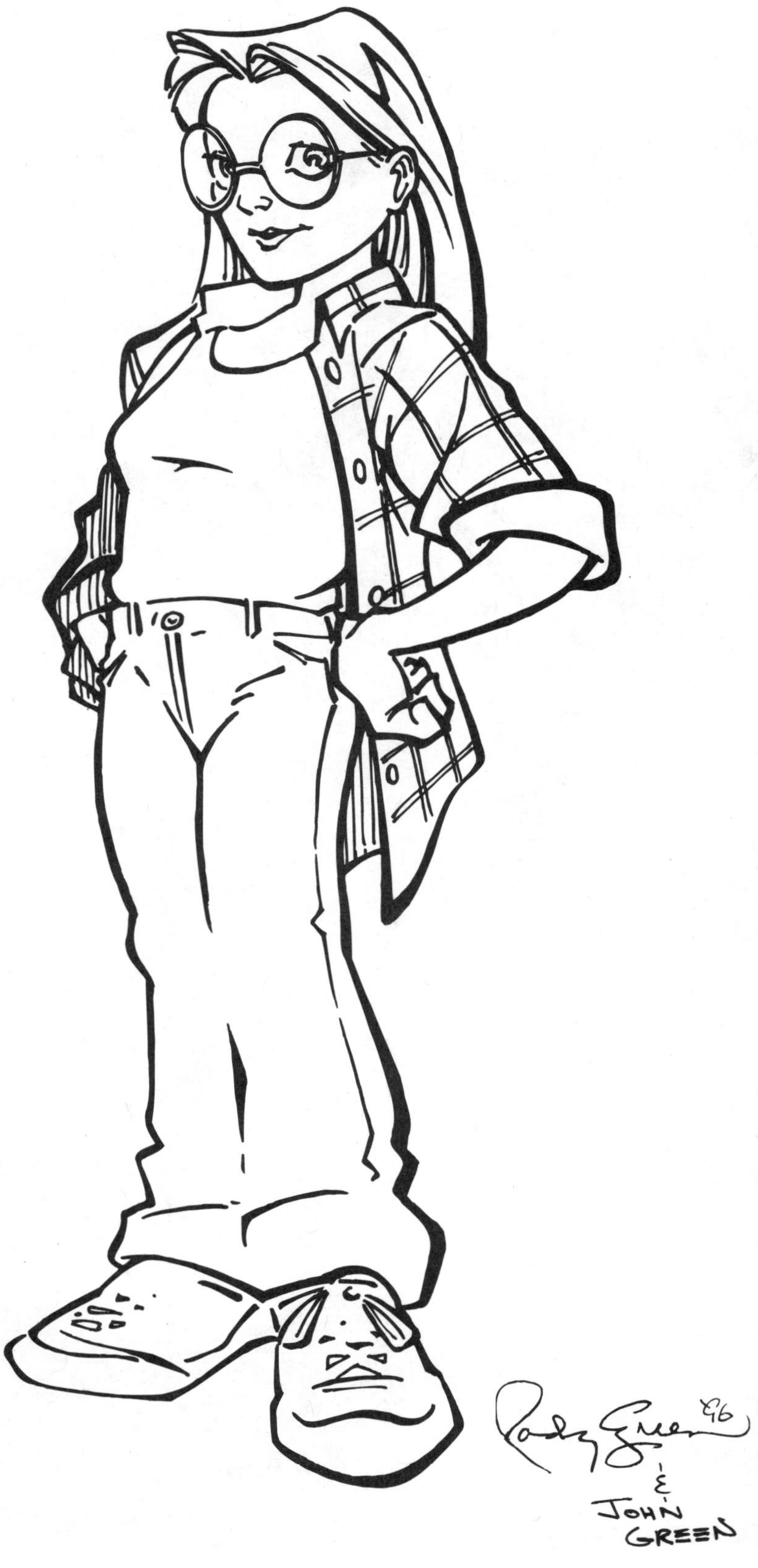
'96
&
JOHN
GREEN

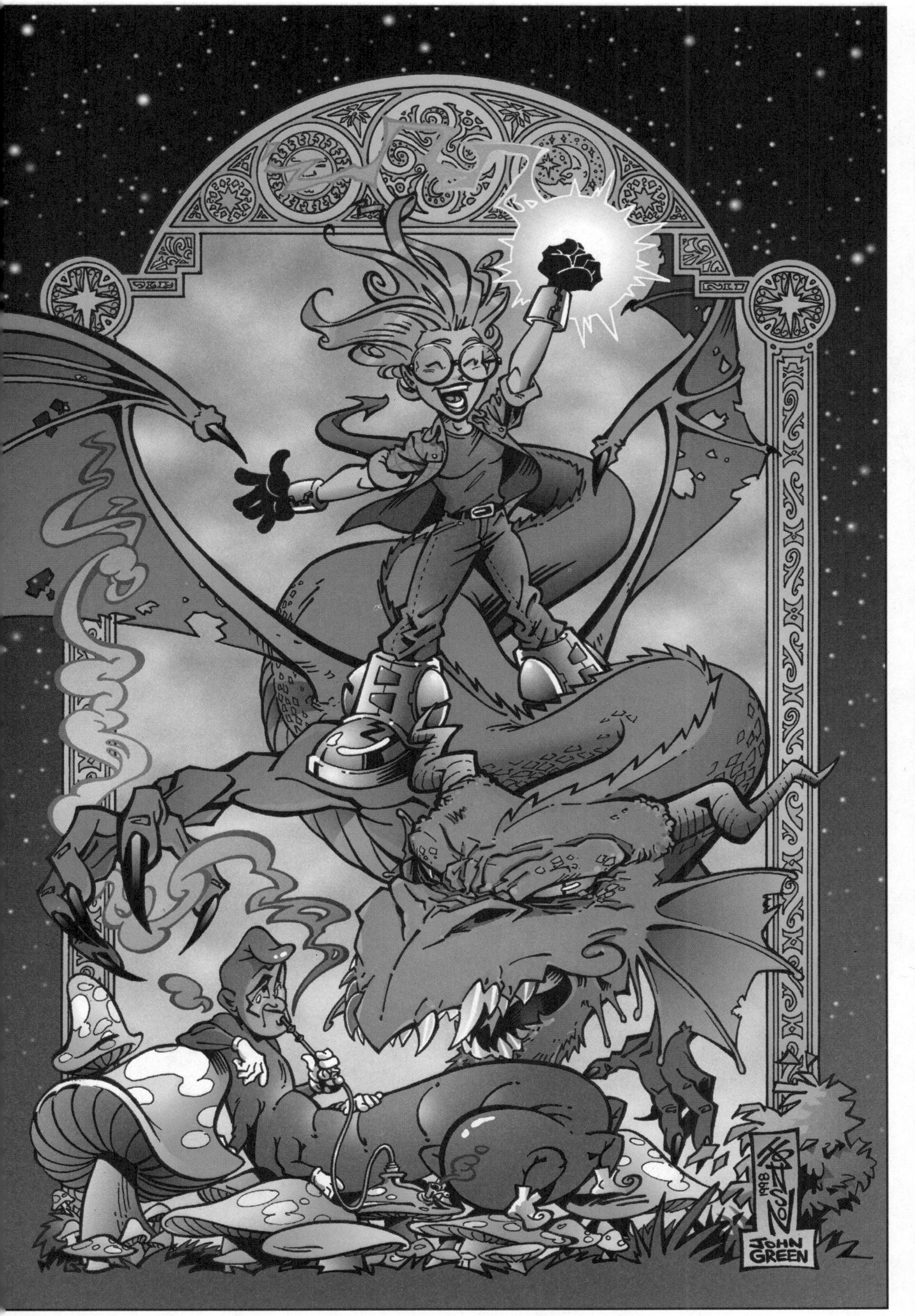
JOHN
GREEN

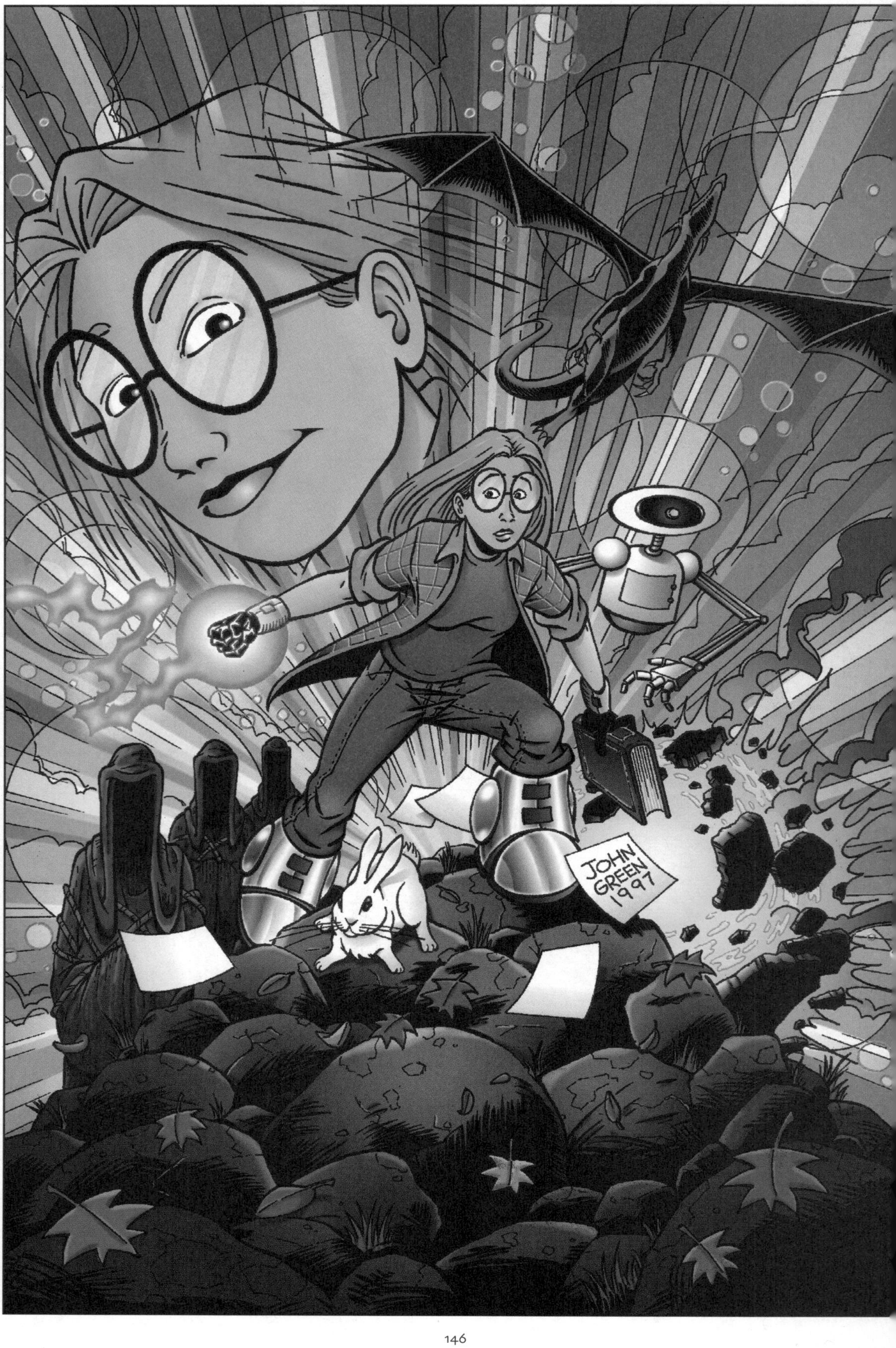
JOHN GREEN 1997

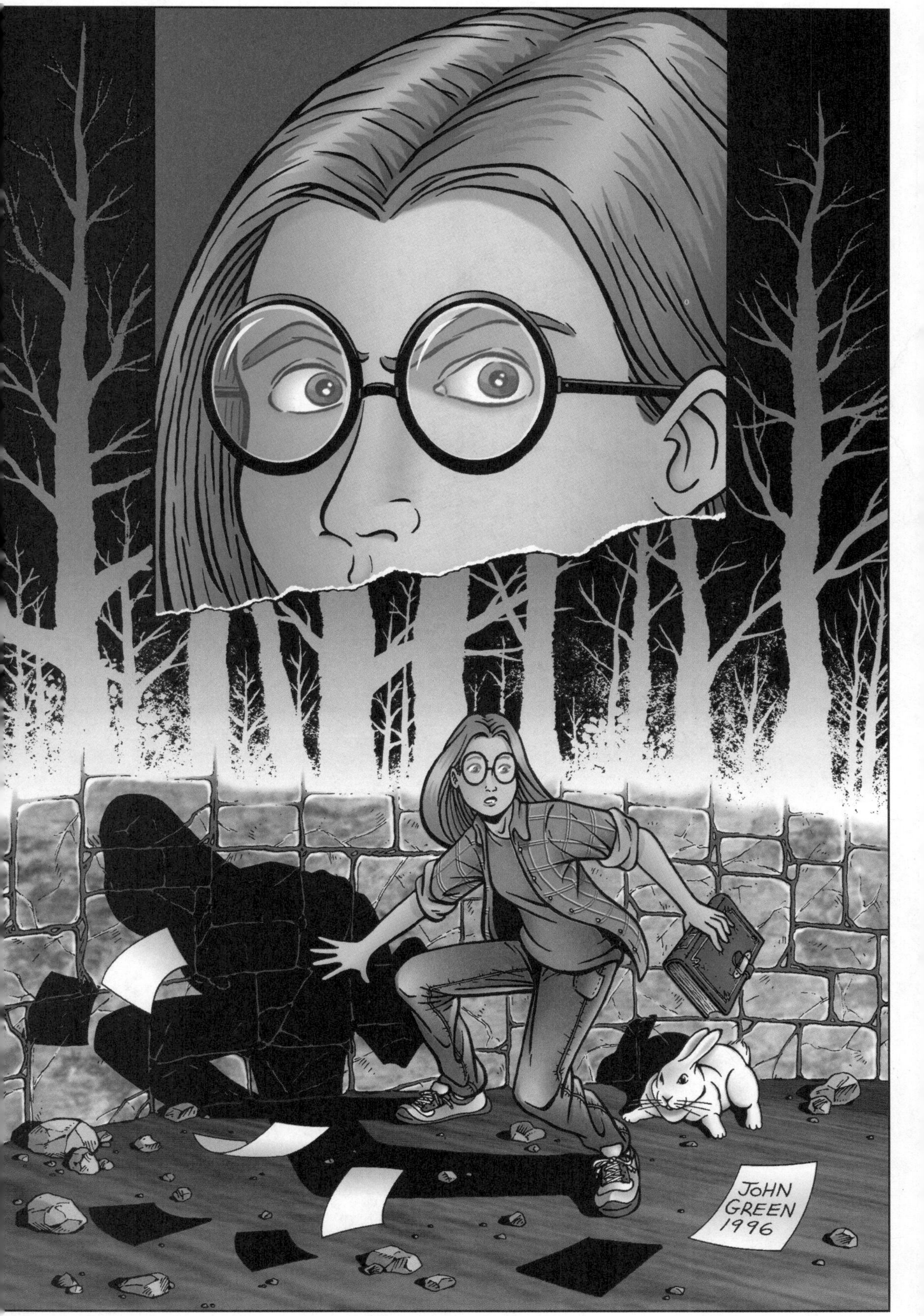
JOHN
GREEN
1996

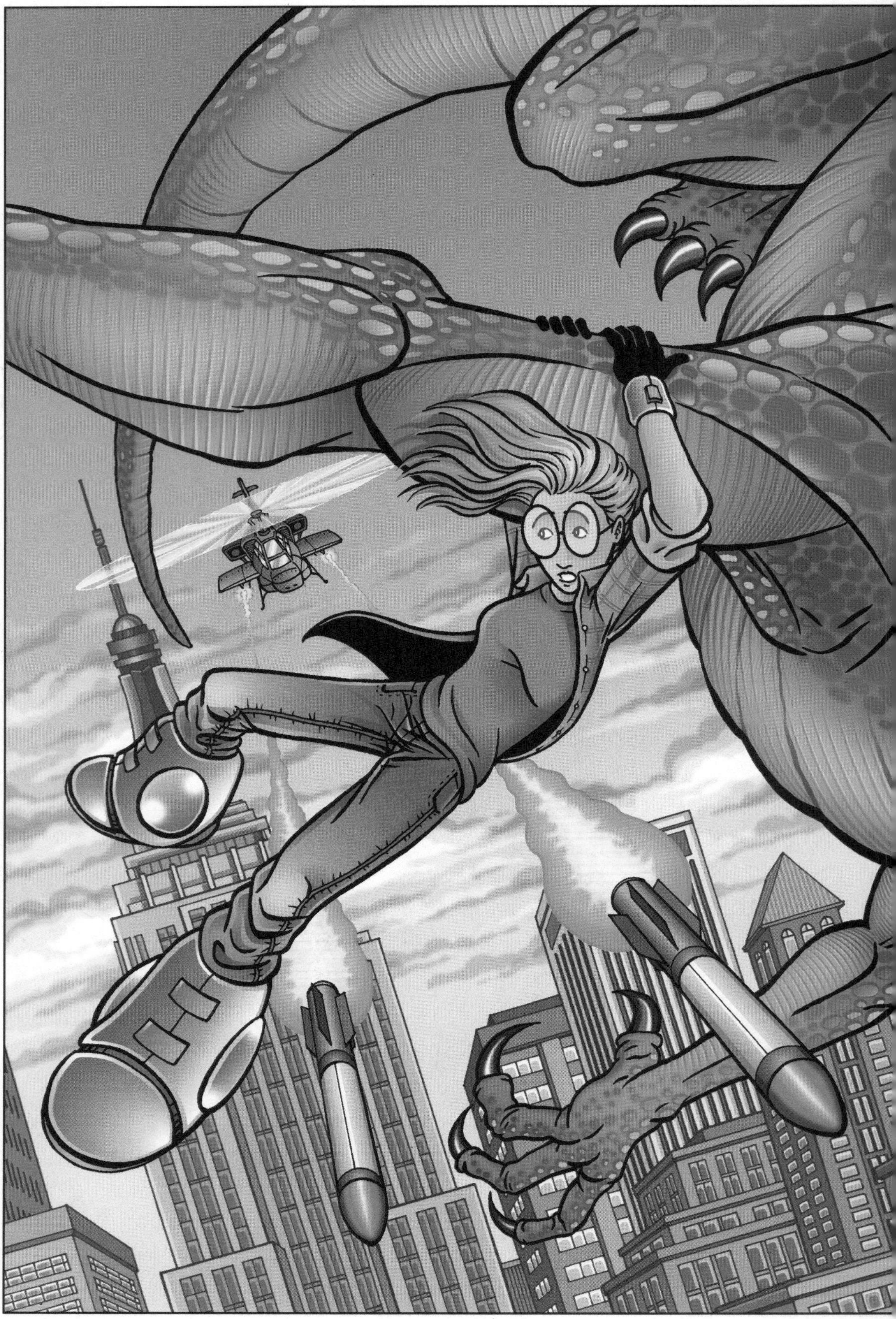

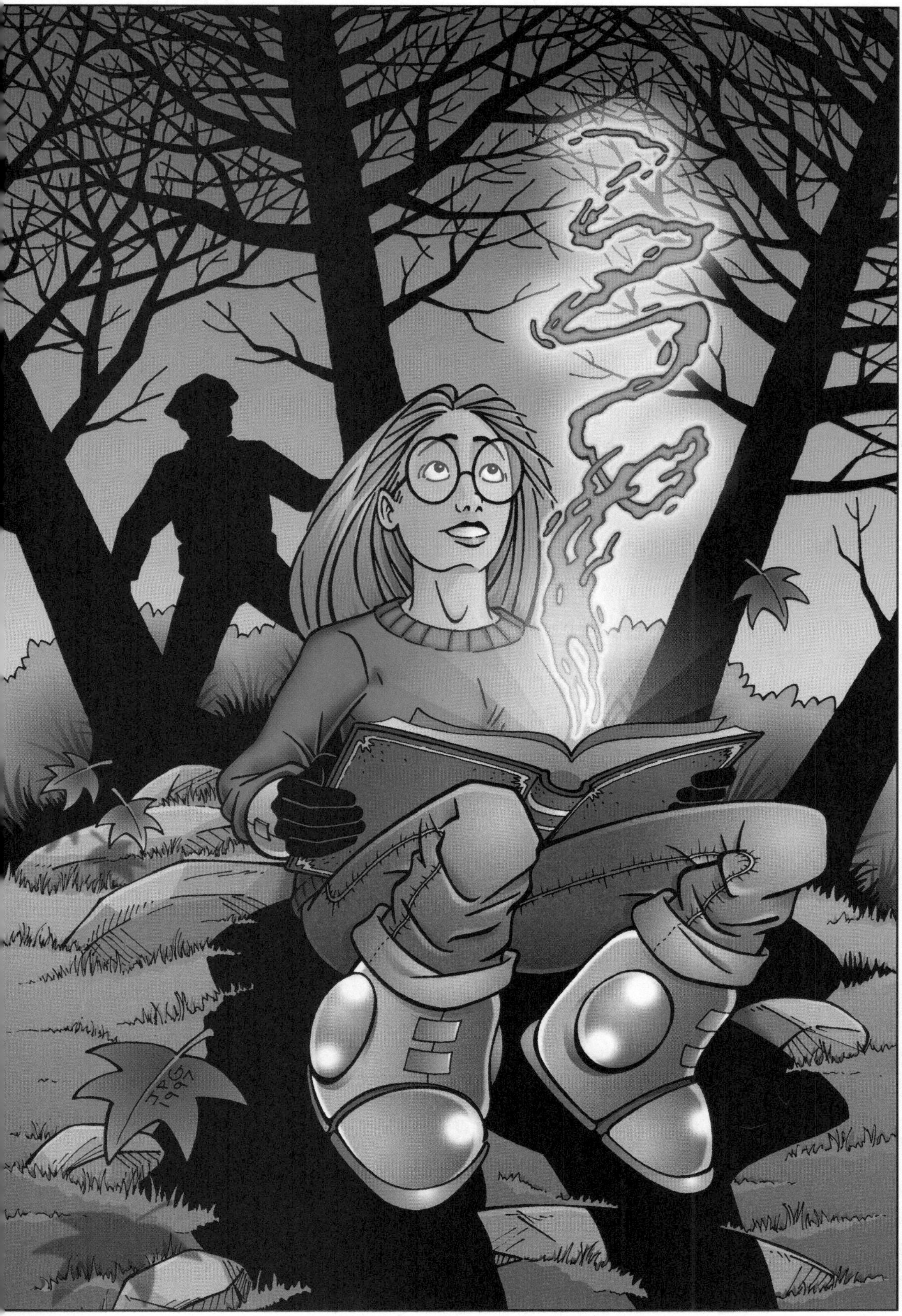

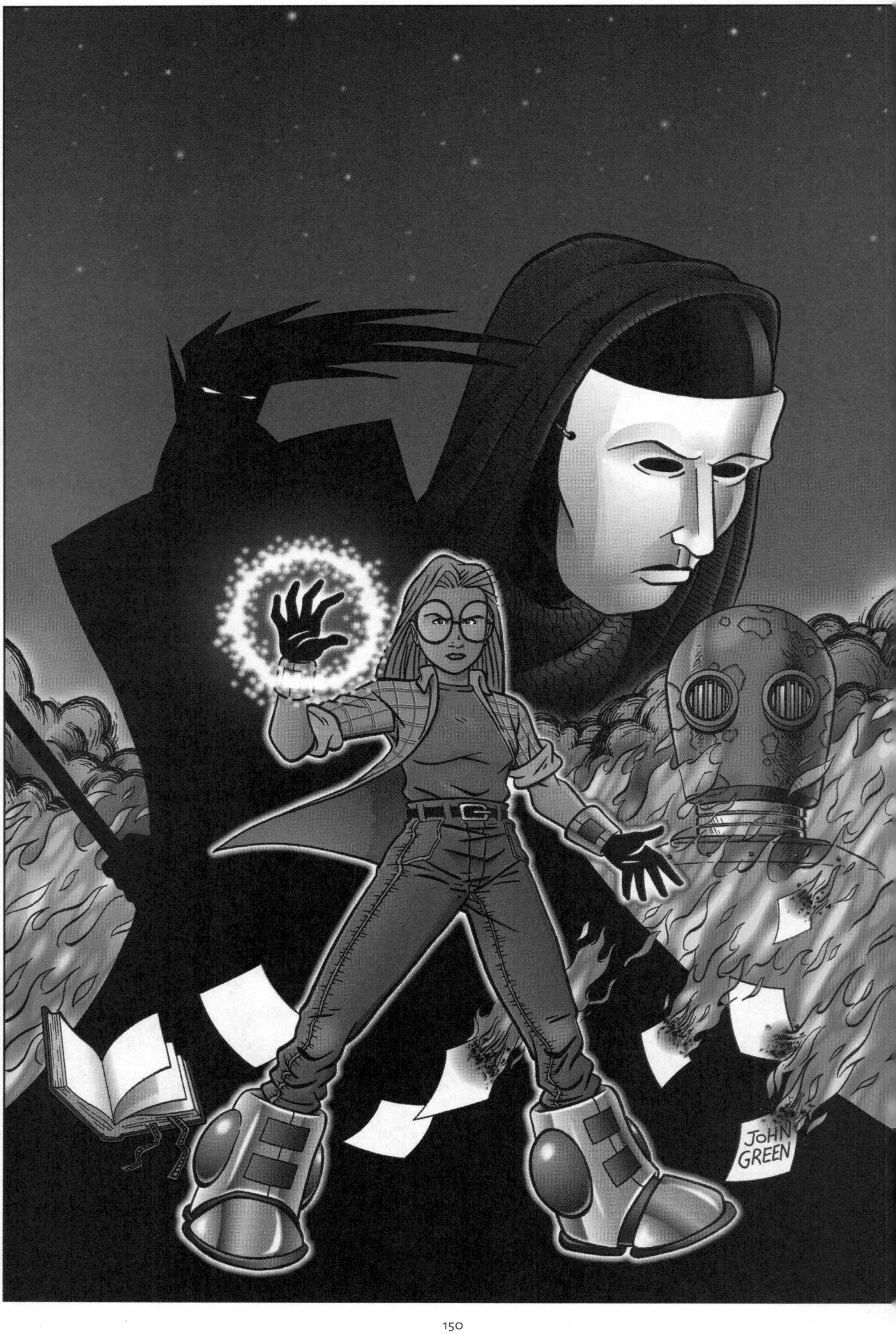
JOHN GREEN

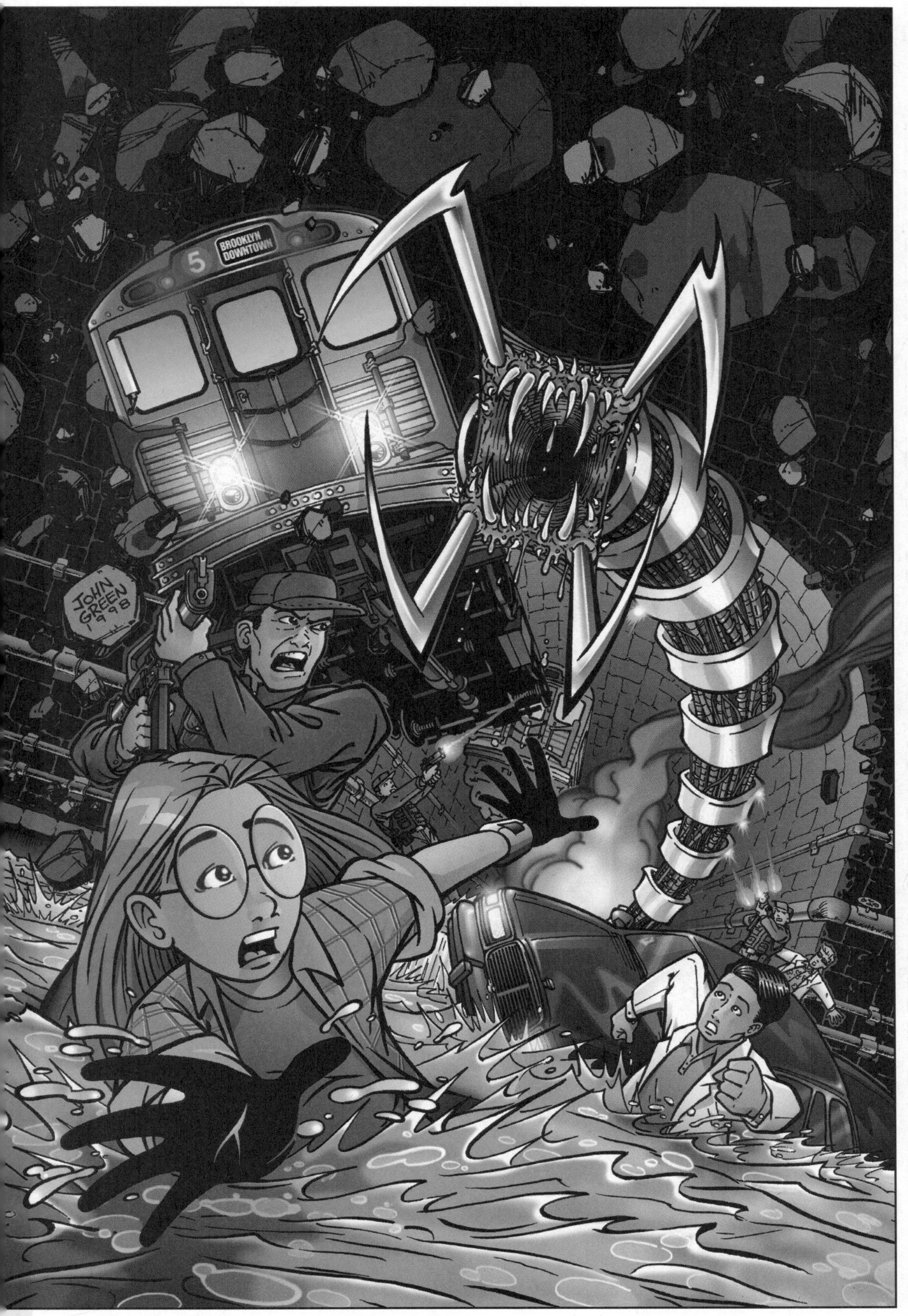
5
BROOKLYN DOWNTOWN
JOHN GREEN 1998

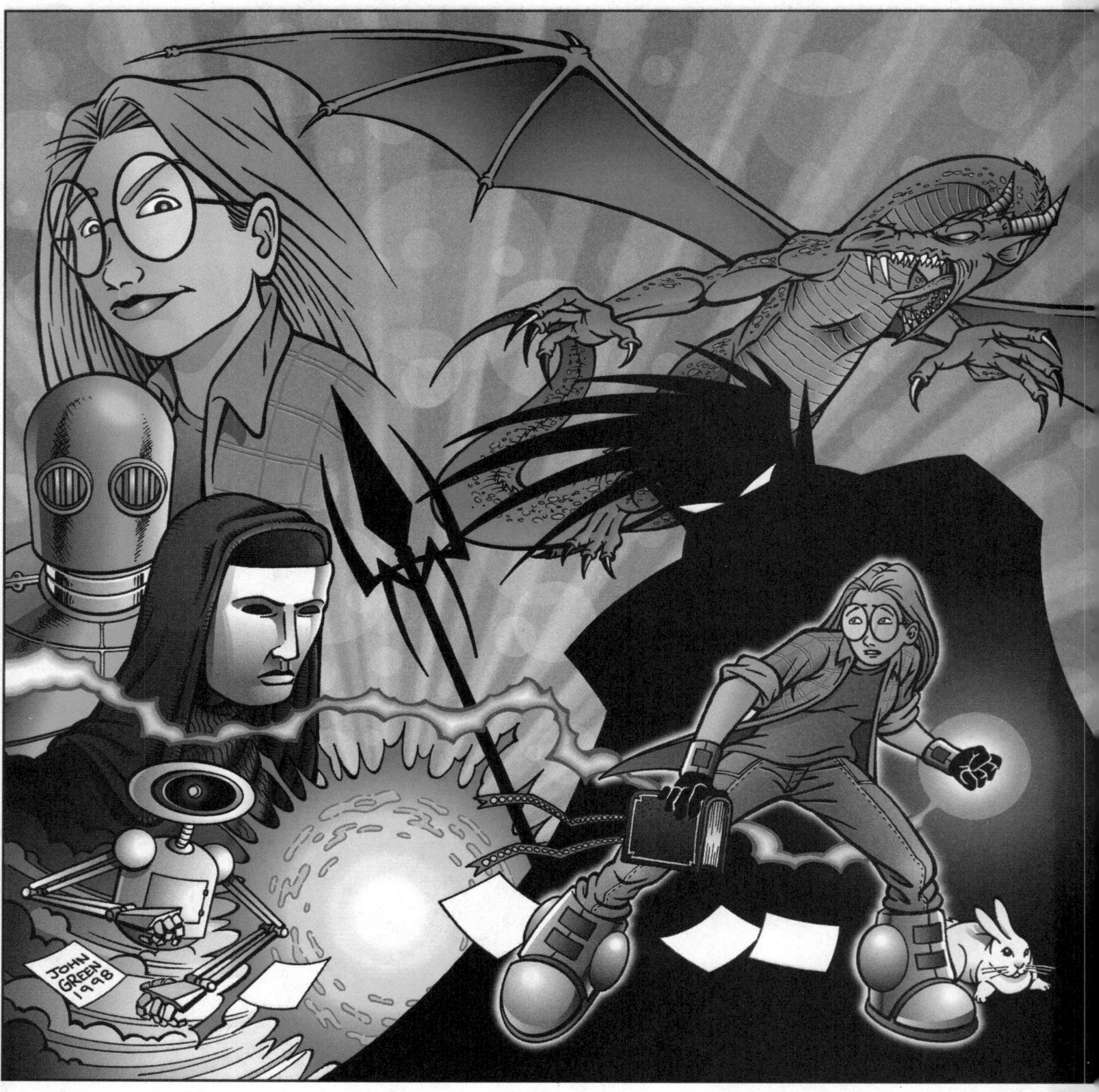
JOHN GREEN 1998